Poverty to Peaches

The Joined-up Life of

Terry Gasking

To George → Angela.
Keep Dancing - Smiling -
Best Wishes

Cover by **Rebecca Slough**
D5 Design,
www.d5-design.com

Tedy G 2022

Poverty to Peaches
is dedicated to family, friends,
the many wonderful folk with whom I have worked
and all who helped me along the way.
***

'Poverty to Peaches
The Joined-up Life of Terry Gasking

First published in 2013 by TwigBooks
Paperback ISBN 978-1-907953-54-5

Available from Amazon, EBooks, Kindle
Leading Bookshops
&
TwigBooks
1-2 Biggs Lane, DINTON
Aylesbury, Buckinghamshire
UK, England HP17 8UH
www.twigbooks.com

<u>Introduction</u>

In 2011 a super guy named Roy Blass with whom I was at school found his way through the internet to contact over 60 of the lads who first attended Hackney Downs Grammar School in 1951. He suggested a 'Reunion Dinner' and 54 of us turned up to an incredibly nostalgic and hugely enjoyable day.

Roy had suggested that we each might circulate a very brief email defining our life prior to, and in the years that followed 'HDS'. The emails showed that a real sparkle and cracking humour still existed in these 71 year olds (their emails would make an excellent book in themselves).

The goodwill I received from my peers as a result of my story really surprised me for they appreciated that my life really had been from *Poverty to Peaches*.

John Hardcastle was researching how English was taught in the years that followed the Second World War. He came out to interview me and convinced me that I should write my life story. In his words -

'Not only is this a cracking good story from a very good story teller but it is a socially historic document that mustn't be lost'

In writing this book I hope I have achieved his vision!

Throughout the book I have been entirely truthful and not embellished or exaggerated any situation or event. I have told the story of my life as it unwound.

Life for me has been a terrific adventure that I hope goes on and on. Now, at 73 years of age I am delighted if I can wake up in the morning, open the curtains and feel the excitement of all the adventures that still lay ahead of me each day.

Long may it last.

I hope you enjoy the book.

Terry Gasking

Contents

CHAPTER One
Making an Entrance

'How much longer?'
Wally couldn't answer!
'It's baking hot outside and it's sweating the life out of me' all Wally could do is to try and reassure *'Can't be much longer now, it will come when it's ready'*
'But I've been in labour since yesterday afternoon and now it's already tea time. Can't you get the midwife to hurry it along?'
It was 1939 – long before the use of modern epidurals and other pain easing birth techniques. This was a home-birth high up in a block of council flats in Holborn, London. The midwife's complete set of pills and aids had fitted into the basket on the handlebars of her bicycle. There wasn't much there to ease the pain. It was a case of push as hard as you can on each contraction and hope the little perisher finally puts in an appearance.
Wally decided he needed a cigarette and some fresh air. He also wanted to take their 3 year old daughter Julia away from the cries of pain from their mother.
He took Julia by the hand and walked out on the balcony that ran along in front of all the flats.
Wally was by now almost totally blind.
He had poor sight all his life but when it is the only sight you have you do not realise that it is inadequate. These were the days before National Health eye tests and regular medical check-ups.

The first time Wally knew he had a problem that others did not was when he 'answered the call' of those who were shaming young men into 'joining-up' and going to War in the conflict that was World War 1. That was in 1915 when the Generals were taking into the army pretty well anyone who could walk.

Thousands of British and German troops were being killed on an almost daily basis. The hideous trenches of the rival armies were full of mud and the bodies of the shot and maimed but each army faced each other across the killing fields.

The Generals from their safe ground well away from the battle lines had this grand strategy that when the millions of Brits had killed the millions of Germans (who in turn had killed millions of British) the British would still have some men standing and hence win the war.

To achieve this strategy the British were taking anyone who could walk, arming them with a rifle and sending them to 'the front' (hideous lines of trenches). The new soldiers were known as 'cannon fodder'.

People back home had no idea of the hideous conditions their sons and husbands were being sent into. They caught the patriotic fever of the time and shamed anyone who did not sign up for the trenches, presenting those in civilian clothes with a white feather to signal their 'cowardice'.

Even leading music hall artists were persuading them to 'take the Queens shilling' (you were paid one shilling if you signed up into the Army) many young men volunteered not knowing what horrors they were about to face.

There was no television in those days transmitting the horror of war into the nation's living rooms. The excitement of having signed up and 'gone to war' soon evaporated as these young men entered the horrors of the trenches. No wonder so many couldn't face going forward into the guns of the Germans and almost certain death on the 'push' and stayed in the trenches only to be shot by a firing squad on their own side for cowardice.

The public back in Britain knew nothing of such horrors and the young Wally like so many of his age group had reported to the recruiting office to sign up and take the queen's shilling. He was 16 years old.

The Army rejected him because his eyesight was so poor they couldn't be sure he would be firing at the enemy – he could only see a shape without being able to distinguish what it was wearing. It was the first time he realised that other people could see better than he.

Rejected by the Army Wally became a van boy. In those days deliveries and even house moves were made by horse and cart usually driven by a hardy old man – too old to be called up in the Army – assisted by a boy – the van boy.

Wally learned a lot of wisdom from his driver and though his wage was too low to visit the silent cinema of those days or the Music Halls he found a way of 'bunking in' to both via a back door. He became fascinated by the tap-dancers he would see on the screen or on the halls and he would practice for hours the tap-dance steps in the back yard of his parents rented house.

Eventually he felt brave enough to try his luck busking the cinema and theatre crowds in London's West-End and was soon earning far more busking than he was on the van.

He managed to get bookings as a tap-dancer at working-men's clubs and entertaining the crowd between bouts at Boxing Tournaments and finally in Theatres and Music Halls.

He met a nice young lady who was in the theatre long before Wally had progressed to that level. She had been Bud Flanagan's stooge long before the revered comedian and entertainer had become a top of the bill act.

She had the contacts and the dance ability. Wally had the flair and was a magnificent entertainer through his dancing. He also had the organisational ability to secure bookings at Music halls all over the U.K.

Wally and Joan Bo-Dell came into being as a dance partnership that was to last for a number of years in the 1920s. The two of them toured all over Britain playing just about every Music Hall in the land.

Wally's eyes were deteriorating but the bright lights on stage and especially the foot-lights allowed him to keep his orientation and to play to the audience that he could not see.

Wally and Joan Bo-Dell were a very successful partnership until silent films were replaced by films on which people could talk and sing and dance and not have conversations by means of statements typed on the screen as still seen in some of the old silent movies.

The wonder of the 'Talkies' lured people away from the Music Halls and into cinemas and this and deteriorating eyesight effectively put an end to Wally and Joan's partnership.

Wally went back to busking but even then was having a great deal of trouble seeing when it got dark. He was facing a very bleak future when he called in on his sister who was working as a waitress in a coffee shop in the London suburb - West Green Road, South Tottenham. There he met Mary Anne Elizabeth.

Mary Anne Elizabeth had an awful upbringing. Born a few years before the First World War as a result of a liaison between her 14 year old mother and one of the many men to whom her mother sold her body for the night.

Little Mary was unwanted and though her mother was to have 6 more children of dubious parentage it was always Mary's job to clean up the home after her mother's night time activities. There would be a beating for Anne as her family called her if the home wasn't to her mother's satisfaction.

Mary still slept in her childhood cot and suffered almost daily beatings until she ran away into service at the age of 14. Unfortunately she landed up with a family who demanded that she did all the household duties, worked from 6 am to 9 pm on 6 days a week and from 6am till 2 pm on Sundays. All for 5 bob a week (25p in new money)

The family she worked for had 4 teenage boys and Mary's sleeping accommodation was the same bedroom as the boys with her bed separated only by a curtain. They peeked around it every night and it was a grim time for the young teenaged Mary.

She eventually returned to Tottenham but this time into her Grannies one-up and one-down cottage opposite the Spurs ground. Her Grandmother was very kind to her and Mary found work in the local Coffee Shops and cafés clearing tables and washing-up.

She met a cracking guy with a motorbike and enough money to take her out once a week to the local pubs or cinema. Suddenly she started to enjoy life but her new found boy-friend was in the Army and got called up into the British Expeditionary Force to India. The absence coupled with the inability of either of them to write coherently ended the romance and she was back staying with her grandmother.

At one of the coffee shops she worked in she was confiding to another waitress called Maude that she seemed to have little prospect of a good life after all she had been through when Maude's brother Wally walked in. He was still immaculately dressed even though his sight was now almost non-existent.

Within a couple of weeks he had proposed to Mary Anne Elizabeth.

Mary was uncertain but Maude persuaded her that her brother Wally was a good man and as neither of them had much prospect of finding someone else, what was there to lose? Six weeks later they were married and living in a 2 roomed flat in Hoxton.

Mary did not like Wally busking and was even more fearful him going back on stage. She could not reconcile her upbringing with that of the theatre people or their way of life.

She did not want him continuing to tap-dance for a living and persuaded her husband to go to the National Institute for the Blind to get checked out to see if the Blind Welfare people might be able to help him find a job. She also wanted to ensure that if they had children then his blindness would not be passed on or affect them.

Investigations at Moorlands Eye Hospital in London revealed that Wally's blindness was caused by a degenerating disease on his optic nerves from which there was no cure. What little light he could now see would gradually fade into unremitting greyness.

Moorlands described the disease as one that could be passed on but only by a female who would not seem to be affected by it. The disease stops in a male who might or might not go blind. Thus Wally's children would be o.k. but Maude's would still be carrying the disease.

Suitably reassured Wally and Mary begat Julia in 1936.

The NIB (National Institute for the Blind) had trained Wally in the art of basket making and then employed him making baskets at the Workshops for the Blind in Tottenham Court Road in the centre of London. It was a very low wage but it was regular in that as long as he was fit and worked then a wage packet arrived every week – a first in Wally's life. He had earned very good money in his days in the theatre but that was long gone.

The NIB also helped them to get a council flat on the 6th floor of Lenard Buildings in Holborn just to the east of the centre of London.

It was the first time in either of their lives that they had a key to their own front door. They had both previously lodged in rooms in someone else's house or flat (apartment) or had lived with their parents, aunts or grandparents.

Mary managed to get some cleaning jobs in the block of flats and enough money came in to fulfil Mary's cherished ambition – to have enough money every week to put food on the table and a roof over their heads (i.e. pay the rent on the flat). A lifetime of struggling to do either had made these cherished ambitions for Mary.

Everything was going well for the Gasking family until Mary went into labour with their second child. It was a baking hot July and the baby just wouldn't come out.

The midwife had arrived and parked her bike at the bottom of the stairwell that led her up to the 6th floor.

'How much longer?' came the cry once again from the bedroom.

Wally could hear from the balcony his wife struggling to give birth. He drew on his cigarette and heard the Bells of St Mary's le Bow (Bow Bells) ring out the hour of 5 pm. He walked little Julia (now nearly 3 years old) to the end of the balcony and back and as he neared the flat his wife's voice cried out.

'Wally - Wally come quick, I think it's coming!'

At 5.10 pm on 15th July 1939 on a glorious sunny day Terry Gasking finally made his entrance into this world.

Eight weeks later the British Prime Minister - Neville Chamberlain declared that Great Britain was at War with Germany and as a consequence World War Two had started.

*

CHAPTER Two
Evacuation

The First World War 1914-18 had resulted in the killing of a huge proportion of able and intelligent young men, sacrificed to feed the foolishness of the great strategy dreamed up by the Generals.

Great Britain and Germany lost the best part of a whole generation of brave, able and frightened youth and young men killed in the trenches and the aftermath.

The First World War had been declared to be the 'War to end all Wars'.

Now in September 1939 – just 21 years later - war had once more been declared.

In the 21 years between the end of the 'War to end all Wars' and the start of World War II science and technology had developed apace and the twisted minds of the weapons scientists had developed greater and greater killing machines, weapons and germs with which to annihilate mankind.

Warfare was no longer to be a matter of sending young men to almost certain death in the hideous trenches for now they could be killed whilst sitting in their own homes.

The competing sides had developed aircraft that could travel great distances, bombs that could cause mass destruction, and incendiaries that could set fire to cities and towns. The British Government didn't want to wipe out another generation quite so soon after the last disaster.

They reasoned in some obscure way that the adults were expendable but the generation of children that lived within the range of the German Bombers should be saved.

They had a plan!

Take all the children that lived in the vulnerable region of the country away from their parents, herd them onto trains and send them out into the parts of the country they did not know but that were thought to be outside the range of the German Bombers.

They were to live with people they did not know and had never met in who knows where, for when the trains set off the parents they left behind had no idea who their children would be lodging with or even what town or village they would end up in. There was no guarantee that they would ever see their children again.

So in a few weeks in September 1939, one million, eight hundred thousand children were moved out of London and the South East of England 'to safety'.

Because of Dad's blindness the Gaskings were being evacuated as a family.

Their few belongings – furniture and bedding had been taken into a government store, their front door key was handed back to the Council and they were evacuated to the village of Rickmansworth – 30 miles West of London.

My cockney Mum (who was at a loss outside London); my Blind Father who was a magnificent man who let nothing phase him; my 3 year old sister; and 2 month old me - Terry Gasking.

Rickmansworth is in Hertfordshire and only 20 miles or so from the Holborn in London where we had been living. It was thought to be a safe haven as German aircraft were not expected to be powerful enough to reach further than London.

I understand that we had stood in line with all the children to find a volunteer family to take us in. We must have presented a formidable problem to the people who had taken on the task of billeting the evacuees. We were lucky enough to find one room in a small cottage with a very amenable husband living there but a sharp and dominant wife.

The only problem with the accommodation was that the room we occupied had formerly been the home of the cats and dogs of the owners and had not been 'de-flead' very often, so all our legs soon had flea bites up to our knees.

Mum daren't lay the baby, me, down on any surface near the floor for by the time she got me up again I was covered in flea bites.

Dad loved the countryside in and around Rickmansworth. He couldn't see it but the smell of the blossom in the gardens lifted his spirits in the many walks he and Mum went on – Mum pushing my sister and me in the pram, Dad hooking his white stick over the front of the pram and helping by tugging up all the hills.

The people in the house we stayed in allowed Dad to sit on their small front lawn and make baskets that were sold to the locals. The money supplemented the almost non-existent welfare payments Mum picked up from the Post Office.

For Dad – life in Rickmansworth was super – despite the cramped accommodation – but the drying up of his income once everyone in the village who wanted a basket had bought one, along with Mum's earnest desire to return to the East End where she was comfortable, and the fact that no bombs were falling during the 'Phoney War' (in the first 18 months or so of the war no bombs fell on London or any other part of England) resulted in our return to London and into one room in an Aunt's house in Tottenham.

Dad could now work at the National Institute of the Blind's Workshop in Tottenham Court Road even though it was a hell of a journey involving buses and underground trains– making baskets - and could supplement his income by 'working the clubs' (tap dancing in his own act on their Variety Show Evenings).

Dad had been a top tap-dancer in his early 20s and played nearly every Music Hall in the U.K. The bright lights of the stage would augment his failing eyesight and he could dance with comparative safety, even when registered as a blind person, provided the stage had footlights to stop him tipping over the edge. He could still perform and the Working Men's club circuit in London at that time paid 7/6 in old money with and extra half a crown (2/6) for an encore which Dad normally achieved.

Ten bob today (50p) is a miserly amount but in 1940 it would provide a week's food for our little family.

It is someone's 'law' that seems to dictate that no sooner did our family in keeping with many other children returned to London - the bombing began!

There was a munitions factory at Enfield (5 miles up the road) that the Germans kept trying to hit and put out of action. The result was that our family along with many others were continually spending their nights in a public air-raid shelter.

Every night families grouped around the radio (no TV, mobile phones, or laptops in those days) to listen to the news and to listen to 'Lord HawHaw' (an English man claiming to be from the aristocracy who broadcast propaganda on behalf of the German enemy)

'Tonight – all you people who live near Enfield go out and look at your Munitions Factory. Tomorrow it will be raised to the ground by German Bombers' the nasal-toned of lord HawHaw crackled over the radio.

'Oh Wally, that's just up the road from us' said Mum – ever the worrier but this time with good cause.

'Don't worry. We will just have to make sure we are all down in the shelter when the sirens wail' said Dad reassuringly.

Poverty to Peaches

The Air Raid Sirens wailed their warning – a wailing pitch that sent every sensible person scurrying for cover in whatever Air Raid Shelter they could.

Many families had built a 'Morrison Shelter'. This was in-house and a bit like a big very solid table with a very solid top that was big enough for children to sleep under with adults crouched next to them. Others dug a deep hole in their garden for an 'Anderson Shelter' - a bit like a glorified ditch in their garden which they covered in corrugated metal propped over and covered that with earth. Many Anderson Shelters were fitted out with benches and bunks. Some were carpeted and had Oil Lamps and heating.

Many victims of wartime bombing took their sleeping blankets, suppers and breakfasts (food was very scarce during the war so these were of subsistence level) to the Underground Stations and spent each night there. The Underground Railway Platforms would be covered with sleeping families that you had to step over if you were to catch the underground trains that came and went throughout the day and evening. Yet others got themselves to the deep Public Air Raid Shelters that housed dozens or even hundreds of people for the duration of the Air Raid.

The Gaskings had access to the latter and when the Air Raid Warning Sirens started Mum gathered up the children and with Dad carrying the baby (me) and with sister Julie taking his hand, off we went to the shelter. Mum was by now well into a pregnancy with an unborn sister or brother to Julie and I so progress was not fast.

As in all wars the accuracy of dropping bombs is hugely exaggerated by the side that drops them and many sticks of bombs fell across the surrounding area or even miles away from the intended targets.

That night there was apprehension in the Air Raid Shelter after Lord HawHaw's warning made worse by the sound bombs hitting the ground close by but all seemed safe in the Shelter.

Dad and probably many others in the shelter were worried. They had heard that the German Air Force sent in a first batch of bombers to drop fire bombs and flares to light up the target for the heavy bombers who were following. They all hoped that they were not hearing the sounds of the fire bombs. They sat in silence not daring to speak their thoughts for fear of frightening all those around them.

Then came the crunch of very heavy bombs falling very close by. The bombers were off their intended target by a number of miles and hitting Tottenham instead of Enfield.

The bombs would fall in a row. Suddenly the shelter shook as two fell very close before all hell was let loose and the ceiling came crashing down putting all the lights out and causing pandemonium.

A bomb had landed right on top on the shelter but – by the grace of god – it did not 'go off' (explode).

Air Raid Wardens arrived on the scene almost immediately trying to get people out and to safety using only the torches they carried.

'Wally – I'm bleeding' – it was Mum's Voice – *'I think I am losing the baby. I'm in real trouble'.*

'Warden we need help' shouted Dad *'I think my wife is miscarrying'*

'Stay where you are guvnor' came the Warden's reply *'there's a bloody big bomb between you and me. I'll try to get you around the bastard as quick as I can. For God's sake don't let it explode while we are trying to get you all out.'*

It didn't – otherwise I would not be here to write this book.

It caused massive damage and casualties. Mum was carrying what would have been my younger sister or brother but had immediately miscarried.

The lights had gone with the bomb and parts of the shelter had collapsed inwards. It was pandemonium as the wardens tried to get people out – knowing that there was an unexploded bomb in the midst of the damage.

There were a lot of casualties in the East-End that night and Ambulances struggled to cope – often with no knowledge of which hospitals had any empty beds to take casualties to. Mum eventually got taken off to hospital but no-one knew which one. Dad was left behind to look after my sister and me and get us to a place of safety.

'You got anywhere you can go?' asked a Warden of Dad.

'I have an Aunt living about a mile away'

'Which direction?' asked the Warden

'Down Northumberland Avenue'

'You should be ok there; the bombs have fallen North/ South but be careful there are an awful lot of houses down'

With that Dad, carrying me in his arms and led by my dear sister (now nearly 4 years old) clambered through the broken masonry with Julie guiding by responding to Dad's memory of the district from before his eyesight had deteriorated to its present state.

He somehow got us back to our Aunt's home a mile away from the wreckage of the shelter.

Nothing could be done until the morning and the stress Dad must have felt that night not knowing if his wife had actually survived the bombing and with no knowledge of where she had been taken can only be imagined.

In all the chaos there was no-one available to look after sister and I the following morning and no-one knew where Mum had been taken. The wardens were able to tell Dad the names of the Hospitals they thought the ambulances had gone to so Dad had no alternative but to set off with me aged 18 months in his arms and my 4 year old sister taking his hand

and steering him around all the fallen masonry from the many houses that had been hit that night. He eventually found Mum at St Anne's Hospital in South Tottenham – quite a few miles from where they had set off that morning. She had lost a lot of blood and the baby, her nerve was shattered, but she was alive.

Amongst all the tears of relief at finding each other alive Mum was to say *'Wally, I've lost the baby'*

Their sadness was alleviated in part by the fact that all the family were still alive and they were together in all the chaos that surrounded them

As soon as Mum was fit to travel our family were boarding a train at Paddington Station along with hundreds of evacuee children on a journey to Wales and far away from the London bombings.

Mum had virtually no education. She was seldom at school as she was required to clean up each day after her mother's mess left from the previous evening and night on the game. Dad left school at 14 years old and was self-taught as a tap dancer.

It was hard enough to get evacuee children placed but a family of four with a blind father and two very young children had no chance and so we finished in a disused barn on a hillside of deepest Rhonda Valley in Wales.

My sister has memories of that time that are particularly sad.

'The family had occasion to go to Ton Pentre to meet a cousin who was coming in on the train. The train from London pulled into the station and as the doors opened, hundreds of children stepped out onto the platform.

They were children of all ages from tots to teenagers. Each one of them was carrying a little suitcase. Many of them were crying uncontrollably. Their chaperones did the best they could under the circumstances but how would any of us feel

being separated from your father, who was away at war, and your mother, who worked in the munitions factories supporting the war effort and trusted that some stranger miles away from home would take good care of you'.

There were people in those days who were willing to take in one or even two children into their homes and a few who would accept families but a blind father, an East-End mother and children ages 18-months and 4 years old presented a formidable problem.

The train from Paddington had been specially arranged by the government to evacuate children and some families and it had made a number of stops along the way. At each stop a number of children disembarked and were often herded into cattle pens alongside the track whilst local adults came to look at them to see if they would be acceptable to move into their houses for an unknown duration of time.

Many such families were incredibly kind to the children they took in – some were cruel.

The selection process in the cattle pens (or the equivalent) was incredible stressful for the children as they heard the adults discussing them.

'Don't like the look of that one!'

'That one might do'

'She might be alright but I am not sure about her brother'

'What four brothers and sisters – we can't possible take four, we will take those two and the WRVS will have to find someone else to take the other two.'

'I'll have that one but not those with her'

'He looks all right, we'll give him a try'

'I don't like the look of any of them but if I have to have them I'll take that one'

This and similar scenes were taking place along each stop on the train's journey.

We were tagged to go to Ystrad Rhondda in the Welsh Valleys and disembarked along with a number of children.

On arrival at the station the local mothers came to select the children for whom they were prepared to offer homes for the duration of the war but perhaps not unexpectedly - no-one wanted a family of four with a blind father and an 18 month old baby.

All the children were found homes but we were left standing on the platform for an interminable length of time.

Eventually the local welfare lady contacted a local farmer who had an empty barn up the side of the Valley and that was to be our accommodation until 'something could be sorted out!'

There was water at the barn to feed the cattle troughs but no sanitation, light or heat. Someone found two mattresses that could be put down on the straw the farmer had provided and that was that – our accommodation in Wales as evacuees.

Well that would have been that except that my mother needed to go to the toilet in the night. She had always been afraid of the dark so lit an oil lantern that the farmer had provided. She started for the door to use the field outside as a toilet when she recoiled with horror. The heat of our four bodies had brought out every cockroach in the barn and the wall and floor was black with them.

Next day mother tramped up and down the high street in Ystrad looking for better accommodation until she found a disused and closed provisions shop that had 3 decrepit rooms behind. Without asking permission our family moved into the rooms as squatters just as fast as my mother's legs could get us there.

It was wartime so it seems no one acted to get us removed and we spent the rest of the war there.

To us children it was fine. There was a back door onto an alley that ran down to the Blacksmith's Forge about half a mile away. Morgan the Milk used to bring the horse and cart he used on his rounds for his horse to be shod at the smithy (milk was ladled out of a large milk churn in those days into whatever jug the householder brought to him).

The milkman was a very jovial man and used to allow Julia and I to ride down to the Smithy on his cart – a real pleasure for both of us.

One day towards the end of the war I was playing with a pal in our disused shop doorway. I had a toy that was a lump of wood shaped like a toy car.

We were in shop doorway at the front of the old disused grocers provisions shop in which we were living when a rat appeared from the shop. The leftover spilled grain; oats etc in the disused shop was a haven for mice, rats and other vermin so this was not an exceptional event. I remember we both moved to one side of the doorway to let the rat continue out onto the pavement where it met an unexpected end! A miner – black from head to foot with coal dust - was coming along on his way home from the pit, spotted the rat, told us boys to *'stand back'* and booted the rat way up in the air and across the high street where it smashed against the wall of the chapel opposite and fell dead.

The miner smiled. *'Scored many a point for Llanelli* (one of the Valley's top rugby teams) *in my time boys'* he said as he went on his way whistling happily.

Tommy Farr – a boy from the Welsh Valleys was fighting the American Joe Louis for the heavyweight championship of the world. Someone produced some boy's boxing gloves and our 'alley' became a boxing ring. My sister would sit on a high wall with the other girls and count out loud to 100 whilst diminutive Terry boxed with other lads from the valley.

Food was rationed. That meant that you were only allowed to buy very little as designated by the government. Dad's blind welfare payments hardly covered the cost of food and certainly did not provide for clothing and whatever rent mother had to find to keep us in our accommodation in the back of the still closed provisions shop.

On Saturday evening Mother would beg or buy any meat or bones the Butcher might have left and did not want to leave in the larders (no fridges in the Valleys in those days) and then went to the Greengrocer to do the same with whatever vegetables she could get. All went into the same large pot and this was boiled up every day of the week with more vegetables added to provide a daily stew that sustained all four of us throughout the war. If we were lucky we would also get a lunch of a 'doorstep' of bread and dripping.

Thankfully my father was a gregarious man and encouraged a number of the friends he had made to join him in a 'Concert Party'. They got a number of bookings up and down the Valleys and though they didn't make much money at it – the little they did bring home proved a godsend in feeding the family.

When you do not have enough income to feed the family – you certainly have none for books or papers. There was no TV, Playstation, video games, Nintendo, Wi or even radio to entertain or brighten up one's life.

When it rained – and it often rained in the Rhonda Valley - there was nothing for Terry to do other than sit at the window watching the raindrops rolling down the window pane and longing for the rain to stop so that he could go out to play.

When I hear modern youngsters complain of being bored when they have a house full of gadgets of entertainment, books, comics etc., my mind immediately puts me back to sitting at the window watching the incessant rain drops rolling down the window pane with no way of alleviating the boredom.

Dad's income from the Concert Parties helped feed us and the handout clothing Mum managed to scrounge helped to clothe us. This was a time of War so scrounging clothing and shoes was an acceptable way of life in poor families where many fathers were away fighting the war.

It was certainly a way of life for us. Mum's obsession was to make sure she begged enough clothing to ensure her children were clothed and shod – she hated the thought of Julia and I having to run around barefoot for lack of shoes – it reminded her of the children in poverty in her childhood who she feared would almost certainly finish in the Workhouse.

Sadly it was 60 years later that we were to discover that I would have been better off running barefoot. Somewhere in those war years (perhaps for all of them) I had been kept in a pair of handout shoes that distorted the growth of my feet. I had never been able to balance on one foot at games and 60 years later my feet collapsed. The Consultant described my feet as 'Chinese Ladies Feet'. They had effectively been bound up in hand-me-down shoes and not allowed to grow. In my 60s I was finding it exceedingly difficult to walk for I seemed to be walking directly on the bones in my feet.

The only cure seemed to be to have them stretched and so after a lifetime of taking size $8^{1}/_{2}$ size shoes and boots, including RAF Boots, I had my feet stretched over 2 years and now take size 11. It was a long and painful conversion.

Back in the Welsh Valleys it was wartime and the Concert Parties did a great deal to cheer the people left at home. As long as there were bright footlights Dad could perform and dance and keep his orientation. Although he could see almost nothing his eyes remained open and clear all his life (it was the optic nerves that had failed) so most audiences had no idea he was blind.

One of his friends had a battered old van that they all piled into along with the props they needed for their shows and drove to the 'gigs' in various towns along the valley.

Poverty to Peaches

The van was so old and decrepit that it could not get up steep hills (and there are many steep hills in the Valleys) so they all had to get out, unload their props and push the van up the hill with its engine straining its heart out to make it. They would then walk back and pick up their props – back to the Van – all pile in until the next steep hill was reached. Really steep hills needed the same treatment but the van also had to be turned around and backed up the hill as its Reverse gear was lower geared than its First.

My sister also has a number of memories that escaped Terry as he was too young at that time.

'We walked to school and had two trips out of the Valley in the 7 years we were evacuated in Wales. We went to the 'seaside' and along the way there were German prisoner of war camps. The Germans would stand by the barbed wire fence and wave at us as we passed. They were obviously well treated and happy to be out of the war.

I made friends with a girl my age in the small town of Ystrad in the Rhondda Valley. She was Welsh and her family lived in a house behind us.

Her father worked in the coal mines which were all around the area. It was a normal sight to see miners going home after a shift covered from head to toe in coal dust.

I remember one day when I was playing at her house, we ran into the living room (parlour as they were called). There, in the middle of the room, in front of a roaring fire was a bungalow bath (a tin bath that could be hung outside on the shed wall when not in use). Sitting happily in it was her Dad. He had finished his shift at the mine and had come home to take a bath in the blackest water I have ever seen. I never figured out how he got clean.

Welfare payments scarcely kept our family alive and Dad's concert party bookings were a key to the Gasking family being able to afford food and shelter.

Sadly the Concert party broke up in disarray and in a way that I don't think my mother ever forgave my father for.

The players in the Concert Party were getting a reputation with the ladies in the Valleys and many an illicit affair was rumoured.

Many wives had husbands away in the war and were 'lonely' and they also had a lot of females of easy virtue who were 'camp followers' or groupies. Many were of uncertain age and at one event there was a police raid backstage in response to a local parent's anxious call that their underage daughters were having sex with the performers after the shows.

As the police burst through the door everyone fled, apart from the blind man who was arrested.

At the subsequent trial all his companions swore that he did not take part in the sex sessions and he was found not guilty and discharged but mother never went to court in support of her husband. I only learned of this event when recording my mother's life when she was 80 years old.

Courts, hospitals and officialdom really scared Mary Ann Elizabeth (my mother) but the thought of my kind and wonderful father having to go through the trauma of a trial with no support from his family (Julia and I were far too young to know what was going on or even if anything was) saddens me greatly.

I never heard about the trial or of the occurrence until the 1990s - just before my mother died but it was clear that this was the incident that made her determined to leave Wales and get back to London.

That was in 1947 – the war had been ended two years earlier and we were still living in the back of the disused Grocers Shop in Ystrad Rhondda. Mum wrote to Dad's Mother to see if she could put us up in the house my Grandma rented in Hackney. This would give Mum time to find somewhere we could live. Grandma agreed. The few belongings we had in the still disused grocers shop were to be left behind along with Peter the mongrel dog we had that I absolutely adored.

I had developed an affinity with animals that I was too young to realise at that time. In later life I was able to stroke a fully grown wild Lion, have a wild Cheetah purr at me, feed and ride a semi-wild elephant, and have a wonderful rapport with a herd of wild Ostriches.

In 1947 I was nearly 8 years old and loved this dog with all my heart but was equally at ease with other people's animals, Morgan the Milk's horse and any other animal I met.

I was numb with fear for my beloved dog when Mum said we couldn't take him with us - he would have to be put down or left behind. The fear turned to horror when my parents said there was no alternative – Peter the dog will have to be shot!

The dog so adored me that my parents did not think it would settle with anyone else and they were running out of time to find it another home. It would have to be shot!

I begged them not to get the dog shot. I insisted that the dog had done no wrong – he couldn't be killed.

My parents insisted that the dog couldn't go with us so this broken-hearted the boy searched desperately for another home for his beloved dog.

I ran out of time. Whilst I was still begging people to give Peter a home my parents without telling me took the dog to a local farmer and Peter my beloved dog was shot dead.

I never got over it.

Knowing nothing of the court case and Mothers determination to leave Wales with immediate effect I had never believed my kind parents could act so cruelly and kill our beloved Peter.

The effect of this event was to stay with me for the rest of my life.

It has given me a lifetime's aversion to any cruelty to people and animals and a hatred of war that I considered was the reason for people I loved dearly – my Mum and Dad – to act so callously and cruelly.

In 1947 with my beloved dog dead the Gasking family returned to Hackney in the East End of London to one room in my Grandma's house.

*

CHAPTER Three
'Return to London'

In 1947 the Gasking Family – Mum, Dad, 11 year old Julia and 8 year old Terry - bodged into a single room with Grannie in Olinda Road, Hackney, London, England.

We were to stay with her for more than a year.

I had never before met Grannie Gasking. She was about 70 years old and only had one tooth in her head – in the front of her mouth. The others had long since disintegrated and she was nicknamed by the family 'Central 'Eating'. A fit in years gone by had distorted her face and the left side had dropped giving it a droopy appearance.

She lived in one room of the house with her husband – Granddad Gasking – living in one room upstairs. The rest of the house was effectively unused.

Granddad and Grannie were miles apart – temperamentally and in every other way. Granddad was a staunch member of the local temperance society. Grannie was pickled in Guinness (a well known alcoholic stout).

They lived their own lives.

Granddad would give Grannie enough money to take her away to Southend (a seaside town East of London) for the summer in the hopes that he wouldn't see her again until the autumn.

Granddad was a very private man and I never really got to know him. He would come home from his job as a cabinet maker and confine himself to his room - only going out to his Temperance Society.

Grannie was a totally different kettle of fish. She had a great sense of humour and giggled a great deal. Mum said that it was the Guinness but I just enjoyed her in the time she was at home rather than paddling in the sea at Southend.

Mum questioned how the pair of them ever got together but Dad would just say –

'Look at my eldest sister's Birth Certificate.'

His Eldest Sister was born just 4 months after they were married and at the end of the 1800s the man 'did the honourable thing' and married the girl he had 'got into trouble'.

Life at 24 Olinda Road was therefore very cramped. We occupied one room but it was very entertaining. The largest room in the house was the front room – known as the Parlour. It was never used but kept with the best furniture the family could afford in case they ever got a visitor. The room was never heated and grannie kept it full of stuffed birds under domes of glass and some photos that seemed to be nothing to do with the family.

Grannie lived in a small room with a very small coal stove that had side platforms on which she cooked. I was always fascinated that she would organise her meals in a series of saucepans – each balanced on top of the other so the whole meal was cooked on one small fire. 60 years later I saw a similar system in a modern magazine proclaiming such a thing to be a revolution in the way we cooked.

Lighting was by gas lights with their delicate mantles. I was always overwhelmed by how my completely blind father could manage to light the gas light with a single match without breaking the gas mantle that would otherwise crumble to pieces at the merest touch.

Olinda Road was a street of terraced houses built sometime between the wars. They were occupied by and large by born and bred East-Enders with a few professional people here and there. Most of the fathers worked in factories in the East End or in the timber yards that lined the bank of the River Lea some mile or so away.

After the Second World War the lot of the factory workers was improving under the Labour Government that had unexpectedly swept to power in 1945. In the late 1940s they were bringing home a wage that my mother could only envy.

 She hoped that her Terry would get a good enough education to get a job in a factory somewhere and earn a regular wage that was sufficient for him to bring up a family and live reasonably well on – something she had never experienced in her life. If he could achieve that then her expectations of him were complete.

Her Terry – me - had been to school in deepest and darkest Rhonda but they taught in Welsh – a language I never mastered. So as an 8 year old enrolling at Craven Park School in South Tottenham my educational acumen was non-existent.

Even at that age I never fancied spending my life in a factory and I had discovered football when my Granddad took me to watch Spurs Reserves play at White Hart Lane.

Granddad never watched the Tottenham Hotspurs first team as the crowds (up to 52,000 strong) were too rumbustious for him so he used to watch all the home games of the Reserves.

The sheer magic of the stadium, the game, and the fact that footballers could earn as much as £6.50 a week appealed to me immensely. Even at that young age I set the goal of getting myself out of the life of poverty I lived in by playing professional sport.

I was not aware of the word 'poverty' then – even though I lived at a rate that was much poorer than all the mates I made amongst the other boys who lived in Olinda Road. I just accepted that my family were poor.

My house and upbringing was so full of love and support from two very caring parents and a sister who's worst insult to me was *'You are a soppy fool and you stink'*.

Probably both were true for we never had warm water to wash in and the water could be very cold indeed in an unheated house in winter so a wash was just a quick flick of the face with a wet flannel.

No-one in the family swore or had a row, or raised their voice in argument so life was good and money or our lack of it did not matter.

There was a bomb damaged house further up the terraced houses of Olinda Road that had a resident old man living in a back room. It was in a very poor state and needed a lot of repair and renovation but the landlord held off from doing anything until he could get fully vacant possession. They were not letting the rest of the house but were waiting for the old man to die so that they could renovate and sell the property with vacant occupation thus enhancing the price.

The property needed a lot of renovation and repair and had no electricity but Mum squatted the four of us in it at her earliest opportunity. It had no hot water or bathroom and an outside toilet. Only the downstairs had any lighting and that was lit by gas lights.

The outdoor toilet close to the back door that let out into a garden that was completely blocked by a brick and concrete Air Raid shelter leaving a few square yards to be shared between a concrete base and a garden.

The loo (toilet) was mighty cold in winter and we could not afford even an oil lamp to take the cold out of it. The torn up Radio Times (used as toilet paper and hung from a bent wire) could be mighty rough.

There was no heating or hot water in the house and the only fireplace we could afford to use was in a minute room that became the living room. The rest of the house was unheated and also mighty cold in winter.

The house was big enough for Terry and Julia to have separate rooms but it needed a candle to light your way up the stairs and a stone hot water bottle filled from the kettle to take the extreme chill off the bed. However it was the second home for which Mum had a key to her own front door and she was happy to be back from Wales and amongst the Cockneys (Londoners born within the sound of Bow Bells) where she felt safe.

Dad got his old job back making baskets at the National Institute for the Blind workshops in Tottenham Court Road and Mum scrubbed the floors of local shops so the 'wolf was kept from the door' as far as the provision of food and shelter was concerned at least until the children started to grow up and needed regular re-clothing.

In our early days in Hackney Mum walked with me the mile or so to my primary school but as an 8 year old I was soon capable of managing that on my own.

My biggest interest was not school but the games of football we could play in the playground and over at the Rec (Recreation Ground) after school.

The Rec was a wide area of grassland with a football pitch drawn out on it and a cricket pitch cut along the side. Its problem was that there was a sewage plant alongside the children's swings and roundabout section that discharged untreated sewage into the River Lea that ran alongside the 'Rec'. It never bothered me for I was too old for the children's playground but I must admit that the obnoxious smell of the untreated sewage would often drift right across the Rec. Goodness knows what we were breathing in as we played football or cricket but in those days nobody cared.

I was a wow at fixing up impromptu games of football on the Rec and later on Clapton Common.

We needed a real football to play with (plastic footballs for kids had not been invented then) and usually played with a tennis or rubber ball. On my 10th Birthday my parents decided to buy me my first real birthday present. We never had birthday parties for we could not afford them and I think mum was ashamed to let anybody into our house at 22 Olinda Road for fear they would see what poverty we lived in.

However Mum and Dad had clearly saved up enough money to buy me a football in the market and that year Mum walked the 2½ miles to Walthamstow market to buy me a proper leather football – a 'T-ball' that was all the range then - and then walked the 2½ miles back home carrying her sons football with her.

Walthamstow was a difficult place to reach from Olinda Road, it needed 3 buses and Mum couldn't afford the fares there and back, she only had the money for the ball. There was no alternative for her but to cross the River Lea, walk across Walthamstow marshes, duck under the very low railway bridge and walk onto the market.

Mum's Aunt Annie lived in Walthamstow and Mum used to insist we visited her 2 or 3 times a year. This was always a wrench for me.

I had to get dressed up in my 'best' clothes (our most recent clothes from Maurice Jays Second hand Clothing Store were not worn but were kept for 'best') and look clean and tidy whilst we walked to the same route to Walthamstow to visit. I just wanted to be out with the lads kicking a football.

Aunt Annie's children were all married and lived in rented houses in adjoining roads so we didn't just visit Aunt Annie but went on to visit each of her children as well and that was my days football gone. All of her family were very generous and though they had virtually nothing themselves they always found a 6 penny piece (old pence worth $2^1/_2$p in new pence) to give Julia and I.

It was years later when my mother was in her 80s and I was talking to her about her life that I realised why she was so fond of her Aunt Annie.

My Mum's mother was a woman of very easy virtue who was paid for sex – hence mum was born illegitimate when her mother was only 14 years old, a fact her mother never failed to remind her of in days when being a bastard was a massive disgrace. Even when Mum was a little girl her mother used to beat her regularly with a broom handle on the slightest excuse and one of the men her mother lived with along the way joined in this terrible abuse of this young child.

On one occasion Mum fled to her Grannie who told her sister - Aunt Annie of Walthamstow – that the child Mary Anne Elizabeth was black and blue with bruises inflicted by the pair of 'parents'.

Apparently Aunt Annie found out where Mum's step father worked. It was the battery manufacturers at Tottenham Hale and she waited behind a pillar outside the factory gates at the end of the day waiting for the workers to all come out. Mum's stepfather fancied himself as a ladies man and came out in the middle of a group of the factory girls all laughing and flirting. They walked past Aunt Annie without seeing her.

'Bert Bullock, come here' Aunt Annie's voice roared.

They all turned to see who was shouting just as Aunt Annie swung her handbag in which she had secreted a brick.

The handbag smashed against the side of Bert Bullock's head. He staggered back only for Aunt Annie to crash another blow on his head, and then another and another until he crashed to the ground at which point Aunt Annie started kicking him where it would hurt the most.

'Beat up an innocent little girl will you – I'll teach you', she screamed at him. Aunt Annie kept up her diatribe against him

and her attack until he could only just stagger away with the assistance of his workmates.

'If you ever lay a finger on little Anne again I will come and finish this job off. Don't think I won't! Lay one finger on Annie and it's your end! Don't ever be in any doubt about that!'

He never touched Mum again and Mum's mother never again wielded the broom handle to her daughter.

Mum assured me that this was a completely true story and it was incredible to think that lovely gentle Aunt Annie had been so incandescent with rage at the cruel treatment Mum had received from her 'parents' that she had humiliated and beaten Mum's cruel stepfather.

Aunt Annie was long dead before Mum told me of why she was so fond of her Aunt and I regretted all the negative thoughts I used to have of visiting the Walthamstow aunts.

I soon became the organiser of the evening games of football. Boys from all around the district would turn up for a game. It didn't matter what religion, creed, colour, nationality, ethnicity or even age each boy was – they all joined in and had a great time.

In those days east End girls never played football or cricket – they were boy's games.

None of us 10 or 11 year olds had girl-friends. We were all using up every hour of daylight that was left after school playing soccer in the winter months and cricket in summer. Girls never hung around the schoolboy footballers or cricketers for they knew the boys would be playing until dark and they could no longer see the ball, then they would rush home at the double as the time would be way past the time their mothers had told them to be home.

I don't ever remember any of my friends being told off for being late home. Their parents knew they were out with the gang of us that were all sports mad and thus not getting into trouble. They also knew that we had all developed a street-wise attitude that emerged from such groups that were given the freedom to develop their characters away from their parent's constant supervision.

We all ran as fast as we could to the rec or the common to join in the games and then when it was too dark to see the ball and the game ended we would run as fast as we could home as it was past the time our Mums had said to be home.

The game today is supervised by adults. It is a long way away from the super times we kids had on the rec. where we organised and ran our own games. The kit we wore consisted of a shirt, pair of shorts and a pair of plimsolls, mostly not washed for weeks on end. I am not certain that all the modern kit being worn by youngsters today makes any better sportsman. It is certainly more expensive than our year-long kit that was worn until it fell to pieces.

Our coats and pullovers were put down at either end of the pitch where the goal posts would have been and two captains were chosen for the match. Each would choose a player in turn for their side and this would go on until all the boys were included in one side or the other.

It never mattered two hoots to us if there were an odd number of boys and one side had one more player than the other – we just got on with the game. If any latecomers arrived they were put into the sides in the same way as before. We might be playing 6 or 8 a side or 16 or 18 a side – it really didn't matter until the dreaded cry rang out –

'Billy, your Mum's looking for you' then Billy would either ignore the cry or take his leave of the game. We all carried on whatever the balance of players.

We never had a referee or any parental supervision or even in attendance at these games and in the years we played (right up until I was called up to National Service as a 19 year-old) I never once recall anyone arguing over whether it was a goal or not even though we had to estimate if a shot was too high (based on how high we thought the Goalie could jump) or complain that anything was unfair, or a foul. We just got on with the game and loved every minute of it. We would play on until it was dark – really dark. If the distant street lights shed enough light to still just about see the ball we carried on playing.

Our games produced some fine footballers – none more so than the Harris brothers. Alan and Ronnie Harris went on to play for Chelsea. Ronnie even captained them to Cup Glory. He picked up the name of 'Chopper Harris' but was a lovely kind and gentle boy – it was just that all our kick-about games were played hard, living in the East-end of London we didn't know any other way to play the game.

Alan also found fame as coach to Real Madrid in Terry Venables time. They had been friends in his early days at Chelsea and all three have played in our kick-abouts on Clapton Common until Chelsea put a stop to it.

It is interesting to note that Alan Harris and Terry Venables had a parting of the ways when Venables was managing Tottenham Hotspurs and Alan was his assistant. Sadly neither had any real success with their teams after their partnership broke.

Primary school in Tottenham was pleasant but I was far from academic. My sister Julia was always brighter and far more mature than I. I struggled through the studies but loved playing football and cricket with my school chums at every interval and indeed at every opportunity.

At that time my life centred around impromptu games of soccer and cricket after school and tracking with the lads in Olinda Road in the school holidays.

I was the youngest of the lads in the Road. It wasn't a gang as in today's culture but rather a group of about 15 – 20 boys who played together in the streets of Hackney.

One of our popular games was a form of 'he' where half the gang were effectively the quarry and the other half the hunters.

The boys who were the quarry would set off in different directions and in different streets each with a piece of chalk in their hands with which they would mark an arrow on the pavements every 50 yards to indicate the direction they were going in. The 'Hunters' would follow the trail until they caught sight of the quarry and then try to catch them. To catch them they merely had to touch the quarry and a clever sidestepping boy could keep the hunters at bay for ages as he dashed around the streets of Hackney.

It never occurred to anyone to cheat and point the arrow in a different direction for much of the fun was to be had by evading capture once you were spotted. When you were 'had' (touched by a hunter) then you would join the hunters and seek out someone who was a quarry. This would continue until the last quarry was 'had'. It was often late into the evening before this was accomplished. Sometimes it never was. We really needed torches in winter but we could not afford such a luxury so the dim street lights of post-war Hackney had to serve to see the arrows on the pavements

With such games the whole of Hackney became a playground and the freedom to roam without parent's supervision or worry was part of the fun. The excessive concern of today's parents has spoilt all that fun for boys growing up today.

The oft quoted fear of the levels of traffic today made the streets dangerous was overcome in our day by teaching the children traffic sense. Much the same is true of paedophiles.

When you are part of an innocent 'gang' then you share information.

We all knew who the 'dodgy' geezers (men) were in the area and we steered clear of them and any strangers trying to get friendly.

If one of the quarry was vulnerable out on their own they only had to cry out and there was half the gang up the road who would drop everything and run to his aid. The prospective paedophile knew that if he tried anything on the individual then up to 20 boys would descend on him and punch his lights out so we were never bothered.

The fact that we were all aware of such dangers meant that we rapidly became 'street wise', something that would be a great asset to us all for the rest of our lives.

A great part of our tracking included the barges on the River Lea. In the late 1940 they were still drawn by horses and used to transport timber to the wharves at the bottom of Craven Park Road and all the way along the Lea to Stratford.

They would be moored by the side of the river waiting to be unloaded and it was great fun for the 'quarry' to lead the hunters down to the river and then be spotted 'hiding' on one of the barges. The ensuing pursuit all over the barge and from barge to barge was enormous fun.

Another regular haunt in which the 'Quarries' could hide were the bombed out houses. One was particularly attractive. Its roof had been blown off and all the stairs collapsed but the banisters were still in place so we could lead the 'Hunters' to the overgrown and wild gardens of the house and hide there or nip into the house through the non-existent front door that had long since been blown off in the bomb damage. We would then clamber up the banisters to the first floor and watch the hunters from the hole in the walls where the windows had been.

Eventually one or more of the hunters would spot us and they would charge into the house – then the fun really began. There were no floorboards but the rafters were still intact so you could chase across the rafters. The crafty quarry would climb out of the window hole and shin up the remains of the outside of the building to the next floor. Our game could go on for hours dashing across the rafters. We all knew that if we stood on the beams that had been the rafters of the floor below they could snap and break and send us plunging to the remains of the ground floor – 3 floors below but if we ran across them at top speed our weight was never on one beam for long enough for it to break and we would be safely over the other side of the room' particularly if we could straddle 2 or 3 rafters with each stride.

We would continue this pursuit throughout the bombed out house for hours until a roving police cyclist would hear us and push his way through the gap in the fence and shout at us to get down. If we saw him in time then Hunters and Quarries were united in their lightening evacuation of the site and be gone in every direction before the copper had managed to set foot in the house. Our games meant that we knew every escape route.

I only remember being 'apprehended' by the policeman on a couple of occasions. Each time the copper tried to impress on us how dangerous these buildings were but it was in the days when Coppers were regarded as your friends who you went to if in trouble and they let us go with the verbal warning. None of us were ever recorded in their notebooks.

Saturday morning cinema was also a great wheeze. The Super Cinema in Stamford Hill used to show Cowboy and Indians films every Saturday Morning for an hour or so and charge children 6d (2 ½ pence) to enter. 6d was more than many of us got for a week's pocket money so we would pool all our money so that one of us could go. As soon as the lights died down and the first picture started the one would go to the toilet that just happened to be next to the fire exit outside which stood the other 14 boys. He pushed the fire door open (there were no alarms on them in those days) and in a trice 14 boys had secreted themselves in seats all over the cinema and gradually moved up together as soon as they were sure they had not been spotted. Roy Rogers and his horse Trigger along with Hopalong Cassidy and all the other Cowboys became our screen heroes.

We never visited each other's houses except to knock on the door and ask whoever answered –

'Is Jimmy coming out to play?

We never played in our back gardens for these were terraced houses with very small back yards rather than gardens. The bungalow (tin) bath would hang and bits and pieces such as bits of old bikes or implements etc were kept in the back yard.

Why would we play in a back yard about 10 metres by 10 when we had the whole of Hackney, some of Tottenham, a mass of bombed out houses, and the River Lea with all its barges as our playground. We also had the green areas of the 'Rec' and Clapton Common.

It was all vastly different to the way children's recreation is perceived today with its compulsory adult supervision and organisation but it was brilliant for us kids and with no adult involvement whatsoever we learned all the organisational, communication and teamwork skills we could ever wish for – and all this before I was 10 years old!

Lenny Allen was one of the older members of our gang and he came up with a terrific wheeze that might earn us enough to buy torches so that we could continue tracking long after darkness fell through flashing our torches on and off.

Walthamstow Marshes bounded one side of the River Lea and during our playing on the Marshes Lenny had noticed an area where bulrushes were growing quite profusely.

He persuaded half a dozen of us to go across the Marshes and cut armfuls of bulrushes.

He had explained that some geezer in Egypt long ago called Herod was killing all the babies and one Mum put her new born baby called Moses in a basket and floated him into some bulrushes to hide from the evil git that was trying to do him in. She succeeded and this Moses grew up to lead his people out of Egypt and have a chat with God who gave him ten lumps of stone with commandments written on them that we are all supposed to obey 3,000 years later.

It all sounded awe inspiring but the thing that really interested us lads was that ever since then the Jews remember that event at Passover and buy bulrushes!

We all knew of Passover even though nearly everyone in the gang and the majority of people in Olinda Road were non practicing Christians. Living in Stamford Hill we all had lots of Jewish pals and envied them every year when they had extra holidays to celebrate this thing called Passover.

Lenny reckoned we could knock on the doors of the Jewish Houses (they far outnumbered the non-Jewish houses in the other streets of Stamford Hill) and flog them some Bulrushes.

All went well and Passover was approaching.

We soon found I was the most successful at selling the Bulrushes at the doors of the Jewish people. It was easy to distinguish their houses from they had a small sliver of metal fixed to the doorpost (I was later to discover it was a Mezuzah and contained a small prayer).

I was very small for my age as a result of near starvation during our time in Wales and back in Hackney so who could resist this blue eyed cheeky faced scamp holding a bunch of Bulrushes.

'Buy me Bulrushes lady?'

'How Much?'

'Two Bob' (10p in modern money but 2 shillings bought an awful lot to a 10 year old kid in 1949)

'Alright' and they would sometimes give me 5 shillings – a fortune for a 10 year old in Hackney – I could get into Spurs Ground boys enclosure for 6d (2 ½ pence in modern money).

Soon we sold out and made a couple more visits to Walthamstow Marshes until we had picked all the Bulrushes and our sales were at an end.

Lenny had kept all our money and bought us all torches and had plenty of money over. He then had another great plan. He spent the rest of the money on a set of garden shears for each of us. I was miffed. Everyone one else had a full sized set of shears but mine were only ¾ size and I had done most of the selling the Bulrushes.

Lenny explained that they had finally run out of money and as I was the smallest and youngest I got the smallest set of shears.

'Anyway,' he said *'you won't be able to handle a full size pair –they'll be too big for you'.*

He was right. I could handle my ¾ size and off I went again knocking on the doors of houses that had overgrown hedges against their small walls that fronted the pavements.

There were plenty of such hedges for wartime had claimed all the metal railings that had originally been on top of the small walls and had used them to be turned into tanks, guns and other armaments.

Hedges had been planted inside virtually all the houses except Olinda Road where the front walls were only inches from the fronts of the terraced houses.

The Scouts used to operate 'Bob-a-Job week' in those days and I merely extended their calendar throughout the year for the next four or five years. (Bob being slang for 1/- (5p) in today's money)

The hedges were full of dust and dirt and this put most of the rest of the gang off, especially as they were older and meeting girls. I was terribly shy with girls so half-a-dozen 'Bobs' were worth the dirt and grime and I could always have a wash when I finally got home. It was a cold water wash but that is all I had ever washed in so it was ok even if it is not the most efficient way of removing the grime.

The worst job I had was when I was trimming one chaps hedge and he asked me if I would use my hedge clippers to cut his lawn. It was hard back breaking work that was easier on my hands and knees. I cut through the top of a red ants nest. I had never seen ants before but by god I felt them. They bit me to pieces and even when I finally got home and collapsed onto my bed a little blighter was still on me and boy did he take revenge on me for breaking up his home.

I was still besotted with football and two of my neighbours would walk me the 2½ miles to watch Tottenham Hotspurs play football and back home again after the match. I began to think of myself as a potential Ted Ditchburn – the Spurs Goalkeeper but whereas he was 6 feet 2 - I was about 4 feet 6 but a guy can dream.

On one occasion I had gone with my sister to watch Spurs play. We were in the boy's enclosure when a group of boys a few years older than me started to get fresh and nasty with Julia. We moved away but they followed us in the crowd until we stood next to the wire separating the boy's enclosure from the adults. They then left us in peace for the rest of the game but as we left they saw us and shouted *'let's get the little runt,* (or words to that effect).

Julie and I took to our toes and dodged back away from the flow of Spectators going home and fled down Northumberland Park towards the River Lea with the gang in hot pursuit. Luckily Julia remembered that our Uncle lived near the bottom of the road and we banged on their door. They were in and we were saved.

I was shaken and Uncle wrote to my Mum & Dad (there were no phones in common use in those days) to suggest I go to Boxing Classes to learn how to look after myself. The next week Dad and I were off to a Boxing Club (me leading a step ahead of dad - Dad with his hand on my shoulder as usual when we walked together responding to all my *'kerb coming – DOWN; kerb coming –UP'* with not a pause in our step as we crossed each side street.

We arrived at The Enterprise Working Men's Club where they had a Boxing Club with tuition once a week.

There started a weekly boxing club that I was to attend for the next 7 years of my youth right up to the time I cracked a bone in my hand when a left jab made contact with the bony forehead of the instructor.

Mum was very anti the idea of me going to a boxing club, she couldn't bear the thought of her gentle Terry getting hurt or becoming brutalised but signing me up for the boxing club was one of the wisest decisions my Dad ever made. It gave me the skills, and more importantly the confidence that I could look after myself in any situation. A state of mind that has lasted with me throughout my lifetime and continues to be with me now I am into my 70s.

We were terribly poor at home but very happy.

However somehow I knew I should strive to get a way of life that would at least allow us electricity in the home, hot baths, indoor toilets, heated bedrooms, and so on, and the joy of watching television that had now entered the homes of some of my friends.

My school pal Derek Dear kindly invited me to his house to watch the Cup Final which was about the only match that was televised in those days and we started to play Subuteo Table Football at his house, mine was far too cold with only candle lighting in the bedrooms and outdoor toilet. His parents were wonderful for letting this scamp called Terry into their house so often and I enjoyed the warmth of the house and their affection.

As my football improved I began to think that sport really might be a way out of the poverty we lived in but first there was the 11+

*

CHAPTER Four
'The 11+'

In 1951 education it Britain was centred around the '11+'.

At the age of 11+ every child sat a National Test/Exam to see what level of education they could aspire to. Those that came into approximately top third in the exam could be interviewed by the Grammar Schools, the rest to Secondary Modern Schools or to Technical Colleges.

Over the many years after the war we only knew 2 boys from the 200 plus houses in Olinda Road who had qualified for a grammar school place, It thus didn't really come into consideration as a possibility that anyone from the road would pass and I had no ambitions of success. As virtually nobody from my neck of the woods passed the 11+ it was no big deal to fail.

Poor Julia never had a chance. She was far brighter and more mature than me but was 11 years old when we returned to London from Wales. She had been taught on a completely different curriculum and often in Welsh. In her first year back in England with different teachers, teachings and subjects she had to sit her 11+. She had no chance of success and was off to Secondary Modern School.

Secondary Modern Schools were perfect for the child that would have been struggling with the academic requirements of a Grammar School. Most of the children from the deprived areas of the East-End of London had not the resources or the encouragement to be academically bright. Nor did they have the academic opportunities in their younger lives to succeed in the 11+ tests.

It was an incredible success for the two boys who had passed to get to 'Grocers' one of the most prestigious Grammar Schools in London but sadly they were both to die at a very young age.

Johnny Lovelock was a few years older than me but still part of the gang until a year or so after he had gone to Hackney Downs Grammar School (known as 'Grocers').

Hackney Downs School was very prestigious Grammar School that stood and looked magnificent in a fork of the Great Eastern Railway line that came into Liverpool Street from Enfield in one direction and from Essex in the other.

It had originally been founded by the Worshipful Company of Grocers of the City of London in 1876 and was known as 'Grocers' a name that stayed with it long after it passed into the auspices of the LCC (London County Council).

Johnny was very much part of the gang when he was younger and once went rushing home crying to his Mum -

'Mum, I've just killed Terry Gasking!'

We were about 9 years old and were playing in the small rough garden that surrounded the Methodist Church in Ravensdale Road. Johnny trod on the base of a broken bottle without cutting himself and tossed it over his shoulder out of harm's way. Unfortunately I was walking across the back of him at the time and the jagged edge of the glass hit me in my left temple. The result was spectacular.

Blood spurted horizontally from me for about a foot (30 cm) before curving gracefully to the ground. Thankfully somebody produced what I thought was a handkerchief (a rarity for most of us wiped our noses on the cuffs of our sleeves) Years later I was to discover that my sister Julie had quickly torn a strip off her under slip and pressed it to the cut to stem the bleeding.

The bleeding eventually stopped without soaking me but I did go home even though the house was empty – Mum was out scrubbing the floors of the shops in Tottenham High Road and Dad was working at the NIB basket making Workshop in the centre of London's West End.

We didn't rush off to hospital in those days and anyway the bleeding had stopped and I don't ever recall telling Mum about it when she got home. She only found out when Johnny's anxious Mum knocked on the door to see if I was alright.

At 'Grocers' Johnny had got deeply into his studies and gradually dropped out from the gang as he became more and more academic. He began to nurse the ambition of becoming a Fighter Pilot in the Air Force. We all wished him well and the thought of an Officer walking down Olinda Road thrilled us all – we had never seen one before.

Johnny's GCE results were first class and he made it into the 6th Form. His subsequent exam results were good enough to get him into the RAF Officers School at Cranwell and he could see his way out of poverty and into a whole new lifestyle as a Flying Officer in the RAF.

Sadly – catastrophe was around the corner. Johnny was extremely fit – as we all were in those days.

As an example of that - by the time I had made it to the 4th form I was doing a paper round every morning (up at 5.45 even in the depth of winter brrr!) and playing impromptu soccer or cricket or tracking each evening.

In winter I would start the week-end with a match for the school on a Saturday morning, rush home to get to Spurs to stand on the Kid's terrace for the afternoon, deliver papers and collect the money on Sunday Morning. It was all done at a rush to be sure to get to Hackney Marshes for my game in the Hackney and Leyton Football League in the team that had emerged from the Methodist Youth Club that Derek and I used to attend, and then get to my afternoon game for the Egerton

Road Synagogue Team organised by a friend of mine from school.

Had there been time and a Muslim team to play for I've no doubt I would have turned out for them as well. There was no room for colour or religious prejudice in my childhood – not if you wanted to live life to the full.

There were no such things as regular medicals or health check-ups in the East-End in those days so Johnny's RAF Medical was the first he had ever had. They found him to be superbly fit <u>BUT</u> - he was colour-blind.

A person who is colour-blind would never be allowed to fly an aircraft and Johnny was devastated.

There was nothing else he wanted to do! This was to be his way out of the poverty we all lived in. To be a fighter pilot was all he lived for.

He could not get over the shock and shortly after the disastrous medical he took his own life with his head in his mother's gas oven.

Clifford Mancey had also made it through his 11+ and got to 'Grocers'. Clifford stayed with the gang right up until the time he found his good looks and manners in his teens had a devastating effect on girls of the same age.

Grocers was a boys-only school so the sudden adulation of females he met in his teens somehow seemed more preferable to Clifford than going for a kick-about with the boys. He still managed to turn up for the occasional game however and even turned out for Ravensdale FC (a team I was to form with my great pal Derek Dear) that played in the Hackney & Leyton League on the renowned Hackney Marshes.

Hackney Marshes had 112 Football Pitches all cheek-by-jowl. Hoof the ball into touch and the opposition player was forced to chase across 3 football pitches to get it – dodging the other players as he did.

Poverty to Peaches

You needed to book a pitch for a Saturday afternoon or a Sunday morning game weeks or even months in advance. All 112 pitches were fully booked. At 11 a-side, plus referee, plus three or four spectators a game and a few odd bods the Marshes were covered by about 3,000 people all playing or watching football. No wonder it was a Mecca for inexpensive football for many years – probably up to the 2012 Olympics that I believe commandeered the football pitches for other uses.

Clifford became an electrician after he left school and his skills were further honed in the RAF as a National Serviceman. When he had completed his 2 years in the RAF he got an excellent paid job as an electrician at one of the largest Exhibition Halls in London. The job paid well enough for Clifford to marry and buy a house in the relatively expensive area of Enfield. With everything going for him and a young wife and children Clifford was electrocuted to death at work.

Both deaths – Johnny and Clifford – were an appalling waste of two really lovely talented boys.

These tragedies happened in my late teens and we just got on with life, but back at the age of 11 I still had to sit the 11+ to see what school I would end up in.

I don't remember much about the exam except that there was something to be written, some Maths and a lot of questions that had multiple answers of which I was required to choose one. I had never met that type of question before so just plunged to the one the answer that seemed most logical and didn't worry about it. My chances of passing were infinitesimally small so there was no stress or worries.

When the 11+ results came through we were still in the Primary School and we were told to stand on the seats of our desks if our name was called out by the teacher so that the whole class could admire those who had passed.

Poverty to Peaches

It was grand to see one or two of my pals had passed including my close friend Derek Dear and then I thought I heard Mr Jackson our teacher say Terry Gasking.

I knew that couldn't be true so I sat still.

My name was called again with Mr Jackson looking straight at me. Still I sat.

He called again quite strictly and told me to stand on my desk seat. I did so with complete disbelief on my part and to this day I feel sure that someone made a mistake. They surely must have marked someone else's papers as mine!

Mum was so proud – I had passed the 11+.

Because my birthday fell in the middle of school summer holidays in July I was sent to the Grammar school for an interview a year ahead of all of my pals who were just a month or so younger.

In our part of London 'Grocers' was the Holy Grail of Grammar Schools - only for the brightest of lads.

The Head Master interviewed the applicants who managed to get recommended to him after they had passed the 11+ to see if they were admissible to his school. Somehow I had managed to get an interview.

Again to my astonishment - I was accepted by 'Toby' Balk the headmaster as suitable for 'Grocers'.

Welfare paid for my first school uniform blazer (my first ever new jacket which I was sadly to grow out of within a matter of months) and I relied on hand-me-downs from older pupils for the rest. We did get more welfare cheques but one of the shops Mum scrubbed was Maurice Jay's Second Hand Clothing Shop and he was somehow able to accept the cheque and exchange it for second-hand clothes for all the family.

Immediately we had to do homework. In a house without heating, hot water, electricity or any form of lighting upstairs this was going to be very difficult.

Poverty to Peaches

In the one room in which we could afford a coal fire and in which we all lived was the radio driven by an 'accumulator'. The accumulator looked like a 12 volt car battery and was nearly as heavy. It was somehow my job every week to walk it a mile or so to West Green Road and exchange it for a freshly charged one. It really was heavy and I was forced to put it down every 50 yards or so and change hands. No wonder my arms are a few inches longer than normal!

The need for me to do homework completely floundered Mum who thought it was all too much.

'It will hurt his brain doing all this study' she would tell all and sundry.

We had no heat or electricity in the house and only the money to light one fire in the evening in the very small living room of the house we had managed to squat in. It was empty when we squatted years after the war apart from one old man living in the back room. It had been severely bomb damaged and all through my early school days sleep was interrupted on rainy days by the sound of drips or water running into various buckets or saucepans around the room.

I didn't realise then that my sleep was also very spasmodic due to suffering from Sleep Apnoea. I was suffering severe breathing problems. They tried to cure it by removing my tonsils, then my adenoids, and then I had to spent days trying to stop the scouring liquid from pouring down my throat as the hospital pumped it through my sinuses.

I spent quite some time in hospital being treated or recovering at home and still I couldn't breathe properly. 60 years later and we are thinking that throughout my life I may have been an undiagnosed Asthma sufferer but was never tested. My breathing problems persisted through the first 3 years of my early teens and returned in my late 60s.

As my breathing problems had caused me to miss so much of my first year at Grocers the teaching staff decided I should restart my second year in the first form. Instead of being the youngest member of my class I suddenly became the oldest by a month or so but years of poverty eating had left me half the size of most of my classmates.

The restart to year one allowed me to meet and join a marvellous group of kids. I still suffered breathing problems but they seem a little easier when you are surrounded by friends.

Sleep Apneoa wasn't discovered then but when they tested me in my 60s they discovered that when asleep I stopped breathing 29 times an hour. Thus my sleep period was never more than 2 minutes before the brain automatically kicked me back to consciousness.

Had they discovered that 50 years ago my energy levels at school would have been vastly different and who knows what might have happened. On the other hand - was my constant illness brought on by my inability to keep up with the teachings and my difficulty of trying to do my homework in an unheated home and a room lit only by a candle? We will never know.

After the scarcity of food and the diet we were forced to live on throughout the war I was only just over half the size of the largest lads in my year at Grocers. I got a welfare grant for school dinners to cover my lunches at school and school meals were the first regular dinners I had ever had.

The additional nutrition they provided undoubtedly gave me extra energy. I was desperate to get picked in the school football teams but lads much bigger than I were selected ahead of me.

Joey Duyts was in goal and he was so much bigger than me in those days that my head never even came up to his shoulder. Another lad who towered above many of us lads was Albert Richards was the hero of us all – he swam Butterfly – for the England Youth Team – and he was even taller than his great friend Joey – and both had strong and fit physiques. We smaller chaps were very lucky that the bigger and heavier guys at our school were such nice kids. Never once did they try to inflict their superior strength and size to bully the rest of us into any actions we didn't care for.

It was the fourth form before the regular school dinners began to let me develop and catch up in size and I began to break into the school football team as my strength and brawn developed.

Academically I was well behind. I had missed an awful lot of school in the first 3 years and my inability (and unwillingness?) to do any homework in the freezing room and candle light was leaving me well behind in all subjects.

I suffered greatly from Bronchitis, had sinus wash-outs in hospital, tonsils and adenoids removed but still I would be down with illnesses most of the time.

I would devour every mouthful of school dinners in a way that could only be understood by someone who had existed thus far on the minimum diet my parents could afford.

By a lucky co-incidence the mother of the pig-man was a dinner lady at Grocers and had got to know that I was the lad he used to chat to on his round.

After the War no household threw away any food but gathered any left-overs into the 'pig-bucket' from which they were collected by the pig-man on his rounds and eventually fed to the pigs.

Interestingly we seemed to suffer fewer foot and mouth and related problems in those days with such a crude feeding system that we do now that all the hygienists, health and safety officers and veterinary scientists have had their say in how pigs should be fed!

There were never any left-overs at my house but the vegetable and potato peelings used to go into a bin and be collected once a week by the pig-man. He had obviously talked to his mother about the lad on his rounds who lived on skeleton rations and she started to feed me extra-large helpings of dinners at school and I would devour every mouthful. For the rest of my life I have been unable to leave any food on my plate (or anyone else's plate) at the end of a meal and many a meal has been held up whilst I devour every mouthful – grateful to be blessed with sufficient food on my plate.

As school dinners began to help build my strength I began to compete for a place in the schools soccer and cricket teams. My dream of allowing sport to see me out of poverty was still alive and I was beginning to enjoy the companionship and friendship of my class mates. Academically things were improving but then Mum went down with problems of internal bleeding that led to a hysterectomy.

One of my aunts had died under the aesthetic whilst having a Hysterectomy operation and Mum was terrified. She was terrified of all officialdom and of hospitals per se, and neglected to have anything done until it was almost too late.

By the time she had the operation she was so weak that she had to go to a Rest and Recuperation home away on the coast of Kent to recover leaving Dad, teenage Julie and I to cope. I was often at home trying to cope.

I thus lost an awful lot of time from school in my first 2 years at Grocers. Somehow I seemed to keep up in Maths but very little else.

French was a disaster! Miss a lesson and then you don't have a clue what the words mean. Miss a whole load of lessons and it is impossible to catch up.

Monsieur De la Feld taught us French. He had no sympathy for the frequently absent Terry Gasking. His way around the problem was to set me extra homework.

Extra homework – learning French words and grammar by the light of a candle in an unheated room - in an unheated house - in the middle of winter - without the money to buy sufficient clothing to keep warm - was not conducive to success.

When I arrived back at school each day having failed to learn the words or master the French grammar De la Feld would have me out in front of the class and humiliate me for my ineptitude and for failing to do my homework. He had a nasty habit of twisting the hair just above the ear and it was extremely painful. None of this encouraged me to come back to school each day and I am sure it contributed greatly to my absences.

60 years later as I write this autobiography if such an event was repeated I would have had the confidence to respond to such treatment with an invitation to De la Feld.

'Let me set you a load of work on a subject you have never met before and isolate you in a bedroom on a freezing day without heat or light save for one candle and let's see what your homework was like the next day! Then let me twist your hair for revenge!!!'

He would be bald in no-time!

Of course as a 12 year old in those days you were scared out of your wits to make any reply and I was forced to suffer the indignity and the pain in silence.

De la Feld was cruel and enjoyed inflicting pain and humiliating boys under the subterfuge of 'discipline' or a method of teaching.

Thank goodness at Grocers there were teachers who were dedicated to helping and encouraging their pupils as a way to success. They helped me immensely and to two of them I owe a lifetime of thanks. The two were Les Mitchell and Norman Pass.

When I was 15 years old Mitchell got me into the under 18s London Army Cadets Representative Football side as a goalkeeper. The 18 year old public schoolboys in the defence intimidated me with the feeling that I was socially unacceptable but nevertheless the numerous matches around the country and the tour of Holland & Belgium in company with the school journey (which Mitchell got me sponsored on) all helped to build confidence and give a glimpse of a different way of life.

Mitchell was head of P.E. and encouraged and developed so many young athletes at the school that Hackney Downs Grammar consistently won all 4 shields (under 13s; under 15s; under17s and Overall Winners) at the North London Athletics Championships held at the White City every year.

In the second form he also took us for English. He was a very wise teacher. There was never any swearing in my home but we were East-End Boys and all went through the age when it seemed grown up to use swear words when out with your mates and they began to become endemic in our speech.

I remember a group of us boys on our way to Enfield Station to catch the steam train back from Hackney Downs School Sports Field came across a group of school girls of about the same age going in the opposite direction. The ensuing rapport was littered with profanities and swearwords. Derek said as we walked away *'The adults passing-by looked so shocked at our language, we might be in dead trouble tomorrow when back at school'*.

When tomorrow came there was no 'request' for us to report to the Headmaster's Study but Mitchel set us a homework – 'Using swearwords in everyday language'

It made us think about the use of swearwords and I remember becoming very puzzled as why some words in the English Language were deemed to be swearwords and thus unacceptable whilst others having precisely the same meaning were not swearwords and thus acceptable in conversation. If there were acceptable words why not use them?

From that day I have never sworn. I use the word 'bloody' sometimes to emphasis a point in my lectures and have been heard to exclaim *'Oh Poo!'* or *'You silly boy'* addressed to myself when committing a silly error but have never found use for swearwords since that essay. It really does illustrate the wisdom of Les Mitchell for had he forbade us to swear or allowed the headmaster to punish us I feel sure that all our East-End pluck would have welled up in resentment and we would have just carried on swearing.

One of the unusual aspects of P.E. at Grocers happened every Summer Term. The Gymnasium had been designed with a floor that was taken up for the summer term to reveal a 20 metre swimming pool below. This was filled with chlorinated water but it appeared that the post-war swimming costumes used by the boys would break up and fibres blocked up the draining and purification ducts of the swimming pool leaving the water unfit to swim in There were only 2 alternatives – no swimming or swim without costumes.

The latter was chosen so all the boys and occasionally some of the masters would swim in the nude. There was never any rumour of impropriety but every class seemed to report an event when Mitchell had them all lined up on the side of the pool and the School Secretary walked in to consult with the head of P.E.

The School Secretary was a lady in her late 30s. Public sex and intersex nudity was unknown or certainly not talked about in the 1950s and was so hugely embarrassing in those days so most boys dived, jumped or fell in the water. Many say it was the day they learnt to swim so maybe Mitchell had a hand in the apparent innocent entry of the School Secretary!

In the third form Norman Pass became our Form Teacher and helped develop my interest and competence in maths that he also taught.

This was much needed for the previous year we had a well-intentioned Maths Teacher who just couldn't teach. He was apparently one of the best qualified Teachers in the school but his teachings went right over the head of all of us boys.

I was keen on Maths but could see no logic in calculus, logarithms, signs and co-signs and so on. I tried desperately to get my head around them. The greatest problem I faced was that when I said I hadn't understood or asked a question he went over the subject in exactly the same way – word for word – as he had just taught it.

I didn't understand it first time, and I never understood it second time. If I then persevered and asked again he would go over the subject in exactly the same way again and seemed to find it impossible to divert from his script to answer the particular question I had. As I came joint top of Maths that year in our 'C' class with 40% (less than 2/3 of the mark the top boys should have obtained) I could only conclude that the other boys were finding his teachings just as difficult.

This particular teacher had a habit of severely pursing or pouting his lips and Alfie Dodd used to run a book at a penny a go paid before his lesson started to guess how many pouts he would make during his Maths lesson. Soon we were all finding this much more entertaining than the contents of his lesson. I have no idea how Alfie decided on the correct number of pouts to pay out and suspect he learnt more about Maths from finding some kind of mean average than ever he did from the lesson.

Norman Pass was a totally different sort of teacher and character. He was much less formal, had a brother who was a core member of England's Water Polo Team, and was much more 'one of us' in his style. He wore a gown as did all our teachers at Hackney Downs but was very relaxed in his teaching style and much more effective.

I got thrown out of Woodwork for talking. I was always talking! I guess in the days before Television, Computers, Tablets, CD Players, portable radios, mobile phones, phones in houses and a radio that pulled your arms out of their sockets every time you had to change the accumulators (weekly or more often if you listened to a lot of radio) then talking was your only form of communication or entertainment.

I was never any good at Woodwork or any of the other practical subjects. I have often thought that this might be because Dad was blind so no jobs around the house, or handicrafts were ever done at home but then I guess little or no handicrafts might have been the case in many lad's homes and they seemed to cope.

Warburton – the Woodwork master was always telling me off for talking and one day he said *'I'm not going to tell you to stop talking again'*. With that he hit me over the head with a file and threw me out of the Woodwork Shed and told me not to come back.

Norman Pass was my Form Teacher as well as taking us for Maths and asked me what I had done to upset the Woodwork Master. I replied and he just smiled and asked what I was going to do in future whilst my classmates were doing Woodwork.

I didn't have a clue but he came up with a solution. He found a couple of old GCE 'O' Level papers ('O' Level was the minimum standard acceptable by offices and businesses). The papers were Maths questions and he set me to answer them during the time the others were doing Woodwork.

He marked the papers after school and was most encouraging about my efforts – taking time to explain where I had gone wrong and putting me right. He was teaching other classes as well as ours so the time for his review of my work was very limited. He then suggested that I took myself up to Charing Cross Road in Central London and at a shop called Foyle's Bookshop I could buy binders of old GCE 'O' Level Maths Papers for very little. If I brought those back with me and answered the questions as best I can during the time the rest of term whilst the boys were doing woodwork he was willing to spend an hour or so on a Sunday morning when I collected his paper money working through the questions with me.

He lived on my paper round and I used to collect the money for the week's papers off every house I delivered to. It wasn't a chore for I used to get a lot of tips that when added to my hedge cutting eventually allowed me to buy my very own bicycle. It was the cheapest bike I could find in any shop – but it was mine and I became even more mobile than my legs had allowed me previously. It also allowed me to increase the size of my paper-round and earn even more money to pay off the remaining costs of the bike.

I also got a job at Cohens (Wet) Fish Shop in Stamford Hill at the top of Olinda Road. We had a Stanley Cohen in my class at Grocers (Hackney Downs School) and I believe his immediate family had a Wet Fish Shop in or near Ridley Road. (My) Cohens was I believe owned by his Uncle and whether or not he ever had a word with them I never did know but they were extremely kind to me. They employed me every Friday after school to deliver the Fish orders to houses in Hackney and South Tottenham. They also gave me employment on Saturday Mornings in Summer before I went off to play Cricket in the adult's team I had got into. We had no bathroom at home to clean off the smell of wet fish – just a cold water tap so I must have gone off to cricket on my bike smelling to high heaven but the adults in the team were far too nice to complain.

I delivered the fish on the shop's bike. It was exactly like the one ridden by Granville in 'Open All Hours' on TV and was often loaded nearly as high as his. The front wheel was very small and a platform on which the orders were stacked lay just over the top of the wheel. Everything was most unstable particularly when a Bus or a Lorry whizzed past. The air displacement of the large vehicles would cause the whole of the front of the bike to tilt and it was a battle for this undernourished 15 year old to keep upright.

The bike only fell over once and that was as I was getting off it to make a delivery. It was in Elm Park Avenue. The road had a deep camber and fell away into the kerb. I pulled down the front forks that supported the platform over the front wheel and the whole bike tipped sideways spilling all its contents over the pavement. I tried to guess what fish belonged in what newspaper wrapper and hoped I had got it right. Luckily nobody complained so I kept my job on a Friday evening at Cohens until I left school.

I still had to finish my cash collection for the papers I had delivered in time to get to Hackney Marshes for my Hackney & Leyton League match on a Sunday morning but now I had a bike I could get there a lot faster so I could take Norman Pass up on his kind offer of taking me through the exam papers at his house on a Sunday Morning.

The bike also allowed me to get to cricket matches in the summer. This led to my only accident on my bike and it was nearly fatal.

I was cycling to a match that was south of the River Thames at Wandsworth and had persuaded my friend Kenny to play as the adult team was one man short. We were just cycling along the busy main street by Liverpool Street Station when a coach swept passed us and cut into Kenny's path. Kenny swerved inwards towards the kerb and his back wheel hit my front.

Over the handlebars I went falling outwards into the road. In mid-air I managed to glance back and saw another coach coming straight for me. Blessed be my days on the football field as a goalkeeper for I was able to twist in mid-air and hurl myself into a forward roll toward the kerb. The second coach ran over the front wheel of my bike and Kenny told me that looking back he was sure the front wheel of the coach had run over my hair. I certainly remembered looking up as I hit the ground and seeing the front wheel hurtling past me seemingly an inch or so away, an inch closer and what a lifetime of adventures I would have missed.

Interestingly the passengers were all Walthamstow Avenue Supporters on their way to a match and looking as though they had a bevy (drink) or two before they set off. All they would say is *'Come on, we're late for the match, we're going to miss the kick-off now. The kid's allright so let's get cracking'*

With that they all got back into the coach and set off leaving this 15 year old at the side of the road, shaken and with a useless bicycle.

As luck would have it before Kenny and I could work out what we could do along came the battered old van that 3 or 4 members of the cricket team used to go to matches. By the grace of god they spotted us. So we piled the smashed up bike in the back of the van along with a shaken Terry and set off for the match. It was probably the best treatment for shock I could possibly have had.

Mum banned me from cycling but as soon as I got the bike repaired and she was out cleaning one of the shops she was employed at and I jumped on the bike and took off for school. The wise counsel of my Dad pacified Mum to the idea that I was safe on the bike and I was immediately back on the Paper Round and the fish deliveries.

I was playing men's cricket and the team warmed up for the cricket season by having some nets at the Essex County Cricket nets at Gants Hill.

I had picked up an old fashion flicker series of pictures of the bowling action of somebody bowling leg breaks. It was a series of individual pictures clipped at their base. When you flicked the top of the pad the figure in the pictures appeared to move and bowl a leg break. I became fascinated by it. We used to play cricket with a tennis ball in the playground at school and I was soon able to make the ball turn quite sharply.

Poverty to Peaches

The Essex coaches encouraged me to bowl it at the nets and the following year asked me to bowl in their nets on a Sunday Morning. I was bowling to some of the best club cricketers in Essex who were in the Nets for practice and lessons and soon developed a googly to go the other way from the leg-break. It was good and it was fun.

I was enjoying life immensely and my dream of 'playing my way out of poverty' was still alive.

French had been dropped from my curriculum following an end of year exam result (bottom with $6^2/_3\%$) and thank god that was the end of De la Feld from the teachers I had to face.

The extra food I was now getting from regular school lunches and plenty of sport was building fitness so I used to be absent far less frequently. I even developed an interest in Geography and History and when I was 13 years of age Dad bought me the first book I had ever had (when the family cannot afford to eat on many days it cannot afford books). Mum and Dad had received only spasmodic education and the need for books was never appreciated. The book was an English Dictionary to help cure my appalling spelling that varied between phonetic Welsh sounding words and phonetic cockney.

Mum and Dad were finding it increasingly difficult to pay their way with two growing children to clothe and feed. On a Friday Night Mum would gather all the money together including that from my paper round (but not my tips – they were always mine to keep). She would put enough on one side to pay the Rent Man when he called, and enough to buy the food in the week ahead. Julia and I were given 6d pocket money each week and our fares to and from school for the week. If any was over she would buy Savings Stamps.

She had a series of Saving Stamp books on the table and would put a 6d (old Money) stamp in one saying *'that's for clothing for the family'*; another 6d stamp in the next *'that's for the next coal delivery'* (we could only afford a fire in one room – our small living room) *'that's for the extra food we need in the kid's holidays'*(no free school meals), *'that's for a holiday if we can afford one';* and so on.

In this way Mum managed to save enough to pay for the four of us to have a holiday at Canvey Island most years. Canvey Island is on the Thames Estuary and is a couple of miles long and about a mile wide. It is perhaps most famously known for the severe floods of 1952. It had a Sea Wall of piled high earth and stone but the island lay below the level of the River Thames. When the great floods of 1952 swept up the Thames Estuary the sea wall gave way and the whole island was flooded with severe loss of life.

Prior to the floods it had been an island full of bungalows with many 'streets' that were actually mown lawns. We used to stop at the Travellers Rest – one of the few two-storied buildings. It was a café that had a few rooms on its first floor that could be let out for Bed & Breakfast. How Mum ever got to hear about it is a mystery to me but the proprietor was extremely kind and let us have a discount even on the very low prices that were charged on Canvey Island.

Prices were low on Canvey Islands due to the fact that this small island had a massive Oil Refinery occupying one end of it. It did not have a sandy beach but the 'beach' was made up of shingle and stones. The shingle was very sharp and even cutting on bare feet and the stones were higgledy-piggledy – some as large as a foot stool. Virtually all were black from the seepage of the refinery over time.

The beach had a bricked off part of the 'sea' (the estuary of the River Thames that was so polluted in the '50s that no self-respecting fish would swim in it!) in which you were supposed to swim. I don't know to this day if an incident in this 'swimming pool' almost cost me my life but it certainly scared me to death and made me terrified of drowning until the persistence of our P.E. Master at Grocers finally got me swimming in the third form.

The event that had terrified me started innocently enough. I had seen kids learning to swim by holding a square piece of cork out in front of them – its buoyancy keeping them afloat. I didn't have any cork but I did have a blown-up beach-ball. Going boldly out of my depth with the ball held out in front of me I was ok until I tried to turn. The ball rolled over and I rolled over with it. I was almost immediately upside down under water and panicking. As I went down desperate for breath I hoped I could reach the bottom of the swimming area and push my way back up. When I got to the bottom instead of being a smooth surface on which I could scramble onto my feet and push up – back to the surface - it was all massive stones and rocks making it impossible to get to my feet. I was desperate to breathe and how I finally managed to get my head above the water line and back to the shallows I do not know but it really did scare the life out of me.

Neither of my parents could ever swim and Mum was terrified of any of us drowning. I didn't dare tell her I almost had. If I did I knew she would never let me swim again.

Thank goodness for the persistence of Les Mitchell for getting me through my terror of the water for swimming has become one of the great joys in my life.

The minimum school leaving age was 15.

Julie left School at 15 and got a job at Woolworths. Her contribution from her pay into the household expenses allowed Mum to double the money she put by for holidays. More money coming into the household meant far more 6d stamps in the stamp books and the next year we went to Margate on the South East coast of England. We had Sandy Beaches, cleaner sea (the English Channel) and a terrific Amusement Park with plenty of fun available for a few pence a ride.

Margate had number of a bed and breakfast houses that sponsored a week for the National Institute for the Blind so we had a great week with money to spend on the amusements.

I had started a paper round as a 12 year old and Julie's contribution with my few pence added allowed us subsequent holidays for a week at Ramsgate where Julie and I rode all over the place on a hired three wheel bicycle that was powered rather like a Pedalow and in following years to Great Yarmouth. By now Les Mitchell had got me over my fear of swimming and though I could do little other than splash about it was very enjoyable in the sea.

Great Yarmouth is on the East Coast of England and washed by the North Sea, a very cold sea indeed!!!! I can recall Julia and I coming out of the sea and Mum throwing a towel over each of us. Before we could get dry we were both blue with the cold and had goosebumps all over us. Our teeth were chattering too fiercely for us to say how much we were enjoying ourselves.

I was getting nowhere at school, way behind in my studies with no chance of catching up after all my absences and not enjoying the academic side of school one little bit. I had a great bunch of pals as school mates but Mum, Dad and I thought I would be much happier leaving school and going out at work.

You were allowed to leave school at 15 in those days and as my birthday fell in the middle of the school holidays my parents made a request for me to leave school at the end of the 3rd form so I could go to work and help the family's budget. This suited me for I had no academic prowess and would rather be out earning a living than squandering the next year at school.

Before the school would agree to me going at the end of the Term and thus just before my 15th birthday they requested Mum and Dad attend a Parents Evening.

Poverty to Peaches

Mum and Dad had never attended any event at school previously but they needed the schools permission for me to leave a term early so off they went to Parents Evening

At the Parents Evening they apparently had a long meeting with Les Mitchell and Joe Brearley.

Joe Brearley was a 'queer coot' – an expression used in my young days to signify an unconventional character who did not always appear to be in control of all his senses. The expression had not been kidnapped as has been that lovely word 'gay' to suggest homosexuality and no such meaning is conveyed by the author but he was a 'queer coot'.

He took us for English and we never knew what kind of lesson we were going to get or what kind of content. Brearley used to produce the school plays and these were truly masterpieces. He inspired many boys to act and gave them their first experience of the stage in his productions.

Harold Pinter – later to become the Nobel Laureate in Literature - was one of his finest students and apparently one of the best Romeos seen on an East End stage – be it a school stage in a joint production with Dalston County Girls School. Joe Brearley was very proud of Pinter and Pinter appeared to have the very highest regard for Joe Brearley.

It is odd that the letters Joe Brearley wrote home before, during and after World War II were to lead me on yet another great adventure in my life more than 50 years later. An adventure that was unthinkable and impossible to have even dreamed of as a 14 year old boy.

I don't believe that Joe Brearley was ever a dedicated Teacher in the mould of Les Mitchell or Norman Pass. I think he was really a frustrated Thespian (though I didn't know what the word meant in those days). He seemed to cast himself as a lead character in the school plays and when teaching would fade off into his own world as though picturing himself in the role of a classic Shakespearian character

Alfie and the boys in the class were great at winding him up and Brearley would suddenly lose it. It usually resulted in a class detention but the spectacle of Joe Brearley 'doing his nut' was usually worth the half an hour's detention.

Derek Dear and I never minded detention – for me it was a chance to complete our homework in the dry and the warm (in those days schools did not open after teaching hours for pupils to do their homework). When Joe Brearley was in his 'Psyche Phase' (see 'Fortunes Fool') he would decide that all of us should meditate for half an hour instead of doing any work and though sitting at his desk at the front of class - off he would go mentally in his own meditation.

Derek and I had seen a game called 'Dice Cricket'. On a sheet of paper you made up teams of players you would pick from county or international cricket if you were a Selector and wrote them down in batting order. The first two names then 'went into bat' and you rolled the dice to see how many runs they got from each ball in the 6-ball overs you played. If you threw a 5 then the batsman was out.

It was a simple game but quite amusing for half an hour. If we had played it with a dice and proper team scoring sheets our cover would have been blown immediately but our school pencils had 6 sides. Scratch off the paint and write on a number on each surface and we had our dice. The large blotting paper we had on the sloping desk was perfect for rolling a pencil quietly and writing down the score so Brearley's half an hour's meditation was never a problem for the pair of us sitting at the back of the class playing home-made 'dice' cricket.

When Brearley lost his calm in class he boiled over. This was a common state in many of his lessons to us and may have had as much to do with the content of his lessons and his lack of understanding of an East-End boy's reaction so the soliloquys of Shakespeare as it did to our indifference.

On one occasion he was so frustrated that in the middle of his rage he picked up the nearest boy by his collar and shook him until his shirt ripped from collar to his waist. I never did know the end of that episode apart from hearing that Brearley had been forced to buy the boy a new shirt and his tempers in class calmed down for a week or two.

So Mum and Dad at the Parents Evening had met two Teachers who taught boys in their own vastly different way.

I had no idea what the result was going to be but when they came home my parents sat me down and said –

'Terry – we have just come home from meeting with two teachers who know you well and we almost cannot believe what they say. They have seen things in you that we haven't and didn't know you had.

We told them you were unhappy at school and felt you had no chance of leaving with any qualifications but they completely disagreed. Mitchell pointed out the way you organised the Football teams you have formed, how you arrange all their matches, even getting games against Eton Manor, how you organise your group of pals at school in all the break times and described you as a natural leader.

Both Teachers have begged us to keep you at school if we can possibly manage. They have said that if we can get you to do your homework – who knows what you might achieve.'

I found it difficult to believe that the Teachers had said such kind things about me. The characteristics they talked about and the activities were just the things I do – they were natural instincts - not learned processes, similarly I was always made Captain of the teams I played in simply because I did all the organising on and off the field so it was no big deal.

My parents disagreed with my response and talked me into staying on for one more year and giving my best to all my studies. I pointed out that this was difficult with a candle in an unheated room and they said they had worked that out.

Poverty to Peaches

After we had our tea at about 7.30 pm Mum would shovel out the back half of our one and only fire and carry the shovel of glowing coals upstairs to the fireplace in my room. That would soon warm up the room and last for perhaps an hour when – with three candles I would do an intensive hour's homework.

There was no way I couldn't agree to stay on at school and that was the way it was throughout the next year. With the regular completion of my homework I began to feel much more comfortable with the subjects and in class and life at school did not seem so daunting. I was helped by the wonderful camaraderie that one got from a great bunch of East-end kids I was fortunate to be at school with. Suddenly for the first time in my life school became fun and enjoyable.

Mum and Dad attended a Parents Evening again a year later and received such a confidence boosting report of my progress that belts were tightened yet further at home in order to pay the costs of yet another year at school for me.

They even went to a prize-giving evening when I received a book for being the most improved pupil in my year – it was the only prize I ever got at school so it was good they were there.

At that Prize-giving a boy from my class with the most angelic voice you could ever wish to hear – sang Ava Maria so beautifully that many parents had tears in their eyes.

However, sadly, not all East-End Parents were as caring and loving as mine. Some could be quite cruel. When one of my pals went home after Prize-giving his parents aggressively asked him *'Why can't you be like that lovely boy who sang Ava Maria instead of the little sod that you are?'*

My pal tried to tell his dad that that lovely boy with the angel's voice was in fact the biggest tea-leaf (thief) in the school; and always up to no good. His father wouldn't believe his son. My pal tried to tell his parents that the boy with the angelic voice would return from Woolworths every lunchtime

72

with pockets full of items he had 'nicked' (stolen) and tried to sell them to the rest of his class mates. My pal's father still wouldn't believe such tales and it was off with his belt and another thrashing for my pal. (Years later I saw the name of our tea-leaf with the angels voice in the local paper – sent to prison for burglary and handling stolen goods).

For two years Mum scooped out the back of the fire after tea and took the glowing coals on a shovel with candles up to my room (goodness knows what Health and Safety would make of such an event these days) and for two years I kept my bargain and kept up with my homework.

I still cherished the dream of making it out of the East-End as a footballer and/or a cricketer for I had been playing in men's Cricket at one of the top clubs in Essex for a number of years. But now I might also be able to scrape through enough GCE's to land a good job that would pay enough to cover the costs of travelling around the home-counties in pursuit of stardom in both sports.

I was very happy with life

In the school holidays a pal who had a very posh dropped handlebars multi-geared 'racing' bike persuaded me to join him on a ride to Southend for the day. Southend was a ride of $36^1/_2$ miles so gave a combined distance there and back of about 73 miles plus any local mileage we might do. I thought my trusty 3 geared upright bike could handle that so off we went. The furthest I had cycled previously was 10 miles or so out into Epping Forest which was always a wonderful relaxation after the urbanised Hackney.

The Southend 'Arterial Road' had a cycle track alongside it so we were not bothered by the traffic. The journey is relatively flat but it is surprising how 'up hill' the road ahead looks as you are going down one side of a slight valley prior to going up the other side. My pal began to complain about the (non-existent) hills the further we got from home even though he had about 9 gears to ascend them as opposed to my 3.

We eventually got to Southend and my Pal insisted in going to the Railway Station where we could get a cup of tea in buffet. We had packed sandwiches in our saddlebags (me – bread & dripping and a cake; he – far healthier varieties). We propped our bikes up against the railings of the railway station and pal went in to buy a cup of tea while I sat outside drinking the bottle of water I had brought with me. When he came back out he asked me how much money I had on me. Silly question really as all my money had gone on the bread and dripping and the cake.

He then declared that his bike had a puncture and he would have to travel home by train.

I pulled the Puncture Repair outfit we all carried in those days (a small minute rectangular box containing rubber patches and a little glue) and he made a show of trying to find the puncture to no avail. He went back into the station but the fare was far more than our combined wealth so he led us to the nearest Police Station. They phoned his home (he was wealthy enough for a phone in his home) and his parents agreed to pay his fare. I remember the desk sergeant asking me what I was going to do and I considered it a silly question. *'Ride home of course'.* The thought of my parents being asked to pay for me to ride home on a train horrified me.

'Will you be alright?'

''Of course I will – all the hills go down on the way home' the sergeant laughed but I was serious, I really did believe my pal that all the hills had been against us on the way to Southend so they would be for us on the way home.

'Don't be too sure. Are you sure you don't want me to contact your parents to get you home on the train.'

'No, no, we haven't got a phone and they are both out at work.'

Had I been wiser I would have realised that he was worried at sending this 14 year old all the way back to London on his own but I was having none of it.

'Well if you're determined to go you had better set off now otherwise it will be dark before you get back to London. Your pal here will be on a train as soon as the local bobby has been round to his house and collected the fare'

With that I said cheerio to my pal and set off back home on my bike.

Our trip to Southend had consisted of a visit to the Railway Station and the Police Station. No sea front, no Kursall (the amusement arcade), no fun on the sands.

'*No nuffin*' I thought to myself and with that set off for home.

The sergeant had been right. There were as many hills going up on the way home as there were going down. I did arrive back in London in the dark but luckily knew the way back to Hackney from the end of the Arterial Road at Whipps Cross so my inadequate lights were not a handicap to me.

I was delighted that I had completed the journey both ways but somewhat tired.

I slept well that night!

*

CHAPTER Five
'Grocer's' & Tragedy

Hackney Downs Grammar School was a majestic building with an ambiance that commanded respect and discipline.

Teachers wore gowns and the pupils wore school uniform.

My first school uniform came via a voucher from the Welfare but further vouchers were exchanged at Maurice Jays Second Hand Clothes Shop for clothes for all the family. If I was lucky one of the older boys who had grown out of their uniform would pass me down their blazer but often I would be one of the few boys in the school not wearing a blazer.

One time in about the 4th form the headmaster stopped me in the corridor and demanded to know why I was not wearing a school blazer. I told him I didn't have one and he told me my excuse was not good enough. I was to report to his study at the next break.

Expecting severe trouble I knocked and tentatively entered his study but he must have checked up on me as his tone changed. He objected to the fact I was wearing a windcheater. I explained that I came straight onto school after doing my paper round and I only had this windcheater to cheat the cold and rain in the early morning or my old sports jacket. He preferred the idea of a sports jacket so that is what I wore for the rest of my school days.

One day as class ended Norman Pass wanted a quiet word. He produced two pseudo leather patches from his brief case and asked me to get my mother to sew them over the threadbare elbows on my sports jacket.

'Then you will look like a real academic' he said most kindly.

The 1951 intake was a cross section of about 90 boys from Hackney and a really irrepressible bunch of lads they were. Some were from homes that had been ravaged by war, others had survived the carnage well but whatever their backgrounds they all mixed together wonderfully well with much of the East-End resilience about them.

The school was later to be turned badly into a Comprehensive School with disastrous consequences. It was finally closed under the label of 'The Worst School in England' but that was a title you could never have used in my time there.

Within the decade or two following World War Two Hackney Downs Grammar School produced scholars and sportsmen to grace the world.

A head of the British Atomic Energy establishment was at Hackney Downs in my time, as was the head of Mossad the Israeli Intelligence Service, Harold Pinter was a couple of years older than I and he was awarded the Nobel Prize for Literature. Many boys have gone on to the top echelons of business or to professorships in Universities all around the world.

Many Captains of Industries have been drawn from the ranks of Hackney Downs School. It was tremendously successful at taking boys from all walks of life in the East-End of London and turning them into world class performers in a multitude of professions.

For such a school to fail is a damning indictment of the political games being played in the 1970s by the government verses the Hackney Town Council.

The failure was theirs – and not that of the school. The dreadful slippage in the standards of dress and behaviour that led to the demoralisation of staff and pupils at the school was within the control of the staff at that time but the outcome of their efforts were always going to be effected by the political shenanigans that were never going to give the school a chance of success.

Many years later it was turned into Mossbourne Academy and had £millions of government money poured into it. The Academy achieved a great deal of success in GCE examinations and great credit was taken by the then Headmaster and perhaps justly so. However his frequent boast that he had *'turned around a failed school'* rankles with everyone who was at the school in my time. When you examined the disciplines and methods he introduced and insisted upon - they were precisely the same disciplines and methods we were all brought up with in our time at Hackney Downs School.

I feel that he has not *'turned around a failed school'* but has succeeded in *'restoring the disciplines and methods that had made Hackney Downs such success for the best part of a century until the politicians fouled up.'*

We had all kinds of pupils in my time. Alfie Dodds – one of the great characters in life who – like me - wondered how he ever got to Grocers. Alfie would take on any task and anybody. Woe betide any teacher who incurred his wrath – more than one has been upended or had a waste paper basket descend on his head from the doorjamb as he entered the room. Alfie was fearless and would take on anybody he saw as a threat but was a great pal to those who were not. The only time he met his match when he decided to take on Joey Duyts.

Joey was a great bloke and stood much taller and broader than Alfie. He accepted Alfie's challenge to a fight in the playground. Alfie was an accomplished young boxer and had never failed to defeat any school mate who wanted to challenge him (or any teacher for that matter)

What he failed to realise was that Joey's Dad was a European Wrestling Champion and had taught his son all his holds. The 'fight' was over in a matter of seconds. Joey got a headlock on Alfie from which there was no escape. Typical of all the lads at Hackney Downs in those days there was never any animosity in their fights for supremacy and he and Joey became the best of friends. It was difficult not to be a good friend of both of them and virtually all the other boys that made up the 'Class of 51'.

(Alfie's tale is well told in his Autobiography '**Alfie's Yidl'**)

A group of us lads – Me; Derek Dear; Bob Solomon; Peter Mundy; Joey Duyts; Tony Goran; and others linked up with some of the lads from the flats that had been built at Stamford Hill to replace the houses that had been flattened in wartime bombing and formed 'Ravensdale FC'.

When we were 14 years old we entered our team in the Hackney and Leyton Football League. It was a league for adult players in 5 Divisions that played on one of the multitude of football pitches that were on Hackney Marshes. 112 small football pitches with about 8 paces between the touchline of one and that of another.

We had played school games of football against other 14 year olds and could match them in physical size and power but we completely failed to realise that most teams in Division Five we had entered were filled with middle aged chaps who met at the pub and had a game of football on a Sunday morning. Their figures and fitness were not conducive to running around much so they just ran straight through us lads kicking us up in the air at every opportunity.

We went 4 games and were black and blue before we scored a goal. Our first goal was in a 13-4 defeat, however we stuck at it and even managed to win a few games before the season ended. The following year we won promotion and the year after that in which we also made it through to the Final of the Cup competition and the Hare and Hounds Football 'stadium' in Leyton.

Life was indeed great, lots of Football throughout the winter months and in summer I made up the side in an Adult's Cricket team playing on company pitches in and around London. Life was good but now looming ahead at school was the GCEs.

The General Certificate of Education was a National Examination taken at about the age of 16. The 'O' Level (Ordinary) was recognised at that time by prospective employers as a level of academic prowess of reasonable (employable?) standard. The 'A' level in the 1950s was recognised as a level of outstanding academic prowess.

It is sad that these levels have been distilled over the years since then by the need for governments to keep young people at college or university to keep them off the politically sensitive Unemployment Register. Thus standards dropped and more and more students made it to University. Such was the determination of the Governments from Thatcher onwards that virtually everybody passed the GCE at 'A' Level and nefarious subjects were invented for them to study at University.

I was put in for 5 'O' Level subjects – Maths; English Language; History; Geography; and Art.

Unfortunately a week or so before the first exam absolute tragedy descended on our family.

The news we had been dreading about my Dad's illness was confirmed a week before the exams.

I adored my father. Fate had thrown an awful lot of bad turns on him and yet he still turned up cheerful and caring every day.

Dad had suffered back pains for many years and they were getting more and more severe. At first it was thought that they might be caused by the fact that the workers making baskets in the National Institute for the Blind Workshops sat on the floor all day with the wooden pallet on which they made the baskets on their laps.

When that prognosis failed to fit the pattern of the pain it was diagnosed as lumbago and treated with heat plasters across his back. Dad continued working 8 hours a day at the Workshops but the pain was getting acute. He was admitted to the London Hospital for an exploratory investigation.

Julia had joined the Army a couple of years previously and was tele-printing messages for them from their base high up in Edinburgh Castle in Scotland. I was aged 16 in the 5th form at Hackney Downs Grammar School and Mum was scrubbing the floors of the local shops to keep a roof over our heads and food on the table.

Mum never discussed Dad's illness with me and if she did harbour fears that it might be cancer she never shared them with me. She had a habit of trying to protect her children from the unpleasant parts of life and not burden them with worry.

All of which heightened the immense shock I had when I came home from school in May 1956 to find my mother sobbing in uncontrollable grief. She had obviously been sobbing her heart out all day. When I tried to establish what had gone wrong she was incoherent as she broke down in uncontrollable tears each time she spoke.

I eventually got the news out of her that they had opened up Dad's chest to find acute cancer that had spread to every part of his body and that he only had 6 months to live.

They had no alternative but to sew him back up and he would be sent home as soon as possible to spend the rest of his days at home.

The news completely stunned me. The father I adored had cancer! The father I adored was going to die within 6 months. I had never even given the possibility a thought. I had never realised the complaint was serious.

Mother was inconsolable from that moment until long after he had died. There was no-one else at home so I had to try to figure out how to handle this news and what all the ramifications would be. It was no use me breaking down in tears. If I did then no-one would be capable of even the simplest decision or action.

It seemed Mum had not discussed the possibility of cancer with Dad and forbade me from telling him or discussing it and the outcome with him. We were thus forced to carry out a pretext that all was well and that he was getting better even though we could see him deteriorating and wasting away before our eyes.

This was very difficult for 16 year old me. Dad and I had always discussed everything. We had a wonderful open relationship of father and son and now I must lie to him for the rest of his life.

After a week or so dad came home from hospital but the operation had left him incapable of working and so he was at home full time. Mum continued scrubbing floors – now our only income – and I attended school.

Mum still couldn't cope and burst into tears whenever she was in the house and out of Dad's hearing. She tried to put on a brave face when in the room with him but more often than not had to leave the room whilst she sobbed her heart out in the Scullery. It was left to me to try to keep everything together.

Dad's pain got acute and the only painkiller the Doctor prescribed at that time was Aspirin.

Aspirin verses cancer was no contest and my poor father suffered immensely. The worst day of all for me was when I was alone at home with him (as was often the case) and he was being hit with severe pain. I gave him as many Aspirins as was allowed but they did little to quell the pain. I helped him upstairs where he could lie on the bed in the hope that position would ease the pain. I sat with him and watched his features wracked with pain and him groaning in agony.

Dad never wanted me to see his pain and suggested I left him on the bed and returned downstairs to my homework. I insisted on giving him his white walking stick (carried by blind people) so that he could tap on the floor if he needed me.

I sat downstairs at a loss to know what to do when I heard the rapid taps from upstairs. I rushed upstairs. Dad was in severe pain and neither of us could do a thing to ease it. The situation lasted hours and when Mum came home she couldn't handle it and couldn't even bring herself to go upstairs and see if Dad was alright – that was left to me to do.

That day was the most traumatic day of my life.

Dad survived the day somehow and Mum managed to get a bed for him in St Joseph's Hospice in Mare Street Hackney.

I had never heard of Hospices or the wonderful work they do as they nurse the dying. Had I done so I would have moved heaven and earth to get Dad into one and spare him all the intense suffering I was witnessing every day.

St Joseph's Hospice were able to dispense much stronger pain killers and the difference in my Dad was immense. The relief he got from being out of the worst of the agonies made him realise that the Hospice would be his last place of living.

At long last he and I could talk openly about his disease and how Mum and I were going to manage after he had died. His whole body language showed what a relief this was to him and on occasions during my visits he would return to the merry joking, caring father I had known and loved all my life.

Dad had been given 6 months to live but had lasted a year at home despite the intensity of his suffering and was to last another 5 weeks at St Joseph's Hospice. My visits were generally on my own with mother rarely visiting him at the Hospice. Just before he died my sister Julia got compassionate leave from the army and joined me on my last few visits.

I knew his end must be coming very close with a week or so to go when a putrid smell came up from deep within him on every breath. It was as though his inside had died, but still I loved him dearly and was able to laugh and smile when with him to give him all the happiness I could and to show I was strong enough to take the shock of what was to come.

On the 7th July 1957 my Dad died.

Mum came with me to see his body in the Hospice's Chapel of Rest. It was the first time I had seen a dead body and it was my father – his face at long last free of the intense pain he had suffered over the last few years of his life.

Mum again fell to pieces in her grief. She collapsed on dad's body – stroking his dead face and kissing him.

I didn't know what to do.

Instinctively I felt that mother needed to show her grief in this way but was stymied when she tried to get in the coffin with him. She didn't succeed but continued to kiss and stroke his face.

She wouldn't come away from his coffin.

Eventually I was able to succeed in steering her out of the Chapel of Rest and onto the bus home she still in floods of tears the whole way home.

It had been traumatic.

I told the Hospice (what would we have done without them in those last few weeks of Dad's life?) that I would come in and confirm the funeral arrangements. Mum was together sufficiently to come with me to the Co-operative Funeral Services to arrange the funeral.

The funeral was another traumatic day.

We had two cars for family and relatives. Julie was home from the Army and she, Mum and I shared one car. Mum was in tears from the start and that set Julia off. Auntie May joined in. Someone had to remain intact to get mourners through the funeral and there was no-one seemingly capable but Terry Gasking!

When Dad's coffin was lowered into the ground, Mum wanted to get in the hole with him. Again holding Mum firmly I was able to eventually lead her back to the cars and back home.

It had all been a truly horrific experience!

When the day was over I realised that I had not had a single opportunity to shed a tear for the dad I loved so much.

*

Poverty to Peaches

CHAPTER Six
National Service

I had left school immediately after I had sat my GCE 'O' Level exams and got a job. Julia was in the Army and had a nice posting in Edinburgh Castle in Scotland so we didn't see much of her in this period. The pay I would now earn would have so improved the life of Mum and Dad after all their financial deprivation to keep me at school but that was now shot to pieces by the grim news of dad's cancer.

As a 16 year old it all seemed so unfair to my lovely Dad.

I guess it still does but it doesn't rankle so badly now I have learned that life was never meant to be fair. We all have our own journey to complete be it bumpy or smooth – or in Dad's case be it a severely rocky ride through life. Yet he never complained or moaned about his situation – blind, deaf in one ear – extremely poor – and now cancer.

What was I going to do for work? All I had ever wanted to do was to be a professional Footballer and latterly – a professional Cricketer. Two of my friends - Alan and Ronnie Harris - had been signed up by Chelsea so if it happened to them why not me.

We had all played together since primary School (10 years old) in the evenings and on Sunday mornings on Clapton Common until they went to Eton Manor (one of the top sports clubs in East London) and we played in the Hackney & Leyton League. I did not consider them to be better footballers than me but acknowledged that at 2 years younger Ronny was already at our standard.

Poverty to Peaches

They continued playing in our knock up teams on a Sunday morning and brought a friend from Chelsea boys with them – Terry Venables. In those days sliding tackles were allowed and providing you took the ball first you could also slide through the player. Young Ronny was not spared such tackles and no wonder he matured into the superb player known as Chopper Harris. As teenagers there was nothing 'chopper' about him and all three were as nice a trio of lads you could ever wish to meet and play football with.

However one Monday morning one of them reported into Chelsea with an injury sustained from an over-vigorous tackle on the Sunday morning and Chelsea immediately banned their involvement with us.

At Cricket I had passed on from the Men's team I had played in since a 12 year old and further through Roy Ralph's (the Essex Leg-spinner) old club and onto one of the top club sides in Essex – South Woodford.

South Woodford had a superb batting track and this created a real challenge for a leg-spin bowler in the 1950s. I could turn the ball on its surface as I could on any surface I ever played on (this is one of the great advantages of the genuine wrist spinner) but I couldn't get enough bowling to gain the accuracy of a Shane Warne.

In those days top club cricket was a series of 'friendly' matches against other top clubs from the county and surrounding counties. They started at 2 pm had tea at about 4.30pm restarted at 5pm to finish at 7pm. Invariably on the excellent wickets on which they played the team batting first would not be all out and were expected to declare at tea (hence tea time might vary a little) leaving the other side to bat for half an hour less and try to get the runs.

There thus began an era of 'keeping the runs down' rather than of 'getting the wickets'. If the side bowling first could keep the runs down to 3 or 4 an over then after 2½ hours their opponents would have to declare on about 180 to 220. A score that was catchable if you didn't lose wickets.

Sadly Club Cricket captains interpreted that as setting very defensive teams for their opening fast bowlers and keeping them bowling or bringing on similar bowlers for as long as they could. After about 2 hours the opposition would usually have scored somewhere near 140 for 2 wickets and would start to attack the bowling. With plenty of wickets in hand they could begin to take chances and try to score off balls they were previously blocking. With the score beginning to mount up quickly the captain would throw the ball to his spinner and say 'keep it tight' – the very last thing a spinner needs at that stage of the game. With all those wickets in hand bowling against batsmen who had their eye well and truly in was not an enjoyable experience.

I dropped down to the Second XI and they used me as first change bowler coming onto bowl after one of the opening bowlers had only bowled 5 or 6 overs. This was a huge success. Batsmen were still playing their way into their innings and I was able to bowl in an attacking vein. Also the contrast in the other opening bowler being fresh and fast against my slow spinners bamboozled many a batsmen and their wickets would fall. When you bowl out a team's best batsmen their score is far lower and the Second XI won most of their games. Sadly the message of how to use his spinners never got through to the First XI captain and though I continually played First XI cricket in my teens neither I nor the team had the success that was there for the taking.

About this time I picked up a book from the library 'Ten for 66 and All That' by Arthur Mailey.

Mailey was a leg-break and googly spin bowler, taking 99 Test wickets, including 36 in the 1920-21 Ashes series. In the second innings of the fourth Test at Melbourne, he took nine wickets for 121 runs, which is a record for an Australian bowler against England.

In first-class cricket at Cheltenham during the 1921 tour, he took all ten Gloucestershire wickets for 66 runs in the second innings.

He also holds the record for the most expensive bowling analysis in first-class cricket. Bowling for New South Wales at Melbourne in 1926-27 as Victoria scored the record first-class total of 1107, Mailey bowled 64 eight-ball overs, did not manage a maiden and took 4 for 362. He said that his figures would have been much better had not three sitters been dropped off his bowling -- *"two by a man in the pavilion wearing a bowler hat"* and one by an unfortunate team-mate whom he consoled with the words *"I'm expecting to take a wicket any day now."*

For me Mailey's book introduced the concept of the fiercely spinning ball reacting aerodynamically to the angle of the spin.

The spinner could make the ball drift into or away from the batsman, or dip or even hang in the air all controlled by the way he set the seam and the amount of spin he put on the ball.

This excited me beyond measure and I began to experiment with it whenever I had the chance. What a pity we didn't have cricket nets at school or at our local club in those days. My bowling practice was with an old cricket ball against a concrete wall of Grosinskey's the bakers or any other brick wall that I could chalk a wicket on and that the ball would rebound some way back to me.

Whilst still at school I used to get to cricket matches on my trusty bike. I still did the Paper Round each morning and collected the money on a Sunday morning but I had also been lucky enough to pick up the task of delivering wet fish on a Friday Evening for Cohen's the wet fish shop on Stamford Hill at the top of Olinda Road.

Poverty to Peaches

Stamford Hill had a very large Jewish Community who would not eat meat on a Friday so would order fish. With me now able to ride the shop's delivery bike Cohen's offered me the job of delivering fish to many of the houses in Stamford Hill and South Tottenham. This paid well and also gave me some great tips from the customers. It also gave me quite a few trials and tribulations as only fans of 'Open All Hours' on TV might appreciate.

I did my paper round; collected the money; and kept my fish round, and helped smoke and freshen the bloaters and kippers right up until I got my first job.

Funnily enough my first proper job came out of my Fish Round.

I have always been a talker and a regular customer on my round was a keen cricketer – playing until well into his 60s. He would always ask me how I had got on in the previous week-ends games. When he heard I was about to leave school and had a GCE in Maths and Art he suggested I try out a job as a Draughtsman. Furthermore he was the head of a small Drawing Office in Dalston. He thought he could get me a job there as a trainee draughtsman and sure enough he did.

I was pretty hopeless at the job even when spending 6 months going through the factory to learn how the product was actually made. I was still extremely shy and two married women in the factory used to love embarrassing me until my face glowed so red it could light up the whole of Dalston Waste.

I had just left an all-boy's school and had only ever wanted to be a sportsman. I had been told that girls were a complete distraction and would prevent you from disappearing every weekend to play sport – so there was no room for girls in my life.

I feel sure my embarrassment with the opposite sex was made worse by my mother's insistence that I must leave the room or go out and play every time she wanted to read the 'News of the World' to my blind father. There was obviously something very distasteful or naughty about sex and with no sex-education of any kind in those days – either in the home or at school – I thought it best to avoid girls if I was going to succeed at sport and I could see no other way of getting a life away from the poverty we had endured all our lives.

However – it is a decision I have regretted throughout my lifetime!

How those two women teased me but I had to work amongst them. I needed the job to bring money into the home and no-one was going to pay me for playing sport at that stage of my career

I was in the age group that was going to be called up for National Service so not many employers were interested in starting me – with my GCE 'O' Level Maths and Art – into a career so I was grateful to be a Trainee Draughtsman even if I didn't have a clue what I was drawing.

I still played in goal for London's Army Cadets Representative XI and Egerton Road Synagogue XI but was now captaining Ravensdale FC as an attacking wing half in the Danny Blanchflower style. Our football team was only one division below the top in the Hackney and Leyton League.

Alfie Stokes played in that league and only a year or so previously he had scored 5 goals for Spurs as they thrashed their opponents at White Hart Lane. I really was playing just one step away from the top level. I just needed an opening and I would be there – a professional footballer!

Sadly the only Football Scout I had met wasn't interested in me until I had completed my National Service. He urged me to get in touch with the pro clubs when I finished my National Service.

My dream was still alive but National Service beckoned.

National Service was a two year spell in the British Army, the Navy or the Royal Air Force. It was compulsory – originally from the age of 18 years but that date started to slip back to 19+ as the end of conscription (National Service) drew near. A few boys of that age were let off from this requirement due to advanced studies or exceptional reasons.

Conscription (National Service) was due to end in 1958 and the last age group – born July1 to September 30 1939 – were delayed without knowing when they would be 'called-up'. I was in that group.

Dad had died. Mum was a widow still unable to cope on her own, either emotionally or financially. Julia was now out of the Army with a compassionate discharge just before Dad died and had since auditioned and been selected as a member of a dancing troupe playing the U.K. Theatres.

I was lucky enough to be used as an unpaid 'Net Bowler' by Essex County Cricket Club Nets between my Sunday Morning paper round collection and my afternoon cricket matches. I was thus hoping that given enough bowling I could get the wickets and break into County Cricket despite Essex already having a leg-spinner in Roy Ralph. I was also developing into quite a good middle-order batsman.

Everything seemed to be developing along the right lines and then my 'Call-Up Papers' arrived!

The wage paid to National Servicemen was a pittance and certainly not enough to keep up the regular money I was giving my mother to help her pay the bills and make ends meet now she was a widow. She did get a state pension but this had been reduced to 52/- a week (£2.60 in new money) because Dad had been unable to work in the last year of his life and thus make the necessary National Insurance Contributions in the 13 months he was dying of Cancer.

I therefore signed on for 3 years in the Royal Air Force.

This made me a 'regular' and earned a wage. By sending half my wage home Mum was kept from starvation and I could retain a level of income that was just below the level the National Servicemen earned.

The Royal Air Force fed you, billeted you, gave you a uniform to wear, and provided lots of sporting facilities for your free time. I still hadn't got over my intense embarrassment with girls so they didn't feature in my spending plans so I could exist on less than a National Serviceman wage.

It wasn't that I was rejecting girls – it was just the intense problem about how you ask a girl to make love to you. In the days before 'Women's Lib' boys were expected to make all the running in the 'chat-up' stakes. As a frustrated 18 year old making love to girls, or even a girl, was something I longed to do but just didn't have a clue how to ask.

1958 was just before the 'swinging 60s' and the invention of 'the Pill' that liberated girls and allowed them to have sex without the very real risk of an unwanted pregnancy. Previous to the sixties girls were taught to so NO and I didn't know any technique that might make them say YES!

The sort of girls I wanted to go out with at that time were not the sort to take the lead in sexual adventures. They wanted the opportunity to say NO and maybe say it a number of times before they might say YES. Sadly I never had the courage to get to the first NO let alone get to a YES - so there was I called up into HM Forces still a virgin.

At home throughout my childhood and youth I had always been sent out to play when Mum wanted to read the News of the World to Dad and then the paper was hidden away to make sure I couldn't find it and read it. Sex was never discussed or even mentioned when I was around and there was no sex education either in the home or at school.

I had been to a boy's school and my spare time had always been devoted to Football and Cricket in my quest to use those sports to get out of poverty. Some of the boys at school seemed to have advanced (well advanced when compared with my total lack of knowledge) knowledge of sex and would talk about it to us uninitiated and that gave us the theory but it was a long way from having the practice to put that theory into practice with a real live girl! Like many other lads at that time I had to resort to self-masturbation when I felt desperate.

I hoped that service in HM Forces would give me the chance to meet the girl who would initiate me into the joys of sex. I am sure I did meet a number who would have if I had had the courage to ask them. Somehow my courage always let me down and I 'made my excuses and left' to get to the sports field and training.

After collecting my Uniform at Cardington (Near Bedford) and completing my 8 weeks of 'Square-bashing' (Drilling to perfection!) at Bridgenorth (Warwickshire) I was posted for 3 months Trade Training at Brampton in Huntingdonshire. Although I now ate regularly they couldn't find a uniform to fit my minute waste-line left waste by years of undernourishment and the only way I could go in shirtsleeve order was to hitch the clasp at the top of my trousers into the first hoop made to take a belt.

The RAF (Royal Air Force) had decided to train me as a Tracer (Photographic Interpreter). This suited me ideally. I had always loved maps and as a teenager after I purchased my bike I had navigated myself all over Epping Forest with the use of one old battered map and never got lost or seemingly took the wrong turning.

Now I was to be given maps of various parts of the world where the RAF were overflying with powerful cameras aboard their jets. The photos would come down to me and a number of other Tracer (P.I.s) and we would plot their exact position on the maps. By overlapping two photos we could use a pair of spectacles on a frame about 8 inches above the photos we could get a 3-D effect to enhance the accuracy of our plotting and help the P.I.s interpretation of the photographs.

Mum was unhappy with me going into the forces (the RAF) as it meant I would be away from home for most of the time from now on. Julia was away touring in Reviews in different Theatres and prior to my call up I had tried to give Mum a bit of company by being at home during the week and not going out to enjoy myself. Sport was still my great passion but apart from the Boxing Club and 5-a-side football in a floodlit school playground once or twice a week there was nothing for me to do in the winter evenings.

I picked up a book in the local library that I believe was called 'How to Read Hands' by Mir Basher BA. I had been brought up to totally disbelieve anything about the afterlife, mediums, communicating with the dead, fortune telling, or any other supernatural possibility. I was therefore intrigued that a seemingly educated man with an BA could write a book on 'How to Read Hands'.

A great wheeze crossed my mind that might solve the problem that was ever with me – how to get myself laid!

By now I was beginning to be able to talk to girls without blushing profusely but how could I communicate well enough with attractive young ladies to get into their knickers? If I learnt the basics of what the lines on the hands was supposed to say I could hold a girls hands in private – tell her a load of old rubbish and who knows talk her into bed and end my embarrassing virginity – whoopee!

Then came the great problem. Throughout my life I have never been any good at basing any actions or strategy on sheer fiction or on anything that I just made up. I needed to know what the lines were supposed to say before I could develop a strategy that would bring success at long last in my longing for some kind of sexual conquest. After all I was now 18 years old and had never been laid – was this my way to open up opportunities?

I read the book not believing a word of it even though it was very interesting, particularly the way the lines intersected to tell a story but then came the RAF and a shelving of my grand strategy at least until I had finished my square-bashing and trade training.

I met Ralph Thompson at Brampton.

He was on the same trade training schedule as I and we were billeted in the same room with 4 others. Ralph was a tall (6 ft 6 inches) gentle giant of a man who lived just off Wanstead Flats not far from Hackney. He had a motor Bike and an old, powerful and majestic Jaguar car.

At Square-Bashing we were only allowed one week-end pass in the middle of the 8 weeks. At Trade Training we had most week-ends off but the cost of getting home was prohibitive until Ralph offered me a trip on the back of his motorbike. It was winter and I had my RAF Greatcoat on and wrapped around me but I froze. Every bit of me was shivering when he dropped me at the top of Lea Bridge Road, Hackney.

Mum had written to me that she had moved to a flat in Millfields Road, Hackney – round the corner from the top of Lea Bridge Road and about 3 miles from our house in Olinda Road. She hadn't told me she was thinking of moving but it was all done and dusted in the first few weeks at the start of my Trade Training.

I found the house in Millfields Road – a tall 3 story terraced house and thought Mum must have an upstairs flat. In fact she had just 2 rooms – a Living Room, a large Bedroom - and an indoor toilet shared with the adult daughter of the main tenants of the house.

This would all be hopeless for me for where would I be able to invite friends to call, and where was I to sleep? Mother had rigged up a curtain across the middle of the bedroom to give each of us some privacy and thought it would be ok.

I began to remonstrate when I realised that mother had pretty well lost it emotionally. She just kept saying that she couldn't live in Olinda Road on her own any longer. Everything reminded her of dad. She had to get out into another flat or jump in the River Lea and end it all. I really did believe that she meant it.

With just a week-end's leave there was nothing I could do to reverse her decision or to get her to hold on until I could fix up something more suitable.

The 2 rooms (flat?) had electricity and she had bought herself a small Television (all were black and white pictures in those days) and was loving her first access to TV. She had got herself a job in the launderette at the top of the road and I could see how the flat suited her so stopped any criticism and accepted the situation.

I would have to come home semi-regularly just to make sure she was ok but I would just have to sleep on the single bed in the other half of my mother's bedroom. It was not a situation I liked one little bit but I could see no alternative whilst I was still away in Huntingdonshire being trained for my trade in the RAF.

What really broke my heart was that mother had got a house clearer to clear everything she couldn't take with her from Olinda Road, and that was just about everything. I believe that the house clearer paid her £10 for everything but everything included every single memento we had of dad – photos of his stage career – billboard posters of his Music Hall Shows, programmes, his diary of bookings at theatres all over the country, his notebook of sketches he used in his concert parties, his costumes, his roll up dancing mats, his photos – everything. She had wiped my marvellous father completely out of her life without ever thinking that in doing so she had wiped every memento I had of a wonderful dad from my life.

It was another heart-breaking time for me, again leaving me with no alternative other than accepting the situation and moving forward. If I revealed my true sadness I really did think that Mother would be found floating in the River Lea.

Ralph picked me up on the Sunday Night from the same spot as he had dropped me and we had another shivering ride back to Brampton on his Motor Bike.

We were to repeat this procedure quite often until the weather turned really icy and snowy and then he would turn up in his Jaguar and a comfortable ride apart from one memorable occasion when we stopped in ice on a steep hill. His wheels were spinning without any grip and we had nothing to put under them. We came up with the grand plan that I would get out and give a push and that extra bit of momentum should just help the Jaguar to creep up the hill. It all started well enough and we were succeeding until I came to a particularly slippery piece of ice. My feet slid straight out behind me. The car stopped and started to slowly slide backward towards me. I grabbed the bumper and was almost horizontal as the car and I slowly slid back down the road – giving up the ascent we had just made.

How we got up hill in the end was beyond me but we did eventually get back to camp and on duty the following morning.

Brampton Camp had its own local radio station and the pair of us – and a number of others used to request love songs in the name of some of the lads in the accommodation block opposite dedicated to the well-known girl on camp who was the 'camp bicycle' (a Women's Royal Air Force member known for her very easy virtue) - they in turn returned the compliment so there were all sorts of embarrassed meetings going on.

Ralph worked out a cruel revenge on the block opposite. If we walked into their block last thing at night and wandered into their lavatories he could wedge the lock to that it dropped and locked the door from the outside. In this way all their toilets were locked and in the chaos of getting up the following morning there were some very uncomfortable members of the 'opposition' particularly if there had been a spicy supper the night before.

Life was therefore good and full of innocent japes. Mother's predicament worried me but I could see no alternative but for her to learn to live on her own – with occasional visits from me – and be content with her television – or get herself out to some social clubs or events.

My sister Julia had dropped out of showbiz and was living in a flat in Hunstanton, Norfolk on the east Coast of England. She apparently had a serious boyfriend – an American GI called Butch. On one of my visits home Julie was visiting Mum and called on her with Butch. My sister revealed that she was pregnant and my mother insisted that Julie must immediately leave Mum's 'flat'. Mother would not risk her Landlady knowing that Julia was pregnant and bringing disgrace on the house. It was 1958 and the world has passed by the disgrace of a child born out of wedlock but mother could not forget the disgrace of her own childhood when she was constantly called a bastard child as she was being beaten.

Julie left in tears and I walked with her back to Butch's car. I tried hopelessly to reconcile her to being *'thrown out of my mother's home in disgrace'* but did not do a very good job – how could I for I could not understand how Mother could throw them out just at the time they needed support. Butch had seemed a really nice guy and the fact that he accompanied Julie when she came to her mother to tell her of her pregnancy and their plans to marry should have reassured her if only for the length of their visit.

Poverty to Peaches

Delightedly Julia and Butch have just celebrated 50 years of marriage, have 5 great children and goodness knows how many grandchildren but oh what difficulties I had with Mum over the weeks following their visit as she suffered (or perhaps wallowed) in the imagined disgrace.

As always on my trips home I was delighted to get back on camp and on with trade training and merry japes with Ralph.

So Trade Training passed happily and we passed out as Senior Aircraftsmen – one stage up from the lowest of the low rank we had started on.

The posting to a Unit came up and both Ralph and I were posted to Northolt Airport to the west of London. It would be wonderful for getting home easily but home for me was no longer a place I really wanted to be. Mother was still in need of some emotional support and I still supported her financially with half my airman's salary but a two room flat was totally inadequate to accommodate mother and me.

Another problem revealed itself at Northolt. It was the only base in the whole of the RAF that produced and printed Airport Landing Charts for all the airports around the world that the RAF might land at.

Instead of pouring over maps and plotting Aerial reconnaissance pictures that I so enjoyed we were cutting out little bits of thin plastic showing the required circuit for an airport and sticking them on the landing charts for that location.

I realised that the work was vital but it was also terribly boring and not at all what I was hoping for when I signed on as a Tracer (Photographic Interpreter). I was thus always in trouble for talking but was pretty good at defusing situations with a comic aside or two so generally got away with my lack of application to the little bits of plastic.

Once or twice a week I would hitch hike back home for the evening to make sure Mum was ok and then return the following morning. The chances of hitching a lift in Hackney was slim so I would bus and tube to White City where a lift on vehicles going west along the A4 was relatively easy for a young guy in uniform. (In fact I eventually hitchhiked successfully to many parts of the country when a few days leave was available). My lift would drop me at the gate alongside the A4 and it was a very short walk from there to the Landing Chart Unit.

I needed something to read on the bus and tube part of the journey and remembered the book on 'How to Read Hands'. I managed to buy a copy and it was my companion on all my journeys.

Ralph got the job of Assistant Printer of the maps and collector of the clean laundry (towels for the washrooms and rags for the small printing press). These were collected from the camp laundry on the other side of the air field and somehow he managed to wangle me the task of Assistant Laundry Collector to help him carry the half a dozen or so roller towels etc.

So once a week we would stroll around the perimeter track, wait at the lights just before the landing strip as we watched the rare happening of an aircraft land or take off right in front of us before we continued on to change the laundry before gently strolling back.

On a pleasant sunny day (and Ralph was a past master at finding the need for clean towels when the sun was shining) the walk was a delight. I had never heard the joyous song of the skylark before and Northolt Airfield was a great nesting place for them so the air was full of their songs.

Our weekly walk around the airport was a joy as was the football and later the cricket played against other camps. Both Ralph and I realised we would have to gain some sort of technique if we were going to succeed with the ladies so we signed ourselves into a Dance School in Hackney for 12 weekly evening lessons in Ballroom Dancing.

We found that the RAF would let us sign ourselves onto an ONC in Mechanical Engineering Course at Walthamstow College and claim a mileage fee for getting there. As one of the nights coincided with the Dance Class we were rarely at the ONC class on those evenings. It seemed too good a wheeze to leave to Ralph alone so I bought an old 1938 Austin 10 that Ralph taught me how to drive and then also claimed mileage 3 times a week for 'attendance' at Walthamstow College. The wheeze worked hugely successful for two terms until the paymaster on camp realised that two Airman from the same barrack block were claiming mileage to attend the same college way over the other side of London and quite close to where each of us lived.

One day therefore we were summoned to the Camps Adjutants office. He had clearly seen through the wheeze and warned us that we were '*skating on very thin ice indeed*'. He let us off with just a warning but it was the end of our paid journeys home – and I hadn't even learned the Foxtrot yet!

Ralph and I still didn't have the courage to try out our Waltz, Quickstep or ChaChaCha in a real live ballroom so it was back to Plan A in my great strategy to get laid – How to Read Hands.

There were Waafs (Womens Royal Air Force} at Northolt and some mighty attractive ones too. I had now developed enough confidence to chat to them but not enough to make what I had hoped were the kind of overtures that were still expected from the man in those days to get the girl to say YES.

Now was possibly the opportunity to develop my ploy of holding their hands in a quiet corner or room somewhere – telling them a load of old rubbish under the pretence of seeing it in their hands and convincing them that their lines indicated that they should have a sexual relationship with me.

However - a problem occurred for me in my grand strategy! Before I managed to talk one of the Waafs into having her hands read some of the fellas saw the book on my desk – took the micky (for want of a stronger expression more apt to a load of Airmen at that time) and insisted I read their hands.

By then I had picked up a lot of information from the book about the meaning of the lines on the palms of the hands and even the hand shape and size. I relayed the meanings of the lines in their hands to them whilst still not believing a word of it myself. I always read the hands on a one-to-one basis without others overhearing what I had to say and it was a bit off-putting when many of the airmen would say things like *'How on earth did you know that?'* or *'that was uncanny!'*

I was forced to think hard about what I was telling them. Was it all so bland that it could happen to anyone and thus bluff them that it was true? No, most of the things I was reading in their hands were specific to the hands owners. I just didn't understand where the information was coming from other than the lines on the palms of their hands.

Eventually I managed to get the really attractive Waaf that I fancied into a quiet corner of the Naafi bar and started reading her hands. I was soon telling her how promiscuous she was as a lead-up to my hopes that she would be promiscuous with me as soon as the opportunity occurred when she flummoxed me by telling me that it was all true. She really did enjoy sex and wasn't overly worried by the identity of the man she was having sex with.

This was almost too good to be true and YES she would have sex with me. She had a week-end free in 2-weeks time. Take her somewhere for the week-end she said and she would enjoy a week-end of sex with me.

I was overjoyed! Couldn't believe my luck!

But where on earth could I take her? I couldn't possibly book us into a hotel or a bed and breakfast – I would die of embarrassment long before we got up to the bedroom. I know – I would book my mother's caravan for the weekend!

Mother had bought a very old small 2-berth in a single bed caravan from a stallholder at Ridley Road market for £25.00. We had got it towed down to a caravan site at Wheeley a few miles inshore from Clacton on the East Coast on a very inexpensive site but mother loved it and it gave her week-ends or even weeks away. It was doing a great deal to rehabilitate her.

She only used it about once or twice a month so I reckoned I could borrow it for a week-end when she wasn't using it – invite my Waaf for the weekend and my search for sexual initiation would be over.

I set it all up – telling Mum that a crowd of us boys and girls were all going away for the weekend and arranged the weekend with the consent of my Waaf.

All was going so well until my trip back home for the evening a couple of days before the scheduled ecstatic week-end. Somehow Mother had smelled a rat. Although she didn't actually spell out why she suddenly had to go down to the caravan that very same week-end that I had scheduled to have it but I couldn't help but get the feeling that she didn't want her caravan to be used as a 'knocking-shop'.

It was too late to fix up anywhere else so my Waaf and I put our week-end 'on-ice' for a week or so until I managed to fix somewhere more suitable. To my great misfortune some other feller picked her up on the week-end we should have been at the caravan and gave her such a good time that she told me I would have to wait until she had finished with him – however long that would take.

It took longer than my remaining stay at Northolt for in August 1960 – still a virgin - I was posted to RAF HQ at Monchengladbach in Germany.

*

CHAPTER Seven
RAF Germany

They shipped us by boat from Harwich to the Hook of Holland and then by train down through Holland and Belgium into Germany. I reported to my unit – HQ 2nd TAF (Tactical Air Force) and was allocated a billet in a room with just 3 others in a large accommodation block.

Next morning I reported to the office in which I was to work on the task I had been trained on – that of Tracer (P.I) to be greeted by one of the guys who I had previously met at Northolt.

'You were right', he said by way of greeting *'you got it spot on!'*

I didn't have a clue what he was talking about.

'Who'd have thought we would have had another kid? We were on the brink of splitting up when you read my hands but then along came the baby just like you said and it was a boy just as you predicted. The wife is over the moon and we are right back together again. Let me buy you a drink tonight'.

I was staggered. I had never remembered reading his hands. When I started reading palms it was all a bit of fun and I never took any of it seriously enough to remember what I had said to anyone (with the possible exception of my Waaf – for I wanted to use that ploy again!)

Before my week was out I met 2 or 3 more of my original 'victims' of my early palmistry attempts and whilst not so overwhelmingly enthusiastic they all said that things had happened to them that I had seen in their hands.

All of this was a shock to my system. I really hadn't believed in anything 'supernatural' but now folk were telling me that I had predicted events I couldn't have foreseen in the natural turn of events.

I had been brought up to believe that anything 'supernatural' was false and a con by the perpetrator. Now I seemed to be getting feedback from something that started as fun but that was now causing me to wonder if there really was anything written in the hands that could predict the future.

Before I could give time to deep and serious thought about palmistry and whether there could possibly be any truth in it I was into the thick of camp sport and an attempt to increase my 2 GCE 'O' Levels up to 5.

I had taken myself along to the camp's football training and found myself in both the Unit's football team and the camp's Representative XI. I had also signed myself onto classes for 3 GCE 'O' Levels – English Language, History and Geography, and into an Art Class.

All my evenings were therefore used up and the weekend was all football so life was brilliant.

A lot of people got me to read hands and I tried to define if there was any common theme in my readings but there was not.

It was fun but I was beginning to realise that the lines on the hand were giving me an entry into the psyche and character of the owner of the hands. It was as if their hands were the intro and they led me into somehow reading the person themselves. It was weird and difficult for me to understand how or why it happened but when I stated something about the person, their past, or a possible future event I somehow knew it was true even though the person said nothing and revealed nothing about their lives.

I was really enjoying life on camp but with Christmas coming up I thought I had better try to get home and check that mother was ok. Whilst hoping that it might be the last time I needed to provide the re-assurance she needed in life and that I could at long last get on with my own life.

I got leave just before Christmas, hitched a lift in a RAF aircraft that was flying into Manston Airport in Kent and got a rail warrant to and from London with a promise of a flight back 10 days later.

On the train to London a very pretty girl of about 17 was sitting opposite me. She had both legs in plaster apparently caused by the removal of bunions that had distorted her feet.

She was travelling back up to London after visiting her mother who was convalescing from a serious illness in the same hospital as Mum had been in all those years before. We exchanged names and addresses when the train got to London and off I went to see how Mum was fairing. That would be the 'duty' part of my visit home and might be depressing but my spirits were lifted with the thought that I could meet all my old mates from my teens.

It was great to see Ravensdale Football Club thriving. They were now playing in the league that was just one below the top Hackney and Leyton League – the best league of those playing on the 112 football, pitches on Hackney Marshes. Ravensdale FC had done really well over the years working their way up from the days when we 15 year olds were kicked straight up in the air to massive defeats in the 5th division in the days when Derek and I first started up the team.

Facilities on Hackney Marshes were a long way short of the comparative luxury I now enjoyed after a match in Germany. On Hackney Marshes all 22 players and the referee changed in the same very small dressing room that could perhaps accommodate about half that number comfortably. When you came off the pitch there was only a long trough with 4 cold water taps above it to wash the mud off the players or their kit

and you shared the trough with the players from all the other
matches

Those lucky enough to have electricity and hot water at home
could go home and shower. Those like Terry Gasking would
go home and try to scrub the mud off under a kitchen tap
churning out water as cold as the day.

In the RAF in Germany I could come off the pitch and enjoy
the sheer luxury of a hot shower and then disappear into the
washrooms of the Barrack Block with their many baths. I
could fill a bath up to the brim with piping hot water and then
lay back in it until every bit of stiffness was gone. I often fell
asleep in the bath, woke up when the water was cool, tipped
half the water out and filled it again with piping hot water – oh
such joy for a lad that had never experienced hot water in his
house in the 19 years prior to his National Service.

At Christmas Mum was much perkier. She had made friends
with a number of people down on the caravan site including a
pharmacist who took her out for the occasional inexpensive
meal.

I was beginning to think life was really good. My dreams of
stardom at Football and Cricket were still alive – inspired by
the fact that Ronny and Alan Harris had now made Chelsea's
first team and I knew they were not that far in advance of me
in skill or endeavour the last time we all played together. After
National Service I would try to get a trial with the top teams.

So I caught the flight back to Germany in a happy mood. On
getting back to HQ I was immediately given a funeral duty to
perform. A RAF family was getting all their decorations up
for Christmas when their very young son decided to help Mum
and Dad blow up the balloons. He had sucked in instead of
blowing out and the balloon chocked him to death. I was one
of the two coffin bearers at the boy's funeral and the distress
and feelings of guilt of the parents was heart-rendering.

Thankfully I got back into my football training very rapidly and into my studies for 3 GCEs. If I could pass the exams these would bring me up to the minimum acceptable standard to get a decent job should my sporting ambitions fail.

I had always resisted smoking and drinking as they were reputed to have a very adverse effect on a person's fitness to succeed at sport and – as hard as I tried not to be – I was still a virgin! Contemplating all this after one of my long and wonderful soaks in a bath – I walked back into my billet to be greeted with

'Terry – we need you! Please don't say no! I am playing the front end of the Donkey in the Camp's Pantomime and the back end has injured himself and has dropped out. It is on in two-week's time and we are desperate for a back-end!'

I didn't like the connotations of the words used by my billet mate for though I was still a virgin I had never fancied or participated at any homosexual activity but I realised his plea was genuine and the Pantomime really was short of the back-end of the Donkey.

Always being a lad that could not resist a challenge I became the back end of the donkey. The pantomime was 'Son of Ali' and had been written by the wife of an Air Commodore (one of the very top operational brass in the RAF) who was based at 2nd TAF. His wife therefore directed the pantomime based on the fictitious son of Ali Baba and great fun it was.

My front-end and I rehearsed a few steps and rehearsed a run across the stage being chased by the two Villains. We had to stop centre stage whilst the front-end spoke a few lines to get the children warning us if they see the Villains approaching when the Director decided that the front-end did not have a loud enough voice to be heard under the donkeys head so got us to swap over.

It was an inspired swap. I have been a talker all my life and captained umpteen football teams that needed me to get my voice heard all over the pitch whilst my pal was the cleverest back-end you could ever wish to see. He could pick up my moves when we were being chased and add all kinds of funny steps.

The result was that at the dress rehearsal the Director had us going down the side steps of the theatre stage (and it was a proper theatre at HQ 2ndTAF) and across the front of the audience, being chased by the Villains and then back up the steps on the other side of stage before rushing off the stage to safety.

Well – the children in the audience so enjoyed the donkey, screamed and shouted with glee when it made its entrance and got so involved in the chase by the two incompetent villains that by the Saturday of the week's run the Villains would chase the donkey all over the stage and fall over him as they tried to catch the animal. The Donkey then took off down the steps at the side of stage rushed up the aisle between the seats, stopped for a breather half way up; sat down and started talking to whatever group of children I could spot, whilst they were jumping up and down with concern that the Villains were catching up with us – before we tore off up the aisle just before the villains got to us. With them falling over as they tried to catch the donkey we had time to repeat the trick along the top cross-aisle and again on the way down the other aisle and back onto the stage. Throughout all of this my back-end was brilliant and his antics got roars of laughter from the adults in the audience whilst their children were enrapt in the fate of the donkey.

You will have gathered from all of this that the back-end and I – neither of whom had ever been on stage before – had so much fun that week that we thought we would add the weekly play-readings into our already crowded schedule of studies, sports and pastimes.

I was particularly hooked as in the pantomime we had doubled as guards in one scene where the donkey was not involved.

There was panic at the Palace and the lead playing the Maharajah called out the guard –

'Guards, guards – call out the guards. We need the guards – plenty of guards' whereupon I was given the line

'These are all the guards we got (there were just two of us – my back-end and I now dressed as guards) *we ain't got no more!'*

Now this line did not seem to any of us in the pantomime to be funny, it was just a throwaway line to add to the forthcoming pandemonium. However Bernard Bresslaw was playing a bit of an idiot in the Army game at that time, speaking in a slow idiot type voice and I imitated his accent and delivery.

The Maharajah would panic and call out the guard, all eyes would turn on the two of us and I would put the most puzzled, dopey look on my face that I could muster, turn slowly to look at my pal, then back to the audience and deliver my line deadpan. For some completely unknown reason the audience fell about laughing to such a degree that it was minutes before – still with a perplexed look on my face I would lead the pair of us slowly off stage. Incredibly the audience gave us a huge spontaneous round of applause every night – and that is all we had to do. What fun!

As the week developed the whole of the cast knew what was coming when my line was due and they were all looking upstage at me waiting for me to speak as I looked at the other guard and back to the audience before speaking. From the Wednesday I noticed that they were all corpsing (desperately trying to stifle their giggles as they had their back to the audience some shaking with laughter) long before I was ready to speak. It was getting more and more difficult for my pal and

I to keep such gormless expressions but somehow we managed it all week.

Gosh – is it any wonder that I was so immediately hooked on the fun of amateur drama and became a member of the camp's drama group.

On the Sunday morning at the end of the Pantomime the Producer/Director threw a party for all the cast. It was a super time and as my back-end and I were treated by everyone in the cast as though we very special – probably for the first time in my life - I fell for temptation had my first drink of alcohol.

The drink was flowing and somehow my glass kept getting filled. It was a great couple of hours. When we came away from the theatre the cold air hit us and our legs just wouldn't go in the direction we thought they were pointing. I recall making our way back down the road to our billet, walking in the kerb one moment and crashing into my chum in the middle of the road the next. As hard as I tried I just could not stop this happening.

When I got back to my billet some of the guys reminded me I was playing football for the camp's team that same afternoon and started pouring coffee down me in an attempt to get me sober. They then got me to the game and explained what had happen to the team's manager and coach. He said that the match was only a friendly to try out some new players so I shouldn't worry – just go on and play my normal game.

He had me playing Centre Half, not my favourite position even though in the ordinary course of events I could organise a defence very efficiently. I did manage to get through the 90 minutes and didn't think I played too badly. However it turned out that the opposing centre forward scored 5 goals, 2 of which were scored whilst I was flat on my back having missed a tackle.

When I had sobered up – long after the game – I feared that was the end of my playing for the Camp team. However at the next training session the coach was a delight. He impressed on me the need to make sure I never get into that state again and in the 62 years since I have enjoyed many a drink but never more than the rule of 3 – I never want to be so out of control again. He also said that he and his family had been at the Pantomime on the Friday Night and had never enjoyed a show as much. His kids could speak of nothing but the Donkey all the next day and the guard was the funniest thing he had seen in a long time.

So I had got away with it. I couldn't wait to act in another play – but drinking myself to obscurity – never again!

The GCE lectures were on 3 evenings every week and the Art Class and Drama Group Meetings would often be on the same evening. Football training was between 5 – 7pm and if I cut short my wallow in the bath I could get to most of the GCE classes apart from Geography. I could also often go on to catch the back half of the Art Class.

I was very lucky in that a guy in another billet in the same accommodation block was attending the same classes. He collected the lecture notes and homework papers on the many nights I missed class and we would find ourselves in the most peaceful room in the block - the room the guys stored all their bags and cases that would otherwise clutter up their billets.

In the quiet of the very small Baggage Room we would spend an hour or so whilst Alex would take me through the course papers. It was so very kind of him and although he swore it helped him as much as it helped me his help was invaluable as I would have been lost in all 3 subjects if he hadn't helped.

I was ever grateful to him for keeping me in touch with all the subjects and particularly in Geography (I almost never got to Geography Class after joining the Drama Class).

Occasionally after my match and my wallow in the bath on a Saturday we would meet up in the Baggage Room to go through the papers. Alex would often suggest we catch the bus and spend the rest of the evening in Monchengladbach.

There was a bar that also served snacks and had an anti-room full of one-arm bandits. The bar was opposite the local brothel and I believe both were popular with the British Forces serving in and around the town. There was often a queue of men waiting outside the door of the brothel and I asked of Alex in all innocence what they were queuing for.

Alex couldn't believe I didn't know. When he explained what a Brothel was I said '*Oh you mean a Broffel*'

'*What the hell is a broffel?*' asked Alex.

'*A place where men go for exactly the same thing as that lot are queuing for!*'

'*That's called a Brothel – not a broffel you cockney idiot!*'

All my sex education had come from my friends at school in the East-End of London and the boy who knew enough about such things had obviously pronounced it his cockney accent as Broffel and Broffel it stayed in the minds of all us boys until we were corrected sometime later in life. I wondered how many other names were corrupted by my mixture of Cockney and Welsh accent.

The Brothel was not for us and whilst Alex and I were sitting at a table having a drink and a snack I noticed that he kept his eyes fixed on the annex that contained the slot machines. He would suddenly get up and go play a certain machine. Usually within just a few minutes the machine would make a big pay-out. He would then return, stack up the coins between us and carry on with the conversation as though nothing had happened.

He would do this half a dozen times during the evening and always won enough to pay the entire costs of the meal and drinks we had consumed and the fares on the bus home and still had some left over. He is the only man I have ever known who genuinely came out on top of one-arm bandits. Everyone else I've known would talk with delight about a good pay-out they had but inevitably they had put or would put far more back into the machines.

Alex had the eye of a shrewd investor rather than a gambler though he did get invited to play cards with the hard core of RAF Police in their Friday night session. Alex had been a Cinema projectionist before his call up into National Service and had been made a typist in the Police Section by the RAF. He had played cards all through his childhood but swears he had never seen the version of Bragg the Police were playing. I guess it made them all the keener to fleece the newcomer to the camp who was an innocent National Serviceman.

Alex asked if he could watch for a little while to pick up how the game was played and then he would like to join in. They asked him if he had any money and he put all the cash he had on the table. They couldn't wait to get him into the game.

As Midnight passed Alex was more than £100 up – a lot of money to a National Serviceman in 1961. They insisted he must play on and give them the chance to win their money back. By 1 am Alex was nearly £200 up. By 2am he was more than £250 up and when the game packed up some time after 3 am Alex had taken just over £340.00 from them. The card school never let him play again and the members never again spoke to him.

Alex and I lost touch as soon as our Service days ended but I do hope he kept up his winning ways. I look out for him whenever I pass the Poker Channel on TV but so far I have never seen him. I hope he turned his unique talent to investments and is living a life of luxury somewhere. Without him I wouldn't have stood a chance in my GCEs.

I had landed a part in the 2nd TAF HQ's Drama Club's next production – an Australian drama that the producer thought would suit its entry into the drama festival. The Festival included drama productions on all the RAF and British Army camps and establishments in Germany and throughout Europe.

I found it surprisingly easy to learn the words of my part and would walk around camp repeating aloud the dialogue that everyone would use when I was due on stage. The adjudicator said some very nice things about us all in the play but 2 weeks later we were knocked into a cocked hat by the brilliance of the Army HQ performance of Thornton Wilder's 'Our Town'

The lead was taken by a young National Service Officer who was a professional actor, appearing in a number of TV shows before his 'call-up' into the forces. He and the production were brilliant and won the Festival by a mile.

Besides admiring the production I found 'Our Town' resonated deeply with me.

As a kid when I was about 7 or 8 years old I used to dream quite often about a house with long corridors and rooms going off each side of the corridors. There were very many rooms and individuals looking quite normal would occasionally enter or leave a room somewhere along the corridor.

Somehow I knew the 'person' I could see acting quite normally and walking into a room was in fact the soul of the recently dead and the persons leaving a room was the soul of a person who had died some time ago and who was now making his/her/its way back to the Earth in a different body.

I have no idea where these dreams came from or why I was certain of my interpretation – it certainly wasn't from my upbringing or education - but they were hugely realistic and not at all scary. Furthermore I knew the reason they were returning to earth was because they had not passed their examinations (finding the meaning of life) first time.

Remember this had nothing to do with school exams or GCE's for I was only 7 and 8 years old and had never heard of such things. I had no books so had never read of such happenings or theories – they were just a regular dream.

Poverty to Peaches

From my dreams, even at that age, I was sure that life on earth was just one part of a soul's journey through the Universe.

Planet Earth was Class One – the kindergarten (pre-school). The difference from school was that you had to pass all parts of the examinations before you could move up to the next class that was somewhere else in the vastness of the universe.

That is what the rooms in my dreams were for. They were the place where your soul reviewed and discussed your recent life on earth and learned from your failures.

Your soul would then go back into another body on earth, start all over again, and try to get it right next time around.

You would keep doing this until you finally achieved a life when you attempted to bring peace love and joy to all around you and those you met throughout your life – treating them all with kindness and love. Only then could you move on to class two but that was on another planet somewhere in the vastness of the Universe as you moved up in the soul's great progression.

The dreams have stayed at the back of my mind all my life and were hugely reinforced when I first saw the night sky on a clear night well away from street lighting.

The stars were dazzling and there are billions of them. No-one could convince me that they were only there to look pretty or be the source of love songs for us down on this small planet of ours. We don't even rate as bright enough to be seen as the millions of stars that are shining down on us. How many of them are surrounded by planets with people looking down at our sun and wondering if there could be people on the planets that surround it?

Every time I look at the sky on a clear night my dreams are reinforced and now here is Thornton Wilder giving a theatrical depiction of precisely the same thing.

Our father's house does indeed have many rooms!

So we got to the end of the football season.

The Unit Team I captained had won the league and were runners up in the cup. We shared the celebrations with our closest rivals but when the cup came around full of drink my mind reverted to the morning after the Pantomime and I found it relatively easy to turn down a drink from the trophy.

The GCE exams came up and I had a problem because the Geography Teacher refused to put me in for the Geography exam.

I protested to the Education Officer who also taught us English language and had been such a great help to my spelling. He had taught me to speak to myself each difficult word I was going to use in a way the slowly pronounced each syllable. I then spelt each syllable as I wrote it and joined up the syllables to make the word. It had worked very well. It didn't help me when my pronunciation of a word was wrong (e.g. broffel until Alex corrected me) but it surely helped my spelling.

It also made me realise the way to tackle any complex problem was to break it down into its constituent parts whilst keeping the overall goal in mind and solve each of those one at a time and then co-ordinate all your solutions.

Hence it led to the joined-up life of Terry Gasking.

The Education Officer listened to my plea that 40% of the marks in the Geography Exam came from the Map question and with my background and trade (Tracer P.I.) I was very confident of getting all or nearly all of that correct. I only needed 7% from the rest of the paper and I would pass the Geography Exam. The Education Officer overruled the heated protest from the Geography Teacher and put me into the exam.

I was delighted to reward his kindness by passing all 3 Subjects – English Language, History and Geography.

With the 2 subjects I had already passed at Hackney Downs Grammar School I now had passes at 5 'O' Level GCEs.

This had been the level teachers there were trying to get us 'C' stream boys at Hackney Downs Grammar School to aspire to. I felt my first ever sense of pride at what was for me was an academic achievement that was thought during my childhood and youth by all of us in the family to be completely out of reach of Terry Gasking.

Summer was approaching and the camp had erected some cricket nets. I bowled leg-spin and was a prodigious spinner of the ball. I didn't have the control of many of the world's leading wrist spinners and have often wondered if I would have acquired that had Nets been readily available to me in my youth. Nevertheless I could impart as much spin on the ball as any of them. In all my senior club and RAF Cricket Teams the Wicket Keepers and slips would tell me that they could hear the ball fizzing as it spun through the air.

I thought it would be great fun to see if I could make the ball drift in the way the book *'10 for 66 and all that'* had described. So I spent many hours with 2 or 3 balls in the nets trying to do just that.

The skills I learned in the Cricket Nets in Germany took me into the RAF Cricket Team in Germany and introduced me to a way of life, confidence and companionship with people of a class I never thought I would ever mix with or could aspire to.

The skills of a quality spinner have eluded the understanding of English Cricketers for generations. I hope somebody persuades the members of the current 'top team in the world' to take this book on their next trip and to read the pages that follow at the end of this chapter. Only then might we see an end to the absolute fiasco we witnessed against Pakistan in Dubai in 2012.

By the end of 1961 I had played in nearly all the RAF Germany matches, was their chief wicket taker. Though I was still a lowly SAC in rank (one off the bottom rung) I mixed with ease and joy with the officers and senior managers who accompanied the team as well as those who were involved with the drama group.

Little Tel from 'ackney Downs – now a not so little Terry Gasking after a decade of school dinners followed by 3 years of regular meals and exercise in the RAF - I had shot up to 6 feet tall –was for the first time in life at ease with anyone I met at any level of society.

Cricket had been a vital part of making this happen.

More wickets followed in the next match and then we had a great trip to Berlin, then still a garrison town before the Berlin Wall was built. We travelled by train along the Allies Corridor that I had seen so often on the Ariel photos I had traced for the P.I.s to check Russian Troop Movements.

I had new papers produced for the journey and was shown as a Clerk. Apparently if my true trade of Tracer (Photographic Interpreter) was shown there was a very real danger that I would have been arrested as a spy by the Russians or East Berliners.

I was flattered that the RAF gone to such trouble for a lowly SAC and was beginning to realise that I might be an essential part of the full RAF Germany team. With most team games and particularly with cricket - rank and file don't come into it. If you have the ability and sufficient civility you are treated as an equal to anyone in the team – be they Squadron Leaders, Air Commodores, Flying Officers or lowly SACs. You don't get the best out of your bowlers by demeaning their rank or your batsmen by undermining their confidence. Fielders will not bust-a-gut to catch a ball or cut off a boundary if they pull rank so the RAF Team really was a team even though it contained ranks from Squadron Leader down to two of us SACs.

The Air Commodore who travelled with us was also part of the team and as easy to talk and laugh with as anybody else. This was a revolution in my thinking and self-esteem and I cannot thank those guys enough for 'taking me aboard' their social as well as cricketing company.

We had a night out at the funfare and onto a nightclub (my first time ever!) in Berlin and I was overwhelmed by how attractive all the girls were. Most of them were on the arms of scruffy men and I couldn't understand how they could pull such attractive girls whilst I was still waiting to lose my virginity.

It turned out that job prospects were very low in a Berlin at that time. It was surrounded on all sides by land that was garrisoned with tanks and troops from East German and Russian so most West Berlin families sent their sons out of Berlin and into Western Germany to study and live. Hence at that time there were approximately 25 girls in the 18 to 30 year old bracket for every chap. The girls had to dress to the nines just to get a feller.

I made a mental note of that statistic and thought that I would spend my next leave in Berlin before my 3 year stint in the RAF was over – that surely would end my virginity!

Alas within one month of our visit they built the Berlin Wall and that was the end of yet another opportunity to get laid.

It was a good match in Berlin – played right alongside the Olympic Stadium with the ghosts of Jesse Owen and Hitler rallying the Germans to his views. We played against the Combined British Forces in Berlin and it was one of the few matches we lost. I got a couple of wickets in each of the two days but also distinguished myself in a last wicket stand with the skipper in the first innings that got us out of deep trouble.

Back at camp and into the Tracer (P.I.) unit I was beginning to get into trouble again for talking. I could not see (and still cannot) why you can't natter away as you are plotting Aerial photos, why must it be done in silence? I was as quick and as accurate as anyone else in the Unit. When we were asked to plot the 'bombing raids; of the competition of all the crack squadrons in NATO I had been the first to discover what bridges on the Keele Canal the Crack allied airforce teams had actually 'bombed' (i.e photographed on a simulated bombing raid). Often the bridge they had was 4 or 5 bridges up or down the canal and miles from their original target. Don't let anyone ever convince you that Aerial bombing is accurate. These were Nato's crack squadrons making bombing runs when nobody was shooting at them. Goodness knows how inaccurate they were in war but then again the misinformation pushed out by governments would never let us know!

We shared the PI unit with the Army and they had a far more rigorous discipline than the RAF. The RAF officers tolerated my natterings and were often amused by them – I have always had a rapid sense of gentle humour – but the Army commander of the Unit decided to discipline me for talking.

'We need to see some work coming out of that desk' he said *'We have had enough of you disappearing for 4 days a time to play cricket* (all our RAF matches were over 2 days and we needed a day to travel to the match and a day to return so my unit only saw me for one day a week most weeks). *'It's time you did your share of work. You will not be released for the next cricket match and maybe the one after that and the one after that'*.

I felt that was unnecessarily harsh. I was still one of the fastest at tracing the location of the Ariel photos and plotting them and since Gary Powers had been shot down by the Russians in his U2 the amount of Aerial Photos coming into the unit had halved.

I phoned the Air Commodore who managed the RAF Cricket Team in Germany and gave him my apologies that I would have to cry off the trip the following day to get to cricket as the Unit Commander had some work I must do. The Air Commodore – who was 'sir' on all our RAF Official conversations but was on first name terms to all of us when we were away at cricket – thanked me for my call – and that was that.

However just a few minutes later I was dropping some traced photos off on the Corporals desk that was right outside the Unit Commander's office when his phone rang and I knew it was someone powerful from all the yes sirs he was giving. I went back to my desk only to be summoned to the Unit Commander's office. *'Gasking – it seems that the RAF team cannot do without you tomorrow so I am releasing you this time. Now for goodness sake when you get back get some work done without your constant talking! That is all for now!'*

I felt over the moon. Little me – *'Little Tel from 'ackney Downs'* (as I was once physically and as I still thought of myself intellectually) was worthy of the considerations of a super chap with the terrifically high ranking of Air Commodore who treated me like a friend and who has just overruled an Army Major to get me back on the team.

It was a terrific boost to my self-esteem and confidence.

We were off to play the Dutch National Team in Nijmegen.

Holland played International Cricket at a slightly lower level than England and were approximately the standard of England A (effectively the England Test Reserves). Indeed a couple of years after we played Holland in a 2-day match the Dutch team we had played went on to comprehensively beat England A over 3 days.

This was so exciting for me and a chance to bowl against one of the best teams I had played against up to that time. The Aussies State Players Touring side we had played earlier in the season had ranked alongside the standard of Holland but we played them at a time I was making my way into the side. Now I felt I was a constituent member of the team I couldn't wait to bowl at them.

All of our team were billeted out at the houses of Nijmegen dignitaries or Cricket Club members. The other SAC and I were billeted at the house of a Doctor who was so kind and treated us royally.

The Doctors family fed my companion and I at a superb dinner and it was the first time I had ever been offered Jugged Hare. In the manner of one who had been brought up on nothing I ate every bit of food they placed in front of me and cleared my plate. His kind wife offered me most of the jugged hare that was left and I ate and loved it to everyone's joy.

Many times in life I have had to pinch myself to really believe what I was experiencing was true as it was so far removed from any expectation I had when I was growing up. Here in this lovely grand house of such a distinguished family who treated us as guests of honour - this was such an occasion.

When we arrived at the ground the opposition was extremely friendly and looking forward to watching a leg-spinner bowling on their matted wicket. They explained that Holland had very few Spinners as the ball would turn very slowly and slightly on the matting so they usually got hit out of the ground. – Now there was a challenge to set before a 22 year old Terry!

Our quickies laboured on the matting and soon it was time for me to bowl. The skipper of RAF Germany side was one of the shrewdest I had ever played with and he knew how to use a spinner in an attacking role.

It took me a few overs of just leg-breaks to gain my confidence and find I was turning the ball (I had always been a prodigious spinner of the ball but it did indeed turn slower than on grass) so I tossed the ball higher with the next ball – a legbreak with a terrific amount of spin. The ball turned sharply, the batsman was on the front foot covering where he thought the ball was when it shot past the outside of his bat and our brilliant wicket keeper had the bails off in a lightning fast action

Poverty to Peaches

The batsman had left his back foot just back inside the crease but the shock of missing the ball and nearly falling forward as he tried to smother it registered straight away on his body language. He thought he had come far enough forward to smother the spin but I had learned from all my practice on the theories of Arthur Mailey that a sharply spun ball moves aerodynamically depending on how you use your wrist and the seam of the ball.

Holland's opening bat clearly did not know where the ball was in the last yard or two of its flight and we soon had him stumped. Batting 3 or 4 were Holland's outstanding bats consistently making big scores. They tried to 'read me' see which way the ball was spinning but failed to read the length as I got the ball to dip or hang. They too were victims of the leg-spinner – me. This was getting to be enormous fun!

I finished with 4 wickets in their first innings and we had them all out for one of their lowest team scores that year.

Unbeknown to me Dutch Radio were reporting on the match and Terry Gasking was being talked of as a Spin King. This got back to the British Broadcasting Association in Germany who covered the game on Camp radios throughout Europe.

We batted well and managed to get a reasonable First Innings lead. Again unbeknown to me the Dutch had an overnight conference on how to play Terry Gasking.

I was on to bowl early in their second innings and had soon got a wicket when in came one of their 'star' batsmen. A man of stout heart and even stouter forearms. His body language shone out with determination and cricketing aggression and sure enough in my second over he smashed a leg-spinner from me way over deep midwicket '6'. Two balls later he did the same – the ball went way across the sports-field to wrattle against a fence in the distance the other side of some football pitches - another '6'. Ouch!

128

Now in all the cricket I have ever played in England – that would be me taken off the bowling attack and banished to somewhere in the outfield. English cricketers just do not understand spin bowling. My captain in the RAF Germany team did. He was brilliant. He came over to me –

'Terry you o.k.?'

'Yep'

'Drop the next ball on that line a little shorter and we'll get him,'

'I had that in mind with a bit of extra topspin'

'Good Man'

… and I was still on to bowl! Oh what a joy. What confidence from the Captain.

I bowled leg-breaks on my next 3 balls pitching outside off stump and turning sharply away. I thought he would leave them as he was setting himself for another prodigious '6' and that needed a ball on middle or leg stump. The 4th ball came out of my hand perfectly directly on that line. The topspin on the ball made it dip late in flight and hurry on to the batsman. He hadn't read it. The dip came too late in flight for him to pull out of the stroke. His instincts hurried his shot as the ball was coming onto him faster than he expected and he therefore smashed the ball on the wrong part of the bat for a big hit. The ball soared higher in the air than he wanted and mid-wicket took the catch running in. Both the Dutch best batsman out for a combined score of less than 30!

I was to go on and get another couple of wickets to finish with 8 victims in the match. 8- for not many against Holland – wow. We won the game. We beat Holland - the Dutch National Cricket Team!

A few years later Holland beat The England A Team – effectively the English Test Reserves and yet we playing for the RAF in Germany had put them to the sword.

We had a few drinks with our opponents to celebrate and they were very kind and hospitable with much discussion on the Art of the leg-spinner. Then it was on the transport back to camp.

Camp Radio had been relaying the details of the match and on my return there were a terrific lot of nods and handshakes of congratulations. It was a great feeling.

Our other games went well but all was leading up to the annual battle between The RAF and the Army teams that were garrisoned in Germany. This was a traditional thrashing for the RAF as the Army had many times more men garrisoned there than the Air Force, and also had a lot of National Servicemen with County Cricket Connections.

We had an excellent West Indian fast bowler bowling at the other end whilst I twirled away and it was his turn to take the majority of wickets. I picked up a few and the old adage remained true. Bowl the opposition out (as opposed to 'keep the runs down') and you have a very good chance of winning the game. This we did and RAF Germany beat the combined garrisons of the Army in Germany.

What a Year! Demob was just around the corner.

I had gone into the RAF and introverted, shy, nervous, underweight individual. I was leaving having filled out physically, supremely fit, confident, contentedly mixing at every level of RAF society and a hugely successful member of top level soccer and cricket teams – my way out of poverty!

That I owe all those who were part of that experience a huge debt of gratitude goes without saying.

Now – with head held high I was leaving the Forces for Civvy Street – but to what?

*

CHAPTER Eight
Marriage 1

Demob into Civvy Street was a shock to the system. I had just spent 3 years in a protected environment of service in the RAF where everything was provided – accommodation, food, work, uniform, sport, leisure. I had not needed to consider any of these options. Now I was out into civilian life – what was I going to do?

I had no savings – I had commuted half my RAF salary to my mother to alleviate her poverty and had lived for the last 3 years at a rate much lower than the earnings of a National Serviceman – and that level was generally thought of as well below the level to save anything – so I had no money for a deposit on a room of my own let alone a flat.

There was no alternative but to move back in with Mum, get a job, and save as much as I could to get a flat of my own. Sadly this meant sharing 2 rooms with a curtain across the middle of the bedroom – an appalling prospect.

I had a month's terminal leave from the RAF and luckily in that time my 5 GCE 'O' Levels secured me a job with Lloyds Bank as a Filing Clerk in their Pall Mall Offices in the Centre of London. The pay was very low – school leavers were earning more but it was a job in an office from which I might progress.

Problem was my Mother thought it was splendid to have me coming home each evening and couldn't understand why I wanted to disappear out straight away instead of staying in and giving her company watching television.

'You're not going out again are you. Your father wouldn't have wanted you to do that. He would want you here keeping me company in the evening'

I was desperate to get away but it would take me a long time to earn enough to get my own room anywhere and I really wanted company of my own age.

I found the address of the pretty 17 year-old I had met on the train back from Manston Airport and wrote. She was working as a typist in Central London at the Ministry Of Housing and we met up for a coffee.

She had just broken up from a serious relationship – engaged to a 19 year-old and was happy to go out on the occasional evening. Problem was she was living with her parents in Dulwich – South London, whilst I was at mother's in Hackney – North London, three buses and a lot of hassle apart.

However at our second meeting at her parents flat they were out and a very willing, attractive and very sexy girl was only too willing to have sex.

22 years old and laid at last!

A whole new and exciting physical adventure opened up for me with virtually no planning needed or seduction. A girl of very easy virtue was allowing, nay encouraging, me to do whatever I wanted with her. The fact that I was too naive to know anything about sex other than that told to me by the boys at school and that was restricted to hearing about the missionary position. I never knew any other position or practice existed.

Today it is possible for a youngster to learn everything they wanted to know about sex from the computer but in my days sex education was restricted to whispers in confidence from the few school chums who had practiced it or heard about it. So into this relationship with an attractive and sexy 17 year old girl I went.

Had my father been alive I fell sure he would have nudged me in the direction of keeping it as an exciting physical adventure but he had died many years previously and I had no-one warning me that early sexual adventures could be overwhelming and before I knew what was happening to me – I was married.

I had recognised that marriage was the only way I could get away from my 2-room accommodation at Mum's (young folk did not live together outside marriage in those days) but all too soon it had happened without me really thinking out the consequences.

My new wife and I had carefully budgeted the expense of taking on a flat at the top of a house in Hackney, furnishing it on hire purchase, and paying our way. Money would be tight but with our joint incomes we could manage.

Sadly for our financial planning my wife fell instantly pregnant. My complete lack of sexual education left me unprepared for such an occurrence.

I had heard of couples trying for years to get pregnant but we seemed to have hit the jackpot almost from our first intercourse together. I was sure it was not my wife's first intercourse – she had been engaged previously and her mother had warned me that her daughter had suffered a fall getting out of the bath when she was younger - I really didn't understand all the implications of that cover-up for loss of virginity symptoms but nothing altered the fact that she was now pregnant.

With the pregnancy came complications.

It appeared that my wife had suffered TB centred in her hips when she was a child and the baby had caused it to return. She was sick every morning and quite unable to go to work so suddenly half our income went missing. We did not have enough coming in to pay the rent, food, and hire-purchase so real problems were building up.

I got invited for trials with Leyton Orient FC at Brisbane Road. Maybe sport would at last be the way out of the poverty trap.

They played me at Left Back in the Trial. Not my favourite position – indeed I had never played there in all the years I had played football. I tried to persuade them to move me up to wing-half but to no avail. They swopped out players during the game but I was still playing at the end so hoped I had played well.

They pulled on a whole load of new players, retained 3 or 4 of us originals and then played a 2nd trial. I was still in the team at the end.

I retained my position through the 3rd trial after which they selected the 3 or 4 players they wanted to offer terms to whilst the rest could go. When they got around to me they said

'Sorry son – you're too old'

'But I am only 21'

'Yes – too old. These days now National Service is finished we can get boys at 15 straight from school and train them up. They can be hardened professionals by the time they are 21. Sorry son – that's it!'

I was devastated – there seemed to be no arguing against their logic but it meant the end of my hopes that soccer would take me out of poverty.

Back to my pregnant wife who was 'too ill' to work and we were getting deeper in debt with each week that passed – knocked back on my heels by the realisation that I was never going to make it at football - what on earth was I going to do now to improve our situation.

If my wife couldn't work because of the recurrence of TB then I must get a better paying job that would cover all our bills. I saw an advert from a highly respected publishing and book company – Caxton Press – for a Salesman. It offered an income that would cover all our expenses so I applied and got the job.

When I turned up for my first day as a Salesman I had expected to be selling publications to bookshops and the trade but the job turned out to be selling children's encyclopaedias door-to-door. It was also no-salary- but a commission only wage. Our finances at home were too desperate to argue and that evening I joined a small batch of 6 men going 'on the knocker' around the streets of Hammersmith.

Now it so happened that I was very good at it. The books were beautifully printed and illustrated and who wouldn't want their children to have access to all the knowledge contained within them. What a huge difference they would have made to me as a child had I had access to the information contained within their pages!

I began to earn enough to pay the bills.

Unfortunately my first wife's physical condition deteriorated the closer the baby came to be due and she was beginning to put pressure on me to stay home as cover just in case the baby came early. This was not helping me earn enough to keep our financial head above water and though I was now paying our bills we weren't catching up on our arrears.

Our baby was born in Mothers Hospital Hommerton November 6th – a girl. Fathers were not allowed at births in those days so I was walking the streets as this lovely lass was born. I loved holding her in my arms and carrying her home. We didn't have much but it was enough to make a baby comfortable.

Prams to buy, cots, clothing, nappies etc so I was back to work 'on the knocker' with renewed vigour but first wife was taking a long time to recover from the birth and found that she could not face changing a nappy and cleaning up our new baby. Baby would wake in the night and I would be up changing, washing and drying her, feeding her from a bottle, and settling her down again whilst first wife recovered from the traumas of birth.

We then got a clash between my mother and my wife.

Mother had called around to see if she could take grandchild out in her pram to find the baby already out in the pram on the front step but crying and in need of a nappy change. She couldn't always get my wife to the door to do anything about it. I was getting harangued by both of them.

I was losing time from work whilst trying to keep the peace and make sure my baby was o.k. when the local shopkeeper refused to sell me some provisions we needed.

I couldn't understand it. He claimed that my wife had run up a big bill for credit that she wasn't paying. Back to see wife who claimed that she had been spending the groceries money on things for the baby. I didn't have the cash to pay the credit but needed the provisions. Back to the shop to see if we could find a solution.

'I can help' he said *'I run a little unofficial book that might help someone like you. You owe me just short of £50. I will pay this bill for you and lend you another £50 cash to tide you over. You will pay me each and every week £10 for the next 20 weeks after which we will be quits and you can restore your credit here'*

I quickly realised that I would be borrowing £100 but repaying £200 in less than 6 months so it was a massive mark up by the shopkeeper but we were in no position to argue so I accepted his terms.

What a financial mess we were in.

To make matters worse my wife was pregnant again. I was still completely naïve about sex.

My commissions for selling the encyclopaedias were excellent when I was able to spend time and effort at the task, but non-existent when I was chasing around the streets of Hackney sorting out problems between my mother, my wife and her physical frailties, and the local shopkeeper chasing us for money.

I needed a steady job that would pay all the bills and saw an advert that would allow me to do just that. 'JOIN THE POLICE FORCE'.

As I thought about it I could see myself making a good policeman. The 7 years at Boxing Club during my youth had left me confident that I could look after myself if a confrontation became violent, I should be able to handle the work of a policeman and I had played soccer and cricket against the Met Police so there would be plenty of sport.

I got through the interview and turned up for training at Metropolitan Training School at Peel House, Vauxhall Bridge London.

We were allowed home at week-ends but not midweek. However half way through the training my first wife announced that her weekly visit to the doctors had resulted in further complications and she was likely to be crippled by this second pregnancy. She would be seeing the Doctor on Wednesday for an assessment of the latest situation and she needed me home Wednesday night for support.

I 'snuck out' from the Police Training College for the evening, got home to discover the diagnosis had been confirmed and that my first wife needed pretty well full time nursing. How we were going to manage this I just didn't know but I had to 'sneak-back into' Police Training College early next morning.

My mind that morning was full of the problems from home when I got summoned to the office of the Police Superintendent in charge of Peel House Met Training College.

'You were out all night last night'

'I'm sorry sir, my wife was ill and I needed to see that she was o.k.'

'You know you are not allowed out Monday to Friday nights. There are no excuses – you have disobeyed an order'.

'But my wife is desperately ill'

'You gave that excuse the previous time you stayed out. There is nothing wrong with your wife – you are lying'

I had never been questioned by a Police Officer before – particularly a Police Superintendent and he became quite fierce with me – trying to get me *'to tell the truth! This is just an excuse to stop out'*

I became more and more insistent – trying to explain what was wrong with her health. In the end I said -

'If you don't believe me – pick up the phone – talk to my Doctor – he will tell you the diagnosis he gave her yesterday'

The Police Superintendent had obviously realised the truth –

'I don't have to pick up the phone to your Doctor. Before I called you in here I had a long conversation with your doctor'

I felt vindicated until the Superintendent added.

'The Doctor has not seen you wife for 6 months. She never has had TB and she certainly doesn't have it now. There is nothing wrong with your wife. Her last diagnosis was just after the baby and she was 100% sound – nothing wrong with her at all. She hasn't been near her doctor since then!

'There must be some mistake! She has had a weekly visit since the baby.

'She has been no-where near your doctor for 6 months! As far as he is concerned she is as fit as a fiddle''

I was devastated! I just couldn't believe it. There must be a mistake!

I couldn't accept that the Superintendent had got it right. He must have called the wrong doctor.

'But she has been seeing him every week. He diagnosed TB and complications with this new baby'.

I am sorry Gasking – but your wife has not visited your doctor for 6 months – there is nothing wrong with her!'

Poverty to Peaches

I had never lied in my life and neither had anyone in our family. We were never brought up to lie to each other – such a thing was unthinkable. How can a wife have told such untruths? There just has to be a mistake. How on earth do I sort this problem out?

'You'd better sort your wife out. You can't go on with this training course while she is lying to you in this way. You will have to resign, hand in your uniform and apply again when you have sorted you wife out'

That was it!

The end of my police career before it had even started. Out of work, shamed by the dishonesty of my wife, no money, a six-month old child to care for – another on the way!

What a mess!

The ride home on the bus was devastating. It wasn't just the lies about this week that devastated me but she had obviously been lying throughout our marriage. She never was ill with TB. She could have worked right up to the time of our first Baby's birth. We need never have got behind on any Hire Purchase or any other payments. She was fit enough to change nappies, do night feeds, clean up the home, take baby for walks in the pram, the whole gambit.

Instead we are deeply in debt, I am exhausted from doing all the night feeds and nappy changes as well as working every hour I can to pay our way, and I have just lost a career in the Police Force.

This was not an age when you walked away from relationships that had gone bad but how the hell do we resolve this problem?

I couldn't face her – I just didn't know what to say.

I walked the streets of Hackney before I went home.

I have never been a violent man so the option of giving her a good hiding was never present – besides which what would it

139

solve? I still have a baby to look after, with another due. I just couldn't work out any solution.

That I must confront my first wife with the facts was obvious but then what?

When I put all the facts to her she broke down, cried her eyes out and confessed that everything the Superintendent had said was true. She claimed that she just couldn't cope. She blamed emotional clashes with my mother, a revulsion at our babies nappies, and an inability to work. None of which was any help to me.

I should have walked away from the problem.

Her lies had completely broken the trust on which the marriage was built and we were now in a desperate position financially, emotionally, and in every other way but I still felt huge responsibilities to my child and somehow needed to try and build something from the wreckage.

I saw an advert in the Hackney Gazette for a holiday cottage let in Cornwall for 6 months. The rent was much lower than we were paying in Hackney and it was a case of trying to start the marriage afresh far from the scene of all our problems or collapsing under the weight of all the lies and deceit.

I decided to try a new start.

I phoned Ralph. He kindly hired a van to take me, the children and first wife, along with what goods and chattels we could manage off to a new life in the West Country.

We were to leave behind the furniture, carpeting et al that we were still paying for on Hire Purchase and I had hoped that the HP company would credit me with the value of the re-possessed furniture and reduce the bill that remained outstanding. A forlorn hope!

So it was off to the West Country with just about all we stood up in as our possessions.

*

CHAPTER Nine
West Country

Penryn is a pretty little village on the outskirts of Falmouth. The cottage was a two-up two-down with a very small back yard - end of terrace that dated back 100 years or more. Very pretty whitened in the sun.

The first job was to search for work. I managed to get a job driving round the streets in an old van that belonged to a local farmer selling his produce door-to-door. It paid next to nothing but it covered the rent and the groceries. Green-groceries we were allowed to take from the van.

My wife still wasn't changing nappies and poor babe was red raw from Nappie rash. A bucket of putrid nappies would be in the yard at the end of the week to be soaked and cleaned. As much as I insisted that she should wash them clean if she didn't actually do so – what could I do but wash them – we couldn't afford to throw them away and buy new?

I went along to a practice at Penryn Cricket Club, got in their team for the forthcoming Devon K.O. match against mighty Falmouth Town. We lost the match but a few wickets from me along with a few runs in middle-order was followed by an invite from Falmouth to join them.

I then began to enjoy my cricket again playing for Falmouth in the South Western League against the powerful sides in Cornwall and Devon.

The football season was started and trials with Falmouth Town led to them putting me straight in the first team as centre Forward. They wanted me to be a 'target-man' for clearances from the defence. Again not my favourite position but one I could handle. Unfortunately 3 games on and a burly defender crashed straight through me and smashed my cruciate ligament and that effectively ended my last remaining hopes of making it into professional soccer and cricket.

With hopes now gone of sport being my future my life needed a re-think.

I had a wife I couldn't trust who seemed to have no love or affection for our baby. I had an income that barely supported our running costs and I was 24 years of age.

I was walking through Penryn when the local Grocer stopped me, told me I could have no more credit and must pay up the bill my wife had run up with him over the weeks.

Oh no! Here we go again.

To this day I cannot work out what she spent our money on. We certainly didn't have any to spare but I could never trace extravagant purchases or clothes or anything yet she would run up credit wherever she could without ever telling me.

In the same way I just couldn't see what she did with herself all day. She didn't get a job, the cottage was minute and only took half an hour to clean from top to bottom, and yet unwashed nappies and clothes would be in buckets in the garden waiting for me to wash them down when I got home.

It was tempting to leave her but whatever would happen to my baby if I did. My second child was now close and I feared that they would die of neglect if I left her.

I needed a higher income to cover these latest debts and spotted an advert in the local newspaper from Caxton's Press. I responded to the advert to be welcomed by the same Area Manager who had recruited me in Hammersmith years previously.

He immediately offered me the Area Manager job for Devon and Cornwall. I would get full commission on my own sales and a commission on the sales of all those I recruited.

I was overjoyed. Was this the opportunity to work our way out of the poor way of life we had and maybe even get a nannie (well a school leaver) to properly take care of my babies.

The new job started well and I had soon recruited half a dozen sales people. The cottage was too small for a 'nannie' and we moved up to a much larger cottage near St Mabyn in North Cornwall.

I had purchased a cheap run-around motor that was solid apart from its headlamps. These would fail from time to time leaving you driving on just sidelights.

The second baby was due and the midwife was going to deliver her at home. Unfortunately my wife decided she didn't want to wait for the baby to define the time to come and started to consume copious amounts of liquid paraffin. Local mid-wife was horrified and shipped her off to Redruth Hospital where a few days later second daughter was born. She would be in hospital for a week or more whilst the damage done by the liquid paraffin recovered.

Redruth Hospital was more than 25 miles away as the crow flies and it was ok driving there but dark when driving home. The headlamps would suddenly pack up.

Thankfully Bodmin Moor road was long and straight so I would meander along until a motor came up from miles behind. I would use their headlamps to steer by dodging slightly from side to side until they had caught me up and then clung to its tail lights for as long as I could once it had passed me.

So we got all our visits done and my second child home. I seemed to have all the affection for my children that their mother lacked – but I still had to go out and earn a living. Income was still commission only and If I spent time at home settling my new baby in – there was no income.

Poverty to Peaches

At just such a time the landlord arrived and told us the next 3 months rent was due. With the time I had missed visiting hospital and settling in the new baby I just didn't have enough to pay him. He agreed to give us a month to get the money together but seized our few remaining assets as security.

Sadly it included all my cricket gear including my Caps that I had received for playing for RAF and every other memento I had.

I somehow knew that I would never see them again.

Two babies, a wife I still could not trust, no money!

What on earth am I to do?

*

CHAPTER Ten
Thank Goodness for a friend called Ralph.

I phoned Ralph and told him that I was at a loss to know what the hell I should do for the best. Ralph still lived in Wanstead, London. His father had died a few years previously and left Ralph his house that he now shared with Bunny, an older friend of the family. Ralph felt that he could move things around to release a couple of rooms that I was welcome to share for a few months whilst I sorted things out.

He again hired a truck, drove down to Cornwall, loaded us all in and drove us back to his place. I dread to think how I could have coped without him.

It was clear I could not go on lurching from crisis to crisis. My first wife was never going to be able to cope. My children were never going to receive love and affection from her.

I somehow had to build a life that insulated me from my first wife whilst allowing me to build protection for my children. My wife and I were still living together and co-habiting as there seemed to be no other way of continuing but somehow I had to break this depressing and debilitating spiral.

My dream of professional sport disintegrated with my cruciate ligament. I did not possess practical skills so Engineering was out. I had always been an excellent organiser until the physical attraction of sex readily provided by my first wife distorted my rational and common sense.

My way forward has to be a career in management! But how do you start?

There were a number of courses such as Ordinary National Certificate in Business Studies but they were either part-time – half day a week plus two evenings, or 3 nights a week.

I needed to be home in the evenings to cope efficiently with my babies and get them put to bed in dry nappies and nightclothes so it was looking difficult. However a friend was a Coach Driver and he suggested that he had the perfect answer.

If I were to get a job as a Coach Driver and then sign up for a Correspondence Course in Management I could fit all my studying in by day and still get home each evening.

He picked up his passengers at 8 am, drove his coach to say Bournemouth for the day, dropped his passengers at the front at about 10 am, and then parked up for the day until 4 pm when he picked his passengers up and drove them home. That would give me 6 hours a day to do my homework in a comfortable coach with an occasional swim if I felt like it.

It sounded an excellent idea so I took myself to Grey-Green Coaches at Stamford Hill to talk to them about it. Yes they could teach me to drive a coach and get me a PSV (Public Service Licence) that would allow me to drive passengers but it would cost me £250. I just didn't have the money!

We meandered on for a few weeks when Ralph had a discreet word with me. He and I were getting along wonderfully well together as we always had but the women were apparently clashing and Bunny was finding my wife's presence difficult.

He had been wonderful in providing a haven for us to return from the West Country – now I must find somewhere else. My wife's parents provided a room in their council flat in Dulwich until we found an upstairs flat in a house in Catford, South London. Whilst there I saw an advert – 'Come and drive a Bus for London Transport' and applied.

I had never driven a crash gearbox vehicle but thankfully at that time the Double-Deckers they trained us on were all

Automatic gearboxes so I was o.k. Ralph had originally taught me to drive when we were in the Air Force at Northolt and the Instructors at London Transport were full of praise for my early road positioning and reading of the road. The only problem came when we went on the skid-pan!

To pass the Driving Test for a double-Decker bus you had to show that you could bring a bus that was skidding out of control back under control and to a halt.

My regular Instructor warned me that London Transport had one Instructor for the skid pan and he had a habit of shouting at you if things were going wrong.

'You are a sensitive lad Terry – don't let him put you off. Just listen to what he instructs and do it.'

I was second up. You sit inside the bus whilst the trainee takes it around the block of administration buildings and approaches the specially prepared skid-pan. The window behind the driver has been taken away so that the instructor can wrench the wheel over to one side, haul on the brake, let go of it, and shout at you –

'Don't touch the wheel until the bus is straight – then its, down; up; up and down quick'

All of which is shouted at the trainee driver whilst the bus is hurtling in a circle and keeling over at a frightening angle.

The first driver had been a lorry driver so was somewhat better equipped to handle all this than me!

When it came to my turn I just couldn't let the wheel go spinning around without trying to steer the bus back onto a straight and narrow path. What I hadn't realise that in stopping the wheel turning naturally I caused the bus to hurtle round in the opposite direction.

'DON'T TOUCH THE WHEEL' was being hollered in my ear *'Up; down, up and down quick'*

'Up; down, up and down quick' referred to the way you pumped your foot on the brake pedal but I just couldn't resist simultaneously trying to steer the bus out of the skid.

It was no good. I finished with the bus pointing the wrong way and going backwards out of control towards the Administration Buildings.

Round we go again – around the buildings onto the skid pan *'DON'T TOUCH THE WHEEL'* was being hollered in my ear *'Up; down, up and down quick'*

I still couldn't leave the wheel to spin out of control, my every instinct wanted to use my hands to get the bus under control.

Round again – this time I noticed that the admin staff had all come out of the buildings and were sitting on the small wall to watch this idiot come around again. It must be their occasional entertainment.

Three more times we went around before I was determined that I wasn't going to touch or do anything.

'DON'T TOUCH THE WHEEL' was being hollered in my ear *'Up; down, up and down quick'*

I pumped my foot and then did nothing – the bus stopped hurtling from side to side and instead hurtled forwards. I was aware of the mass of admin staff diving for cover as a bloody great double decker bus hurtled towards them with some idiot sitting behind the wheel doing nothing!

I finally pumped the brake pedal down, up, up and down quick and the bus came to a graceful stop some yards from their spilt coffee cups. There were a series of ashen faces peering over the low parapet wall at me. I did manage a smile and a wave as though it had all been part of the master plan – which of course it hadn't.

Despite this adventure they passed me and I became a Bus Driver operating out of Catford Garage in South London.

First couple of days on the job and they sat you at the front seats on top of the bus so that you could discover the route each bus took. Not easy when your bus is visiting parts of London you have never been to. Then you are on standby duty to cover for any driver that hadn't turned up or was too late to take his bus out. It was rare for the driver and the conductor to be missing at the same time so the regular conductor can guide the driver around the route.

My first standby duty came a couple of days later and I was suddenly given a number 76 bus to take out of the garage and drive the hugely busy route to Marylebone Station in the middle of London and back to Bromley Station in Kent and then back to Catford. The clippie (conductress) was already on board and I grabbed the route card before setting off. My card was partly obscured so I called to the Clippie *'Where to?'*

'Lewisham Odeon' was the reply so we motored the 3 miles or so up to the bus stand behind the Odeon where we could start our schedule. I was trying to work out how we were to get to the schedule on the parts of the route card I could read when another 76 bus pulled up alongside me.

'What you doin' 'ere? said the driver.

'Starting my shift!'

'I don't think so! I've just come up from Bromley. I don't think you're supposed to be 'ere!'

'Well my Clippie seemed o.k. with it.'

The other driver had got out of his cab and was looking at my route card. *'This is no good – you can't read half of it. What's your Clippies card like?*

The Clippies card was as clear as a bell and shows that we should have started from the opposite direction at Bromley. When the other driver pointed it out to her she said *'Well don't blame me I only started in the job yesterday and I'm on standby.'*

Poverty to Peaches

'*Jeez!*' said the other driver '*they've sent this bus out with a driver and a clippie both on their first day – You've no chance!*

'*All you can do is to take your bus i/d markers out of the slot and motor down toward Bromley. Don't stop for anyone. You should meet your schedule at about Beckingham Hill Road. Turn your bus around, put your i/d plates back in and motor on as though nothing had happened. The Inspector on the route will be none the wiser. I just hope you can remember the route*'

'*So do I!*'

I did just as he suggested having first swapped the route cards with my conductress so I could keep us on route.

I remembered most of the route but there was a tricky right turn amongst some narrow roads. I didn't want to miss it for trying to reverse a double-decker bus back through rush hour traffic did not appeal to me.

I stopped just short of where I thought the turn was, wound the window down behind me and summoned my Clippie.

'*I'm not sure where I'm turning right here. Can you tell the passengers that this is both of our first day and ask if they can help?*'

My Clippie was a lovely bright faced Caribbean girl who bounced the question off the passengers much to their amusement. One of them stepped up to the window behind me. '*Don't worry son, we'll guide you through*' and that is precisely what they did. When he got off the bus he handed over to another and him to another and we got to Marylebone remarkably unscathed.

London Transport Staff Magazine appeared in the Canteen and they had a Drama Group that met in their Training Establishment at White City. They also had a vigorous and hugely successful Operatic Society that met at Griffin House Edgware Road, but singing and dancing was definitely not my lot.

Poverty to Peaches

My wife had finally got herself a job – her first in 4 years of marriage. She worked as an usherette in the local cinema 3 nights a week when I was on early shift and seemed to have made some friends there – again the first in 4 years of marriage.

I decided I was going to take the 2 nights when she wasn't working and could look after the babes to the best of her ability – which wasn't much but at least they had a person in the flat in case of trouble - and I would join the Drama Group.

I was the only 'busman' in the group as all the others came from the LT Offices, nevertheless they made me extremely welcome.

They had a Stage Producer/Director – Gaye – who was a personification of a theatre producer, entering rehearsals in a swirling cloak and full of theatrical mannerisms. However she was an excellent Director who knew precisely what she wanted from each character to build the tension and drama. By day she was a part-time teacher at RADA so we were lucky to have her. She decided that she should improve my diction and for the next few months I could be heard driving my bus quoting little ditties like –

'Are these knees clean knees?
Yes, these are clean knees,
No-one has ever seen knees cleaner than these clean knees'.

It was one of the ditties she used to use to distinguish between the *ee* sound and the *ea* sound. She had lots of such aids to diction and got me to use them all.

So there am I driving my No 1 or No 76 bus repeating the lines of the next play they would be casting and making sure my *'knees were clean knees'*. It is a wonder I didn't get arrested as an idiot.

I got a part in their next production – the comedy lead no less – and thoroughly enjoyed it.

Then my first wife started to fall out with the people who lived in the bottom half of the house and life started to become intolerable. She insisted if she could have a house of her own – a council house – all our troubles would be behind us.

Colne & Nelson in Lancashire were trying to tempt London Transport Bus Drivers to their valley where they had Council Houses standing empty and available for peppercorn rents.

I was now on my last efforts to keep my marriage together. If we were going to move to Colne & Nelson then this was going to be our very last attempt to hold it all together. I made it clear to my wife that if this move did not work then it was all over.

I phoned Ralph – what would I do without him? – hired a van – and Ralph drove us to a council house of our own in Colne, Lancashire.

*

CHAPTER Eleven
Lancashire

The buses used by the Colne & Nelson transport system all had crash gearboxes. I had only ever driven an automatic gearbox bus. With a Crash gearbox you cannot just drop down a gear. You must knock the bus out of gear, rev the engine and let them drop and just at the precise moment when the engine revs match the gear revs you drop it into gear and hey-presto you have changed down a gear.

Now I found the explanation of changing down on a crash gear-box a bloody site easier than accomplishing the same. They let me drive the buses because I had excellent road handling and gave comfortable rides to my passengers but you could hear me crashing the gearbox all along my route – a great grinding of gears as I tried to accomplish the impossible and change down.

Unfortunately Colne & Nelson reside in a valley and it was rumoured that the whole of the valley knew where Terry Gasking's bus was as the crashing gears echoed off the valley sides. If I ever got it into gear first time I would hear a round of applause coming from all my passengers in the bus.

We were paid a reasonable wage as a bus-driver but money was once again tight. It was always tight. I didn't smoke or drink, didn't go out with the boys or the girls, didn't have a social life so I never knew why money was tight but tight it always was. I could never see where the money was spent but we never had enough to pay the bills that would suddenly emerge.

As well as my bus-driving I got an evening job 'Bouncing' in a ballroom. A strange job for such a gentle person but 7 years of boxing in my youth gave me the confidence to handle tricky situations and I was able to calm down the troublemakers with a gentle reasoned approach. Within a couple of weeks I was looking after the stage twice a week when the top pop stars played the ballroom.

I got the job as stage 'manager' as I was the only bouncer unsullied by the under-age sex that had been taking place backstage before I had been recruited. It was made clear to me that my job was keeping the girls off the pop stars and DJs. The only way I could accomplish this was to be quite strict and have no girls allowed backstage. There were lots of other places they could use if they or the musicians needed to but backstage was going to be reserved for performing music rather than sexual gyrations.

This was not as easy as it should have been. The 1960s had a completely different approach to sexual activity. The 'Pill' had just been invented and it allowed women and girls to have full sex without the fear of pregnancy.

An awful lot of girls – over and under the age of consent – threw themselves at the Pop Stars and DJs. If they could return to school the following day claiming they had been fondled by the star they would be treated with reverence by many of their school-friends. If they could claim to have had full sex they had scored a whole lot of respect from those of their companions who were similarly promiscuous.

With about 200 screaming fans at every event my time was spent peeling them off the stars or successfully barring their entrance to the backstage area. This latter activity was made extremely difficult by the quest of many to get access and have sex with their idols and thus to get around any barriers we erected.

Many pop stars welcomed their attentions – many did not want to know but the promiscuous girls still used every trick they knew to get to them. If you look at most photos from that time you will often see the girls with their arms around and all over the stars rather than the other way around.

It was never a case of protecting the girls from the unwanted attention, sex or caress from the pop star it was much more a case of trying to protect the pop star from the over-amorous attention of the girls. There was no knowing if the girls were under or over the age of consent.

My marriage was on the rocks and I was struggling to keep it all together. I had three daughters that I adored so there was no way I was going to accept the offers of numerous girls if I would only let them in with the stars. They made it absolutely clear that I could have anything I wanted from them if only I would let them backstage when the top-ten pop groups were appearing.

I managed to keep the back-stage area clear of the girls most nights and resist the temptations they laid before me. At that time of my life with my marriage on the brink of collapse the risk of accepting their offers was far too high a price to pay for an hour or two of passion.

Today the girls might have been thought of as promiscuous (although I have no evidence that such behaviour has ended) but in the early 1960s the sexual evolution caused by the pill enabling safe sex for the first time in a girl's life led to the need to protect the pop stars from their attention.

I often wondered whether being fondled by a pop star of the day was any worse than the fondling that often used to take place in school behind the bicycle sheds in their mother's day.

Did either activity do any lasting harm and if so to whom – I will never know. Having been to an all-boys school I was never to experience the bicycle sheds or the pop-star idolisation from the ballroom girls.

Poverty to Peaches

Working full time by day and 4 nights a week at the ballroom
by night caused things to go badly wrong in the marriage.

They had never been right since the Police Superintendent
revealed my first wife's life of lies but now she began to try to
provoke me to violence. I couldn't understand why. I was no
different. I was still trying to hold my marriage together for
the sake of the children but it was as if she began to despise me
for it. I wondered if someone was stirring up criticism and
causing massive trouble.

I would come in late at night after the ballroom to have her
criticising, and screaming and shouting at me. I couldn't think
why. I had given her 3 children in three years so virility was
not a problem. It could be that I no longer wished to make
love to her or to have any physical relationship with her that
was causing her to become violent to me. I no longer had the
slightest love for her but I adored my children.

I have never been a violent man and couldn't bring myself to
hit her back. I would restrain her whilst she continued to taunt
and insult me. Eventually one night it went over the top. She
had gone berserk and was screaming and attacking me. I was
so angry. I wrestled her to the ground and so very nearly hit
her with all the anger I had suffered from 5 years of appalling
behaviour and deceit from her.

I knew that if at that moment in time I had lost my temper
and hit her I could have killed her.

I couldn't take that!

This was worse than at any time in what for me had been 5
years of hell. It was no longer a home I could allow my
children to grow up in and by the end of the week I had gone.

I walked away in just the clothes I could stand up in.

Where I was going – I didn't have a clue. I had some vague
idea about working my way around the world. As I was
leaving my wife's close friend suddenly joined me in my car.

Poverty to Peaches

'I've always wanted to get away from Colne and travel the world' she said, *'I'm coming with you'*. I was too confused to respond or resist giving her a lift. She was 22 years old and I guess knew what she was doing

We set off for Dover.

We got as far as Sussex where I saw an advert in a field for 'Farm Labourers Wanted' so applied. It would give me time to work out a solution before setting off around the world.

After a few days I phoned my first wife, confirmed that our marriage was all over. I could not take it any more. I had gone and was not coming back.

She asked what she was going to do with three children and I replied that she must get her mother in to help her. I cannot stay in a house with her a single day longer. If I did I could no longer restrain myself and would start fighting back. Who knows what might then happen – I might kill her.

I have never been a violent man and had never laid a finger on her despite all the provocation of 5 years but I could take no more. The marriage was over.

I got the job on the farm, purchased an inexpensive tent that I could pitch in one of the farmer's fields and started work - getting in the harvest.

My wife's friend was sharing the tent with me when her parents suddenly arrived and took her home.

That was it – life was for me, alone with a tent and the harvest.

These were the days before intense mechanisation on the farm. The tractor baled the hay in blocks and spewed them out behind where there was a labourer – me – balancing on a sledge and piling these great bales of hay – 12 high 4 across - before tipping them off the sledge and starting again.

It was hard and tiring work and I would collapse into my tent each night – often too tired to pick up a pie and a pint at the local pub or have anything to eat.

157

I stayed on the farm for the rest of the summer and it was the hardest physical work I had ever done.

With the harvest over I guessed it was time to pick myself up, dust myself down, and start all over again.

I knew there would be huge debts from the marriage that I had not known about and I needed to find some way of repaying them.

I drove my old van up to London to visit Mum. She had married her Pharmacist and lived in his council flat in Streatham Hill, South London. He appeared to be a refined gentleman but mum said he couldn't hold his drink and would be vile and abusive when drunk.

There was a two-roomed furnished flat advertised in a shop notice board and I moved into it in a house owned by a delightful Indian family. My head told me that my old way of life was over and a new start was on the way, but my body said that there was penance to pay.

I suddenly started to shiver violently. My whole body was shaking. I took to my bed but that didn't help, every part of me was shaking uncontrollably. I just couldn't stop. Hot tea, borrowed hot water-bottles, blankets, coats, nothing made any difference. I was having a complete nervous collapse. This went on for a week before I emerged from the trauma and began to pull myself together.

Another week of hot sweet tea and beginning to nibble at food and I started to recover. I knew I would never be able to forgive myself for leaving those three lovely daughters behind. I equally knew there was no other way for them or for me.

I decided to visit London Transport's Drama Group to see if anybody remembered me and to find out if there was any chance that I might become some sort of trainee in their administration department.

To my unmitigated joy all the people I had been on stage with were at the rehearsal and they greeted me like a long lost friend. Boy did I need their love at that moment in my life. They let me join in their play-reading and over coffee afterwards I told Madge of my predicament and the terrible state I had got my life into.

I hadn't known what everyone's role was at LT when Madge suggested I called in to see her at 55 Broadway (London Transport's Head Office at St James Park in the centre of London).

Madge was a Personnel Officer at LT (London Transport) and – delighted to find that I had passed 5 GCE 'O' Levels in the past. She soon fixed me up with an interview at Griffith House Training Centre (Edgware Road) that resulted in my appointment as an Admin Clerk Grade II (the lowest rung on the ladder – but a rung nevertheless).

Was this the break I needed to start my life again?

I started in the Accounts Office – checking invoices and signed on for a half-day release to study for an Ordinary National Certificate in Business Studies.

A whole new way of life was indeed about to begin.

*

CHAPTER Twelve
SHOWBOAT

One evening at LT Drama Group I was given the message that the Operatic Society had lost one of their minor principles in their forthcoming production of ShowBoat. There were still a few weeks to go before their production but could the Drama group provide them with another 'Steve'.

Steve was only a minor part but he helped to set up the story line so they wanted someone reliable. The Drama Group nominated me and though I felt intensely shy about trying to sing or dance in a musical production Madge (who had a part in Showboat) persuaded me that it was non-singing; non-dancing and I would easily be able to play the part.

The Operatic Group rehearsed on the 6th floor at Griffith House a wide area once the tables and chairs were cleared out of the way. I got there early – not knowing what to expect. I parked myself on a table at the side of the room as the cast, singers and dancers began to arrive. It was overwhelming.

I had been used to Drama groups meeting with about a dozen members but here people kept on turning up I was later to learn that Showboat had 72 players on stage. At rehearsals they also had business managers, scene shifters, backstage helpers etc. all turned up. It was a veritable army of actors, dancers, singers and helpers and this little woman who I realised was the Choreographer/Producer controlled them all with ease and to the evident joy and enjoyment of the everybody.

Madge introduced me to Bertha (Choreographer/Producer) who was busy sorting out a dance routine in which virtually all the cast were moving. She welcomed me – got someone to give me a libretto (the words) and the actors on stage moved me around as I gave my lines to the positions the previous Steve had occupied before his demise.

The whole evening went past in a dazzling array of movement, rehearsal, dance, singing, and was startling. I disappeared to my quiet table top when I was not 'on stage' and became captivated by the whole entourage and particularly by the dancers.

Eight of the most beautiful girls emerged from their 'changing room'. They were not only hugely attractive to look at but they had a verve and drive about them that dazzled and this was before they even danced. In leotards they were stunning!

I was licking my wounds from a 5 year horrific relationship and I had decided it had put me off wanting any relationship with attractive females again but here were these gorgeous girls – full of life and joy. Add another bunch of attractive girls from the Chorus and I was in a state of wonder and awe.

I soon realised that these show business folk had a very relaxed relationship with each other and hugging and kissing was the order of the day both when they met and when they said goodnight and wended their way home. This had to be the way forward for Terry and very soon they had all kindly accepted me as part of their 'gang'.

ShowBoat has a play performed within the play. The ShowBoat was a Paddle Boat steaming up and down the Mississippi. Amongst the nefarious characters aboard were Captain Andy's Touring Players who would put on a show at each port of call. Captain Andy and Crew would rig up a stage and play out a drama for a variable collection of characters sitting in the 'Audience' on the stage.

The play within the play was set in the days of melodrama so the characters were allowed (indeed demanded) to overplay their characters to captivate the audience. This suited me to a tee and soon Julia (my wife in the play) and I were overacting wonderfully with the on-stage 'audience' sighing or cheering every word.

'Miss Julie, as I came across the field I saw the Cattle being driven home by your faithful dog'

Lots of aahs and sighs from the on stage 'audience'.

'Oh Hamilton!'

'Miss Julie, though I wear this garb of a parson beneath these robes is the heart of a man .... And it is beating for you alone!'

Lots of emphasis on key words and the 'audience sighing, cheering and playing a wonderful part.

Suddenly the whole play changes as someone I had a fight with in an earlier scene brings the Sheriff to have me thrown off the boat. I won't give any more of my minute part away for if you get the chance to see ShowBoat you really should make the effort and see it.

It was enormous fun to do and it filled the Scala Theatre London every night for the week – 1,340 paying customers a night and matinee on Saturday - it got a super write–up and I was hooked on the sheer joy the Operatic Group projected to each other and to the audience (on stage and in the auditorium).

During the show according to whether the dancers were part of the crew that were black, or part of the show that were white they had constant changes where they blacked-up or whitened-up. This required them to rush back to their dressing room, throw off virtually all their clothes, black-up (or white-up) throw on all their change of costume and rush back on stage to make their next entrance.

Now guess who was the only character who was not needed on stage during those moments and was thus available to help all these beautiful girls to throw off their clothes, don their next costumes and then rush back on stage. I couldn't believe my luck!

I am sure the girls would not have stood for any improper move on my part and the time limit for the changes were so tight that we all helped each other get back on stage as quickly as possible but the sheer joy of having the trust of these lovely girls stayed with me for the rest of my life.

There were about 6 such changes with Terry helping with every hook and eye he could - removing costumes and redressing the girls as they concentrated on blacking or whiting up. Can you believe the difference it made to my life!!!!

I had come from the most horrific of relationships with the first girl I had ever kissed or had any kind of relationship. I had a few one-night stands (well fumbling-evening stands) as my marriage was on its very last legs and my first wife and I had long ceased having sex but I knew these were not for me.

The break-up of my marriage had left me bereft of any confidence with the opposite sex. When I came along to help out by playing Steve I had sat quietly on a table in the corner of the rehearsal room wondering if I would ever have the confidence to be a part of such a happy group.

Now – just a few weeks later - all these gorgeous, vivacious and lovely girls were showing such wonderful confidence in me that they were allowing me to help their quick changes without fear or favour. They will never know what they did to restore Terry Gasking to a buoyant confident person who has loved virtually every day of his life since with an ease and joy in the company of gorgeous girls or intelligent men.

I was to go on and act and/or dance in half a dozen West End Shows with London Transport Players and ComU.

There was another reason why ShowBoat changed my life.

All the Dancers were vivacious and gorgeous but in the strange way that life unfolds one particular dancer – Jill - was hugely attractive. She was 33 years old, gorgeous with a terrific temperament and I couldn't believe that she had never married.

A few enquiries revealed that she had been engaged or seriously courted a time or two but it seemed that those relationships never worked out to marriage. I cannot think why because she was really vivacious and truly gorgeous.

I remember asking her out to the cinema but she had the car to drive me there and lived with her parents in a secure and lovely house at Winchmore Hill, North London, whereas I still had virtually nothing apart from the clothes I stood up in, a massive debt of nearly £2,000 from my broken marriage, and was still occupying two rooms in Streatham, South London.

Jill was a teacher but her great hobbies were Tennis at a very high standard and dancing in shows of a similar very high standard.

I had never played tennis but I was able to join the chorus/dancers for some of the shows she was in so we not only had huge amounts of fun on stage but against all the odds our relationship began to blossom.

We really liked each other. However when Jill took me home to meet her parents her poor mother wondered what on earth her only child – her beloved daughter was letting herself in for.

Jill could have had husbands from any sphere of life she chose. She had turned down bank managers, sportsmen, outstanding tennis players – some qualifying for Wimbledon - executives, Musical Directors and so on and had taken up with this Grade II clerk from London Transport who only had one suit – the one he stood up in - and had just left a wife and three young children, and had debts of nearly £2,000.

What on earth was to become of her Jill.

Jill's mother adored her younger brother (Jill's Uncle Pete) and was always influenced by him. He insisted that Jill's parents should find everyway they could of getting Jill to end this relationship with this ne'er-do-well named Terry Gasking. And I couldn't blame him.

However well I thought of my intentions I couldn't deny that on paper I was not the most attractive fellow their beloved Jill could fall for. She really could have taken her pick of eligible men so you could imagine how lucky and how privileged I felt that she seemed to have chosen me.

Jill's father was always a well-balanced and fair man so I never knew the full extent of the pressure they put on Jill to end the relationship but the next thing that happened was that they found me two rooms at the home of a friend of theirs who lived in the next street.

Whether it was to give me better and more convenient lodgings or it was to keep a closer eye on me through the family friend I never knew but the accommodation was so much more superior than I had in Streatham and Jill lived around the corner so I moved in.

Jill and I were rehearsing a couple of shows a week so our relationship continued to blossom. Jill had been chauffeuring our producer/choreographer Bertha around for a number of years but now also gave me a lift back from rehearsals.

Her mother continued to hope that I was an aberration in her daughter's life on a temporary basis rather than permanent but the more I went around to their place for a meal the more we all began to develop a healthy respect for each other.

Jill's father began to take a healthy interest on how I was progressing and started giving me some very helpful advice from his experience as a Principal at the Bank of England.

Then I made a staff suggestion at LT to make my job redundant. This shocked all and sundry – at work and in my domestic life.

I was checking invoices to make sure they totalled across (i.e. 144 widgets @ £1.00 each = £144.00) correctly and added down the page correctly. It was essential work to make sure that Suppliers did not overcharge or even undercharge on their invoices.

Trouble was that the Invoices were already checked before they got to me by the clerk in the Purchasing Office that first received them and authorised them for payment. They then came into my In-Tray. I then checked them and passed them to my Out-Tray that also served as the In-Tray of the Senior Clerk who sat to my left. She then checked them, authorised them for payment and sent them to Accounts Payable where a clerk checked them before assembling them all into order for a Cheque-run.

We all put our initials in the nice little boxes attached to each suppliers bunch of invoices. Cheques were then printed to the value of the total of the checked invoices and sent to the Supplier.

What could possibly go wrong?

Yet every month there would be a whole lot of invoices get through the system with mistakes on them whereupon the order would come down from above that we all needed to be more diligent in our checking.

When working in that chain of Invoice Checkers it was easy to see how the mistakes slipped through. The Suppliers knew our Cheque-run was on the 26th of each month. If they included on their invoices everything they had supplied up to the 20th of the month they could just get it through our system in time for that month's cheque-run so only waited a matter of days for their payment. If they sent their Invoices out at month-end they would have just missed that month's cheque-run and must wait a month for their money.

So for the first 3 weeks of every month only a trickle of invoices would go through the system. They could all be fully and meticulously checked by each of the 4 of us involved in Invoice Checking. The day's supply of invoices could be checked in a couple of hours, leaving us with nothing to do for the rest of the day.

One evening at Jill's her father after listening to my sad woe at a system that didn't work said –

'If you are going to marry my daughter there is a book you should read.'

I wondered what the devil he was going to pull out of his bookcase. *'You're too late!'* I thought .

'You need to read this little book' he said. *'I really believe it should be a compulsory read for every budding manager'.*

Jill's father had just introduced me to 'Parkinson's Law' and he was exactly right. No-one should be permitted to rise to the rank of manager or director in any organisation without first having read *'Parkinsons Law'* from cover to cover.

If ever there was an example of his law that -

'Work expands to fill the number of hours available.' Invoice Checking at LT was it.

4 Invoice Checkers would be seen to be busy checking invoices for 8 hours a day when for 3 weeks a month there was only about 2 hours of work a day for each of them.

To me sitting at a desk with little to do is an anathema. I tried all kinds of experiments with the invoices to see if there was any way of finding magic numbers amongst the costs just to fill in the time before checking them thoroughly and passing them to my Out-Tray.

However in the 4th week of the month we would be inundated with invoices as all the regular Suppliers chased their invoices through our system to get them into the cheque run.

The result was an In-Tray that was piling higher than the rate at which I could check them. Inevitably the thoroughness of the check would diminish as I hurried to clear the pile and move them to my Out-Tray.

It occurred to me that all 4 of us were doing the same, so for 3 weeks a month every invoice got meticulously checked but in the 4th week we all rushed the checks to ensure we were not sitting on invoices when the cheque-run was ready to start. No wonder there were so many mistakes getting through the system.

The solution to the problem seemed obvious to me.

We make each checker fully responsible for ¼ of the total number of invoices coming through the system. Thus instead of all 4 checking every invoice, One would check all invoices from Suppliers A-G, the next checker would check Suppliers H-M, the next N-R, and the 4th S-Z. In this way even in the peak week we would each only be checking a quarter of the invoices we currently checked so had plenty of time to get them absolutely correct and through the system in time for the Cheque-Run.

In fact there would be so much spare time if this change was made to the system you could save at least one checker completely and let the others cover A-H; I-P; Q-Z.

I tried to talk this through with the Senior Clerk and the Office Supervisors but they didn't want to know. I then passed an LT Suggestions Box that had a notice on it *'Cash Rewards for Suggestions that can improve the systems you work on'*.

I thus made the above suggestion and popped it into the Suggestion Box. The result was somewhat startling!

I got called into the Accounts Senior Manager's Office to be interviewed by him, and the big boss over him 'The Principal' of the Accounts Office. I had never met either before.

I was praised for my initiative and clear and concise thinking – it was just the thing LT needed from their Administration Trainees – and often someone coming in new to the system can see improvements that are lost on those who operate it on a regular basis.

However on this occasion they couldn't implement the suggested changes for reasons that I wouldn't understand at my stage of training.

They were delighted to make me an award of £10 for my initiative (this was 2.5% of my annual salary so was very welcome) and wished to encourage me to keep thinking.

They also had an excellent recommendation that I should apply for an Administrator I position that was coming up in the Muniments Section (original maps and plans of LT Property) that would give me a salary increase and more time to complete my studies.

So I left my interview feeling delighted. It was only later that I discovered the status and thus the pay of all Senior and Principal Officers at LT was determined by how many people worked in their departments.

I had just suggested making a redundancy and was showing every sign of coming up with yet more such suggestions. If I carried on like this the whole of the Section would become much more efficient and jobs would be saved but that would cause their salaries to reduce so it was little wonder that they wanted me out of Accounts and into the backwater of Muniments as quickly as they could manage it.

There was another interesting repercussion from my staff suggestion. The Staff Union representative was a friendly guy and we used to meet up quite frequently and socialise over lunch at the staff canteen. As soon as he heard about my staff suggestion he had a real go at me for attempting to make my job redundant and thus costing a job of his members that he spent his life trying to protect. I couldn't accept that a job effectively doing nothing was worth 'protecting' but he was having none of it and he never spoke to me again.

I applied for the Administration Assistant Level I position at LT and Jill's Dad suggested that I let him buy me a made-to-measure suit from Burtons. I had never had a made-to-measure suit (in fact I never had a 'new' suit and I guessed it showed). I thought it was tremendously generous of him and guessed that he might be reconciling himself to his only child's choice of fellow. On the other hand he could be just making sure I had the best possible chance in the interview so that I could take a better financial share of expenses that Jill mostly paid from her Teachers salary.

I got the job in Muniments and for the next year worked with the delightful George Hedge and Secretary down in the basement of 55 Broadway was given a half a day a week to study on my ONC Business Studies.

In the Accounts Office you had to be seen to be working even when there were not enough Invoices to check. Working with George meant that we gave instant responses to enquiries and requests from LT Surveyors for plans and maps of areas they were working on. However if there was a slackening in demand then George would encourage me to get on with my studies at my desk in our shared office.

I did and eventually passed my ONC Business Studies with 'Distinction' scoring 96% at Statistics and 99% at Accounting.

Alongside the ONC the teachers had encouraged me to take GCE 'A' Level Accounts; Business Law; and Economics.

I passed all three and suddenly Terry Gasking has educational and business qualifications that were beyond his wildest dreams when he was a kid.

Three good passes at GCE 'A' Level and a 'Distinction' in the Ordinary National Certificate in Business Studies.

Jill and I decided to get married.

It was a hugely brave decision by her. I was earning less than half her salary and still owed £1,200 of debt left from my first marriage.

I had never bothered to do anything about divorcing my first wife but now I had a reason to do so.

Poverty to Peaches

The mother of my first wife had contacted me shortly after I had joined LT – she worked close by as a Principal at the Ministry of Housing.

She had suggested we meet up over coffee one lunch time and it was a surprising meeting. I was expecting a severe ticking-off for leaving her daughter and her 3 granddaughters but it didn't turn out that way. Instead she was quite apologetic for the way her daughter had treated me throughout our marriage.

She revealed that her daughter may not have been as pure throughout her teen age as she had pretended to be and there never was an 'accident getting out of the bath'. It also appeared that on the day I moved out of the house in Colne I had lived in with my first wife her boy-friend moved in.

How long he had been around prior to that event I didn't know but perhaps it explained the aggression I was getting from my first wife in the months leading up to my departure.

Her mother also revealed that my first wife was pregnant again and was blaming me as the father. I assured her that her daughter and I had stopped having sex for some time before the break-up. Her mother had guessed that was the case but warned me that her daughter was going to try to get maintenance for all 4 children – my 3 and the one she was expecting. I was already paying maintenance for my 3 and her mother implored me to only pay her daughter maintenance through the court or else her daughter would create problems over money for the rest of the children's lives.

I took her advice and put the payment into court. The court ratified and set the level of maintenance to be paid and completely rejected her claim for the 4th child who was subsequently born 11 months after I had left the home.

I was grateful to my first wife's mother both for her understanding of my position and her advice.

My proceedings for divorce were made all the more complex by the fact that I had left the home but her boy-friend had moved in same day and was now living with her as man and wife and had fathered her 4th child.

I was no longer poverty stricken as I was managing my own money instead of giving it all each week to my first wife (why on earth did I not think to do that during my 5 years of marriage to her?). I was still repaying Debts from my first marriage and Jill and I certainly did not have the money to buy a house in London, despite all our friends living there.

Jill's parents were great friends with Tom and Muriel in Devon. Tom was a Dartmoor Commoner and the Chief Auctioneer for the top agricultural auctioneers in Devon. He told us of a lovely property at 11 Venn Hill, Milton Abbot, Devon that would just suit us and was inexpensive enough to get a mortgage we could afford.

We drove down to Devon and it was a lovely property, a small cottage with walls 3 feet thick and a garden that was an orchard down the road from the cottage. It needed some work on it but would be ideal. The problem would be me getting work. Jill as a Teacher could get employment but where would I find work? Without me in work we could not get a Mortgage so we spent a holiday trying to find work for me.

Whilst we were searching the jobs market Jill's Mum and Dad decided to sell up at Winchmore Hill, London and move to Devon, buying a plot of land on a new estate being built in Tavistock close to their friends Tom & Muriel.

Pete – Jill's mother's favourite brother lived the other side of Dartmoor in Exeter and her elder brother Cyril (my favourite relative of Jill) lived not too far away at Sidmouth. So I guess it made sense to move with most of the family centred in Devon. It also enabled them to keep a close eye on their only daughter for I was still not fully trusted by them. A lack of trust that was fostered to a greater level every time they visited Pete and Gabriel in Exeter.

Problem was that I never could get a job in Devon that suited someone growing in Administrative ability and experience and we reluctantly had to give up the idea of 11 Venn Hill.

Back in London with Jill's family home now gone to Devon we had to find a flat we could share. Problem with this is that if we lived together my first wife would take every opportunity to drag Jill into the forthcoming divorce proceedings and take her to the cleaners financially. We overcame this problem by finding rooms in two adjoining houses in Hackney and living next door to each other until the Divorce finally came through.

The school Jill was teaching at – Bound's Green – was made Comprehensive and merged with another school a couple of miles up the road. All the Teachers had to re-apply for their posts but we had planned to leave London for somewhere we could afford a mortgage as soon as the divorce came through so Jill took a temporary teaching job in South Tottenham.

I had gone up to Colne in Lancashire for a Court hearing on the maintenance I was to pay for my three daughters and to arrange for it always to be paid through the court.

Whilst I was away overnight Sally Wiggins arrived at Jill's flat.

Sally Wiggins was a scrap of a dog – mostly Collie and Dachshund with a lot of other types of dogs thrown in somewhere in her background. She had been picked up wandering, shivering and lost on the Great Cambridge Road in Enfield by friends of Jill. They took it to the Police but they already had strays staying at their houses and asked Jill's friend to take the dog home with them whilst the Police tried to see if it had been reported missing. Dog went home with them and all went well until scrap of dog picked up friend's own dog's favourite toy then there was a hell of a scrap.

Poverty to Peaches

Jill's friend could see no future for this scrapper of a dog – if it went to Battersea Dogs Home they would be forced to put it down as it was so aggressive.

'Come on Jill, you've always wanted a dog but your mother would not have one in her house. Now you've got a flat – give this scrap a chance – take it on whilst the Police try to find its owner'

So Sally Wiggins entered our lives. Well Jill's life! The dog had been very badly treated, its fur was a mass of tangles, its paws were worn down and it was obviously well under weight. Jill's landlady fed it some steak and kidney she had over from her dinner and the dog woofed it down and then bit the hand that fed it.

I returned from Colne having set up the payments through the court and on my return this scrap of a dog's body language said *'You're not coming in here! I've just found a loving home for the first time in my life and men have always mistreated me.'* And with that she bit me every night for two weeks. She was perfect with Jill.

Neither Jill or I could bear the thought of Sally Wiggins going to Battersea and being put down so we persevered and gradually this scrap of a dog learned that men could be loving and kind as well as Jill. Well one man at least.

It took her a while to trust most men. The first time we took her for a walk across the park she shot off leapt at a boy and swung around with her teeth in his anorak. Clearly little boys had been some of the ones who ill-treated her before she found Jill.

It took patience, kindness and firmness but Sally Wiggins gradually settled down with everyone who was not threatening towards her.

She even began to play football with the lads kicking a plastic football on Millfields as I walked her past and over the River Lea to a walk on the marshes. She would chase the ball and

174

nod it forward with her nose much to the glee of all the lads who tried to dribble it away from her. The only time I ever heard them upset was when she chased the ball the length of the pitch they had made between their coats for goalposts and into the goal. Discussion raged behind me as we walked on as to whether Sally Wiggins could be allowed as a goal-scorer and the goal to count in their game.

At Christmas we were invited to spend the Holidays with Jill's Mum and Dad in the Toll House they had rented on the edge of Dartmoor whilst their bungalow was being built. Jill was having a great deal of trepidation over the fate of Sally Wiggins whilst we would be away in Devon for Jill's Mother was frightened of dogs and would never have one in the house. Jill's Dad sensed Jill's unease at kennelling our scrapper of a dog and came on the phone to Jill –

'Your Mother and I have been giving this a lot of thought and have decided that Sally Wiggins can come with you.'

This was great but Jill – knowing of her Mum's aversion to dogs was really on edge. Christmas Eve and Jill's Mum and Dad had invited to drinks and nibbles their life-long friends and all their relatives who were with them for Christmas. Sally Wiggins behaved immaculately – so much so that no-one could resist giving her a nibble of the bits they were eating. The next morning - disaster.

I was sleeping in the extension (unmarried engaged pairs didn't sleep together in those days especially in the girl's parents house) and Sally Wiggins was in with me. *'Come quick Jill – Sally is throwing up all over the place'*

I managed to get the dog out of the house onto the lawn whilst Jill tried to clean-up before mother got to know what had happened. It was of course not possible but the saving grace was that little Sally Wiggins looked so poorly she captured the sympathy of Jill's Mum.

We kept her out in the garden for the rest of the morning until we were sure that she had stopped being sick and then this poor little scrap of a dog came in with every hair drooping and looking very sad. She tried climbing onto my lap for comfort but couldn't settle, then she tried Jill's lap with the same result and then to all our amazement she jumped up onto Jill's Mum's lap and immediately curled up into a contented bundle.

Jill and I waited for her Mum to get over the shock and heave the dog off but all we heard was - *'Oh you poor little thing – you prefer Grandma's lap'* and with that Mum spent the next couple of hours stroking poorly Sally Wiggins on her lap until our little dog was back to health and contentment.

From then on Jill's Mum was our dog's biggest fan and adored her.

Jill was back to teaching at her 'temporary post' at Gladesmore School in South Tottenham and I was back at London Transport Muniments Section – seconded to the Solicitors Department.

My secondment to the London Transport Solicitors Office had me at the High Court to record progress on some of the many court cases involving accidents on London Transport. Often I would be sent out to different parts of London to witnesses who had been on a bus at the time of an accident. I had to interview them individually in their own homes prior to an accident case coming to court and report back so that the Solicitors could gauge the responsibilities and likely damages.

It was a very revealing time for me. I would never have believed how innocent people with no axe to grind and no financial interest in a case could give such different views on what they saw. The biggest divergence of all were two people – unknown to each other – but sitting next to each other on a bus that ran over a child's foot. Each saw a whole series of scenes leading up to the accident that were totally different from the other. You would think that it couldn't possibly have been the same case yet each swore it was exactly as they described and had no doubt at all in their minds that it was any different. They both appeared to be honest and caring witnesses and it has left me always suspicious of whether events were as somebody described or whether their brains have constructed a scene that must have happened and that they subsequently believe their 'constructed' scene to be fact.

Finally my divorce came through and we arranged to get married at Hackney Town Hall Registry Office. We got all the dates arranged but then found that my first wife had not picked up the Divorce Certificate so we had to wait until she did.

I phoned the Registry Office daily until I could get confirmation faxed to me that the Decree Nisi had been picked up. I phoned Jill and asked if she could get off on Friday afternoon to get married? She could.

'Where're you going Miss? Asked her class as she handed them over to someone else for the Friday Afternoon.

'I'm off to get married'

'No you're not – where you really going?

'I really am off to get married at half-past three'

'No your not – tell us where you're off to'

'Get married' and with that Jill was off to get married.

There were still a few days to go before the end of term so Jill was back in the classroom on the Monday Morning and all the girls in her class immediately spotted her wedding ring.

'Cor blimey – she was off to get married.'

A whispered conversation between all those in her class and – *'Excuse us Miss, we'll be back in a minute'* and with that the entire class deserted her.

They returned later with a set of glasses and a 'Good Luck on your Wedding' card.

Jill's Dad had offered to pay for a grand wedding and reception or we could have £250 to put down as a deposit on a mortgage.

Poverty to Peaches

We would have loved to have had all our friends from drama, operatics, soccer, cricket et al and other parts of our life along to celebrate our wedding (it was our 25th wedding anniversary before we managed to do so) but £250 added to what we could scrape together would just secure us a mortgage on a cottage – Lilac Cottage - we had seen in Beenham, Berkshire.

So it was a wedding with just Jill's parents, and my Mum and the elderly Pharmacist she had married a few years previously all in attendance and onto a dinner at West Lodge, Enfield.

Then it was off to Beenham and our first home together.

*

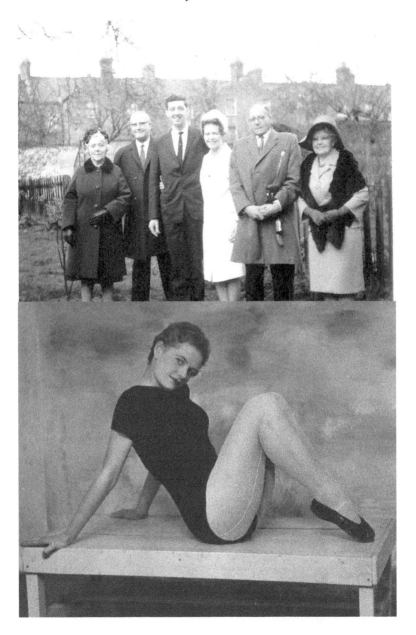

Poverty to Peaches

Above. *Dancer Jill Sanders was given a lead part. Pictured with her are (from left) Herbert Wheatley, Ernie Engeham, Eddie Pontyfix, and Jimmy Nelson.*

★

Right. *Stars of London Transport Players' production of Ivor Novello's hit 'The Dancing Years' were Stephen Marshall (Rudi Kleber) and Christine Mullard (Maria Zeigler)*

COLOUR AND GAIETY IN 'THE DANCING YEARS'

THE London Transport Players captured all the colour and gaiety of Ivor Novello's musical hit *The Dancing Years* in their production at the Scala Theatre last month.

The story follows the career and fortune of Rudi Kleber, a struggling Jewish composer in Vienna. This was the role played by Ivor Novello in the original production, and it was handled with great competence for the Players by Stephen Marshall.

Kleber's rise to fame is sparked by a

Four pretty "Austrian" maids pose for our cameraman. In real life they are (left to right) Angela Robins, Liana Lion, Claire Scudder and Rita Bierman.

deep love for Maria Zeigler, an established star of the Vienna opera, played by Christine Mullord.

Frank Bell, London Transport lost property chief, must feel quite at home in the role of a mid-European aristocrat. After his success as Cosmo Constantine in *Call Me Madam*, he was again cast as a nobleman. This time he played Prince Charles Zetterling, the

suitor and eventual husband of Maria Zeigler.

The Dancing Years also gave Jill Sanders a chance to step into the spotlight. After several shows as lead dancer, she was given the part of Grete Schone, the young daughter of an innkeeper, who grows up into a sophisticated young lady.

A distinguished visitor to the Players' production was Miss Olive Gilbert, the musical comedy star of the 1930s. She played opposite Ivor Novello in the stage version of the play in 1937.

LARGE CAST

The show was not only a triumph for the large cast of eighty. It was also a success for stage manager Joseph Putnam, of the commercial advertising office.

In his first production with the Players he had to supervise four major scene-shifting operations. A hardworking team of back-stage helpers helped the show to go without a hitch.

Other leading parts were played by Madge Royston, Shirley Knight, Nigel Pratt, Yvonne Nicholls, Penelope Davey, Ray Perry, Alan Barber, Ron Veness, and Terry Gosling. The producer was Miss Bertha Peek, and the musical director was Jeffery Bidgood.

29

181

CHAPTER Thirteen
Beenham

Beenham was a small village between Reading and Newbury in Berkshire, England, about 50 miles West of London. Jill would try to get a job teaching locally and I would need to commute to London for work with London Transport by catching the 7.30am train from Aldermaston Station that was situated at the bottom of the hill that led up to Beenham.

The price of houses in London was such that we could not even think of buying a house there – they were all too expensive.

George Hedge – the lovely man who headed the Muniments Section at LT had said that his parents lived out in Berkshire and prices were far less expensive there. He also said that LT (London Transport) had a reciprocal agreement with BR (British Railway) that allowed employees of one organisation to commute free on the other.

There was a fast train service from Reading to London so Jill and I got the local papers and spent a number of weekends out in Berkshire looking at cottages we might be able to afford on our very scarce budget.

A tiny cottage in Beenham - Lilac Cottage - had caught our eye and we made a bid of £2,350. It seemed incredibly cheap to us after all the cottages we had been looking at in other villages but our offer was accepted.

Jill's mother felt we '*had been rooked*' and had overpaid for the cottage but we loved it.

Poverty to Peaches

It really was tiny – two very small rooms up and two very small rooms down - with a minute kitchen and bathroom that had been added at some time. The Kitchen was so small that I could stretch my arms out and touch both North and South walls of the Kitchen. I could do the same East to West. Incredibly in years past a family had brought up 10 children in this tiny 4 roomed cottage.

It was opposite the local pub and in this quiet peaceful village it seemed idyllic to us. I had to pick up my rail warrant and drove down to the station at the bottom of the hill to pick it up.

The station turned out to be a 'halt', i.e. it was completely unmanned, had a platform on the 'up' line and one on the 'down' and a name board 'Aldermaston Station' and that was it.

I had never met an unmanned 'Halt' before but it was to prove to be tremendously useful. There was nothing to stop cars driving onto the platform and right up to the carriages. Something I was to take constant advantage of as Jill and I hurtled down Beenham Hill and along the A4 'Bath Road' as we saw my train approaching the 'Halt'

Earnest flashing of our headlights and the kind Guard on the train would hold it at the halt just long enough for me to skid to a halt alongside and leap out of the car and onto the train leaving Jill to extract the car and return up the hill to Beenham.

Luckily Jill had a strikingly coloured Austin A40 so the Guard knew it was me rushing to catch his train. It was another situation in life where my need to chat to people had paid off as we would natter away as he punched the passengers tickets and kindly chided me for my late arrival. He was a most kind chap and set the journey up to London in a pleasant way.

Now you might think that a reasonable intelligent guy would have thought it odd that this seemingly disused 'Halt' with the name Aldermaston Station had the same name as the Atomic

Weapons Factory that had been the centre of the Greenpeace and pacifists marches that protested against Atomic Weapons being made at Aldermaston but it never entered my head.

I eventually picked up my rail warrant at Reading Station and was telling George Hedge about the 'halt' called Aldermaston Station.

'Don't let that Halt fool you' said George. *'The station is kept looking unused and overgrown to disguise the fact that all of Britain's Atomic Weapons are being built alongside the railway. The Atomic Weapons Establishment has its own railway tracks and internal station that can ship whatever they want in and out, usually under the cover of darkness,'*

Blimey – what have I brought Jill to?

We are sitting on top of Britain's most lethal weapons development organisation. One serious accident and we could be blown sky high or killed by radiation. Best not to tell Jill's Parents about the location of the Atomic Weapons factory!

Back up in Beenham I needed a drink to get over the shock so over the road to the Six Bells Public House.

We got talking to the Landlord of the pub and the conversation got round to recent happenings in the village.

'You're lucky you weren't living here six months or so ago' said the Landlord.

'Why so?'

'This pub was used by the police as their headquarters in their hunt for the killer of Yolande Waddington and two little girls from the village'

'Did they find him/her?'

'Well they have arrested a local lad but the villagers who were born and bred in Beenham don't think he did it. They think it was done by an outsider. Anyone who wasn't born in the village is an 'outsider'.

'So the murderer might still be at large?'

'Could be. There an awful lot of villagers who think so.'

'Jeez, this is not good news. We have only just moved in to discover we are sitting right on top of Britain's Atomic Bombs and there might be a murderer wandering around the village.'

You should have done your homework' said the Landlord. *'The case was all over the papers.*

'VILLAGE OF FEAR' was the headline.

I remembered seeing the headline in the papers but did not realise the village was the one I had brought my newly married wife to.

'I shouldn't worry too much about the murders' continued the landlord of the pub. *The police have combed every inch of the woodlands and fields around here looking for the knife used to kill Yolande. They never found it but they are confident they have arrested the right man.'*

I am not a heavy drinker. A pint and a half of Ale is sufficient for me, but that evening I seemed to have tried to drown out the realisation that – not for the first time in my life – I had failed to do my homework and left my newly married wife and I to who knows what dangers.

We had managed to get a mortgage on Lilac Cottage and had moved in not knowing anything about recent or past history of the village.

At such times there was little alternative other than to grit our teeth and make the best of it.

The rooms were tiny and the cottage had no cupboards.

Jill's Dad had kindly built a cupboard in his garage in Devon and brought it up in pieces to assemble on the day we moved into the cottage.

It was a good job he was there as I had been attending Woodwork Classes run by one of Jill's colleagues in Bounds Green School and with his considerable help had built a double bed from a Stanley Book of Home Furniture Construction. It was made out of the wood he had salvaged from the school just before it was all to be burned in the redevelopments of the school into a comprehensive. I made a contribution of 50p for the materials.

It was my first ever attempt at DIY but it was really DIY+expert Woodwork teacher. When we chose the bed from the book we hadn't found Lilac Cottage or realised that there was no way my beautifully constructed bed was ever going to get up the stairs of our tiny cottage or through its small windows.

Unfortunately it was the first item off the Removals Van so the bed was plonked down on the tiny lawn in front of the cottage and left whilst everything else was moved into the cottage.

Jill's Dad finished assembling his cupboard so items could be stored immediately but the removal men had finished, gave up on our bed, and it was left on the lawn looking forlorn and abandoned.

Jill's dad looked at the construction of the bed and suggested that if we could get 4 metal plates made up with countersunk drilled holes in them then we could saw the bed in half, carry the halves upstairs and then screw it all back together again – if we could also get the screws!

Wonderful idea but where the hell would we find 4 metal plates with countersunk drilled holes and wood screws out here in the middle of the countryside in an area we didn't know at a time that was past closing times for most businesses?

It was then nearly 6pm and we had no idea where we could get 2 pairs of drilled metal plates at that time of night but Lilac Cottage was right opposite the Six Bells pub. A stranger to us was on his way for an early pint and we asked him if he knew of anywhere we could get four metal plates at that time of night. Far from looking at us as if we were mad he said –

'There's a Blacksmith in Thatcham and the Smithy lives above the shop so if you are quick you might just catch him still in his forge before he closes up for the night'.

Into Jill's car we leap and hurtle through Bucklebury and down the hill to Thatcham.

Found the Blacksmith straight away and he was just closing up for the night. I pleaded with him for four drilled metal plates countersunk and screws as my wedding bed was still on the grass outside my tiny cottage opposite the 6 Bells and this was my wedding night. (Remember these were the days before couples lived together so the wedding night was special!!!)

The Blackmith smiled.

'Wedding Night eh! Well we can't let you spend it in bed on the grass outside the Six Bells can we?' and with that he kindly cut four metal plates for us, drilled and countersunk them whilst we watched and handed them to us. He also gave us 8 heavy duty Wood Screws wouldn't charge us a penny for them and wished us well.

It was another of the incredibly kind acts we were to receive throughout our life time.

I was so grateful but he wouldn't take any payment, he just smiled and said *'Enjoy your wedding night'*

I drove back up to Beenham with my precious metal plates, drilled and countersunk and 8 heavy duty wood screws. Everyone at Lilac Cottage was having a cup of tea so I joined them.

Later – just as the trade was picking up at the Six Bells with their customers all wondering why my wedding bed had been abandoned all afternoon and evening on our small lawn – Jill's Dad and I came out of the Cottage and 'ceremoniously' sawed the bed in half.

We often wondered if our new neighbours were running a book on how long – or short - our marriage would be as it started so ignominiously.

Once in half we were able to carry the parts of the bed upstairs in Lilac Cottage and use the metal plates – drilled and countersunk along with the 8 heavy wood screws to put it all back together again.

44 years have passed since that episode and my marriage bed has moved home with us 4 times and is still being slept in every night. If the Thatcham Blackmith is still alive and reads this book then I raise my glass to you sir in gratitude for your kindness all those years ago.

Beenham was a brand new experience for Jill and I.

We had only lived in big towns before and after moving to Hackney where we scarcely knew our neighbours now we were in Berkshire in a small village where everyone seemed to know each other.

We had purchased the cottage without knowing that less than a year earlier the National Newspapers were headlining Beenham as 'The Village of Fear'.

The villagers had been really scared as firstly a teenaged au-pair had been knifed to death and then 2 schoolgirls had their heads forced under puddles of water and drowned.

The 'insiders' who were born and bred in the village were certain that one of the 'newcomers' was the guilty person. The 'newcomers' were all certain it was done by an 'insider'.

Sentiment in the village was split in two until a lad from the village was arrested for killing two young girls. Even then those who had spent their lifetimes in the village were certain the murders were done by an 'Outsider'.

Thankfully the Police had arrested a young lad from the village some time before we moved in so it was no longer the *VILLAGE OF FEAR*' as one lurid headline writer had described it. However there was still an air of suspicion and distrust present.

We had only just moved in but were going to Devon to stop with Jill's parents for Easter. With our lifetime's experience of the risk of burglars in London I said to Jill *'Best not tell anyone we are away and the cottage is empty'*.

Both Jill and I swear we never told anyone yet on our return I was waiting to back into our car parking space on our lawn whilst a stranger to us walked by when he waved and asked *'How was Devon? Did you have a good time?'*

A minute or two later another person unknown to us said from the pub car park *'Gosh you had lovely weather, I bet Devon was glorious!'* and so it went on.

We soon realised that the whole village knew we had gone to Jill's folk in Devon for Easter and our understanding of living in a village was completely wrong. You don't keep yourself to yourself as is the way in most big towns – you tell everyone your business and then the whole village looks after you, your property, and your safety. It is a whole different way of life but brilliant if you embrace it.

Embrace it we did. Jill got a job teaching in the Village School and as such was on the 'Village Hall Committee' as the school's representative.

The Village Hall were looking for ways of raising funds to re-roof the hall. She came back from one meeting and asked - *'Can't you do something to help them Terry?'* and Beenham Village Drama Group was born.

What fun we were to have over the next few years.

***

In 1968 Beenham only had a couple of hundred houses and cottages so I posted a note through every door advising that we were looking to start an Amateur Drama Group and inviting them to the Village Hall to a meeting to discuss it.

Jill by now had got a job teaching in the village school and on the back of the high regard the villagers had for her a number of them turned up to our meeting including a professional TV Producer of Obituaries.

I had never realised that obituaries were actually put together whilst the person was alive and often healthy. It makes sense for if they had an accident or suddenly died there would be no time to film an obituary or a part of one for that night's news broadcasts.

Our 'Obit' Producer was a very nice man but took one look at the village hall stage and lost interest with the comment that it was so small we would never be able to stage anything but a one act play on it. Thankfully he did not discourage the others and we formed into a play reading group meeting one night a week in the houses of the group members.

Eventually we had the courage to attempt a 3-act play on the stage of Beenham Village Hall and knocked at every house in Beenham and Bucklebury trying to sell tickets.

Our first production was 'The Hot Tiara' by Janet Allen – chosen in the main as I could see us casting it from the members of our play-reading group. It was to run for 3 nights and we sold most of our 120 seats on most nights.

It was tremendous fun.

Adjoining the Village Hall was the Working Men's Club and on a Saturday Night they had a keyboard player. The old division between the 'Insiders' (most of the members of the Working Men's Club) and the 'Outsiders' showed itself as the keyboard player was not going to wait until 'The Hot Tiara' finished and our players had to speak ever louder to be heard over the music.

Thankfully we only suffered this problem on our first play. Max who starred as Nick Nielson in the 'Hot Tiara' was a member of both groups and his conciliatory voice was echoed by many of the 'Insiders' who had come to the play.

We had also managed to get Oswald playing a super part as Bracken. Oswald was over 70 years old and like nearly all the cast it was his first attempt at Drama and he turned out to be very good. Oswald was very much an 'Insider' and a growing accommodation and co-operation between both groups began.

With our first night going very well all the lights went out at precisely 9pm. I rushed backstage to see what had happened to find our lighting man John standing on a chair with a torch looking for the Trip Switch on the Hall's Supply panel. He found it and the play continued seamlessly from then on.

However at precisely 9pm every night all lights would black out until we threw the trip switch back in place.

It turned out that the Electricity Supply Company switched supply points at precisely 9 pm each night. The stage lighting we had managed to borrow meant that we were at or even over the full capacity of the lighting supply board and the switchover caused the trip switch to go.

With the aplomb that seemed to accompany everything we did in Beenham in those days all future productions were arranged to ensure that the lighting man could be standing on a chair with a torch in front of the hall's lighting board at precisely 9pm ready to throw the trip switch back on. We got it down to such a precise art that audiences just thought it was a flicker of the lights.

Resourcefulness was the catchword of the group. We knocked at every door in both villages to sell tickets and for 'The Murder of Maria Martin' we even toured the villages dressed in the costume of the time and with a horse and carriage someone had been kind enough to drive for us on the day. We therefore played to sell out nights and squeezed as many extra rows as we could into the hall.

Early on in our plays Gordon saved a lot of wooden beams and flooring from going on a bonfire at the M40 he was in the process of constructing. He managed to get it all to Beenham and for the next play the Drama group had an Apron in front of the curtain that was as large as the stage behind it. Three act plays and even a musical version of 'The Murder of Maria Martin' that I had scripted and written the Lyrics and Stuart Barham had composed the score became possible.

'The Murder of Maria Martin' was played as a melodrama and the villagers really enjoyed booing and hissing the villain

Poverty to Peaches

and cheering the hero and throwing their own comments into the play.

Amongst our members were Brian and Lee. Brian designed covers for one of the country's largest book sellers. He had an incredible ability to make stage props that looked so real they convinced all of us as well as the audience.

A pair of battle-axes he made for 'Wild Goose Chase' were so realistic that I could not tell the difference from the real thing. Seeing them on stage at our Dress Rehearsal I told him they were a brilliant prop but would have to go. If they fell off the wall they would cut somebody's foot off. Brian had to take me right up to the battle-axes and get me to feel the blades before I could believe that he had made them out of papier-mâché. He was incredibly talented.

'The Murder of Maria Martin' was the last play I was to produce at Beenham.

I had by then played in a pantomime and a play in the RAF, spent 3 weeks on a film set and as a temporary stand-in for one of the lead actors in the film 'The Brothers' (which was never released).

I had played in 5 or 6 straight dramas at LT and a dozen excellent musicals that filled the 1,340 seat Scala Theatre throughout each week of the play, played in 'Guys and Dolls' at King Georges Hall where Reg Bundy and I were told off for bringing the house down with our rendering of the Keystone Cops as we chased the villains (apparently the massive laughter of the audience killed the lines that were to follow from the principal actors!) and I had played in or produced half a dozen plays at Beenham.

I had been lucky for all these productions had been very successful but 'The Murder of Maria Martin' was the first I had been involved in that got a standing and prolonged ovation every night.

Poverty to Peaches

The success of the Beenham Drama Group was down to the super group of players who participated on stage, back stage and in support.

Because of the success of the Drama Group I was asked to see if I could resurrect the Beenham Village Fete.

Beenham had held a Village Fete for many years but it terminated a few years before Jill and I came to the Village. Apparently it had never made any money and in its last few years it had positively lost money.

A number of people offered to serve on the Committee and one of them produced the minutes of the previous committees. It was a good job that Jill and I read the previous minutes before I accepted their offers to come on the committee.

Jill described the minutes as reading like a Shakespearean Tragedy and she wasn't far wrong.

Over the years the committee had some wonderful ideas for attractions that might bring people into the Fete but nobody actually did anything about making them happen. Most times they never actually got around to making contact with anyone who could help. Month after month the committee members reported they had been 'too busy' that month to do anything' or that they 'hadn't been able to contact anyone'. This went on month after month until the Fete arrived with half a dozen local stalls and no supervision of the way entrance fees and stall takings were accounted for. It is little wonder it used to lose money and was packed up.

If we were to resurrect Beenham Fete it needed to be drastically different!

If we were to raise enough money to repair the Village Hall roof we needed to attract that money from the surrounding villages and towns. Beenham is situated about 9 miles from Newbury and 10 from Reading. Between those towns there are numerous small villages. If we could attract folk from that whole area we would raise enough to 'raise the roof'.

Poverty to Peaches

Beenham was surrounded by footpaths and bridleways and I had started to learn to ride horses. Jill could ride and found a delightful girl living up on Bucklebury Common who was disabled but had a few horses with which she used to teach riding mostly to children. I think I was one of Toni's first adult pupils. Jill and I would enjoy many a ride across the common with her.

Her sister Merrily and her sister's boyfriend Frank used to ride in 3-day Events and stabled her horse – Sunset (Sunny) – at Toni's stables. Sunset was about 16 hands high; 18 years old; but so full of life that he had a warning on his box – *'Do not go near this horse – he Bites'.*

With my usual approach to all animals I would natter away to the horse and he soon allowed me to nuzzle up to him and I finished up by exercising him throughout the winter. One of the routes I used to ride circled the surrounding area and came up the hill into Beenham via a bridlepath that meandered through the woods to emerge at the village church next to the school.

Sunset liked nothing more than a gallop up the hill and it was always an exhilarating ride for me. Dear Sally Wiggins – the scrap of a dog that was still with us - used to come out on the ride with us and she and Sunny hit up a close rapport. As fast as Sally's legs could go she was no match for Sonny and we would have to wait for Sally to catch us up when we got to the church.

Sally would sit contentedly right under Sunny as I groomed the horse after our ride and Sunny became so fond of our scrap of a dog that she would not go on past the Church until Sally had caught up with us and got her breath back. Sunny would stand proudly looking back at her little friend hurtling along as fast as her legs could carry her until she was back with us.

It occurred to me that in an area with so many riders a small horse show might be the thing for Beenham Gala (we had renamed the Fete to avoid our new concept being written off as the same old fete. Frank agreed to run the horse show for us if I could find a field big enough and could then provide the jumps.

We managed to get the agreement of the owner of Beenham House to use the field on which motor cycle scrambling took place a couple of times a year and we found someone the other side of Newbury who would loan us their jumps and poles.

Dear Jack Larcom – a lovely man who was the farm manager for the Henry Household – lent us his tractor and large trailer. The only convenient time to pick the poles up was the Friday before our first Gala. I drove the tractor to the other side of Newbury and we picked up the poles. Our load was a very much heavier load than I expected and just as we got through Newbury and on the road toward Thatcham and then up to Beenham – the axle of the trailer gave way.

So there I was on the side of the A4 road that was about to get severely crowded with rush hour traffic with a broken wagon full of my fences and poles and unable to contact anyone to help (these were the days before mobile phones). Even if I found a phone box Jack would be now be out on the farm somewhere and out of contact.

I was muttering the immortal lines of Laurel & Hardy but without their humour - *'Another fine mess you've got us into'* when a huge Transport Lorry came out of the small lane opposite and drove up the A4. On the side of it was painted 'Thatcham Transport' and further up the Lane I thought I could see the top of other Lorries.

Hot foot across the road, up the lane, and into the yard of 'Thatcham Transport'. Found a guy who was sympathetic to my plight and to my over-riding joy said –

'That truck is not due out for a couple of hours, I'll use that. Don't worry it will do the trick'

and with that he climbed into the cab of a huge truck and between us we loaded everything into the truck and took off for Beenham 6 miles up the road.

He drove right onto the Gala Field, we unloaded. *'How much do I owe you?'* I asked.

'Nothing'.

'Are you sure?'

'Nothing – you don't think I'd do this for money do you?

I was so grateful. It had turned out that I had spoken to the owner of Thatcham Transport – that is how he was able to divert a lorry from its schedule to help us out. Without his help I was lost.

Throughout my life it is amazing how many really kind and helpful people have turned up to give a hand just as the situation looked desperate and now here was another.

With the load off the Trailer Jack managed to do a roadside repair that stayed together for the journey back up to Beenham and again wanted no payment for the use of the tractor or the repair. Jack was yet another example of the kind, helpful and gentle people who have helped me through life.

Having got the horse show arranged I had been looking for other events that might attract people from the surrounding area. In doing so I discovered a mantra that stood me in good stead for the rest of my life. Do not rely on a person who has plenty of time on their hands to get a job done. Find the busiest person and if they take on the task they will carry it out.

Each person running the event was completely responsible for it. If they needed anything for their event, equipment, or field markings, barriers etc. they came to me and I would find it somewhere and someone to fetch, carry or erect it.

It really was a case of then joining all the events into a coherent show – hence the joined-up life of Terry Gasking.

My 'Committee' consisted of just Jill and I and it worked brilliantly.

I had managed to find busy people to run the events they knew best and others to fill in where we failed to have any experts. They all made a magnificent success of the events we had at our first and subsequent Beenham Galas.

Horse Show & Gymkhana; Dog Show, Archery Display; Stalls and sideshows, Flowers and Vegetables, It's a Knockout, Clay Pigeon Shoot and so on, we had made it a really appealing fair of country pursuits.

Our friends from LT Players: Tony, Colin, Wally, Barbara, Ivor, and Rita (pushing her newly born boys in the pram) came out to Beenham to help run, judge and add a bit of panache to the 'It's a Knockout' that featured teams from the surrounding villages and thus raised the appeal of Beenham Gala to a much wider audience.

Our friends and helpers were wonderful in helping clear up the field after the Gala and sharing in the joy we all had at its tremendous success.

The event attracted many hundreds of people and easily paid off the cost of repairing the Village Hall roof.

Every event went well although each presented a huge learning curve for us and all who were involved.

Before long we were able to attract top line celebrities to attend who all gave their time and efforts at the Gala at no cost to us.

Diana Dors was still gorgeous, still a star of the silver screen and retained the glitter and glamour she had throughout her film career. Out of the blue I had a phone call from her agent saying that she would be pleased to open next year's Gala for a low fee of £250.

Diana Dors for £250 seemed too good a bargain to miss but I had never paid the previous celebrities (Robin Nedwell; Robert Hardy; Nigel Stocks; Hugh Scully; Jeremy Hanley) who had come and joined in the fun of previous Galas so I had to say to Diana Dors Agent –

Poverty to Peaches

'Gosh we would love to have Diana Dors for £250 but we just don't pay celebrities who come to the Gala. No one takes any payment out of running the Gala. All the money we raise goes straight through to the Charity. Please tell Diana that we would love to have her at next year's Gala but cannot pay'

A day or two later he was back on the phone.

'Diana understands but likewise cannot attend for nothing else her fee basis with events that can afford to pay might get watered down. She is willing to attend for £200 but cannot come for below that price'

'I understand her predicament and thank her for doing her best to help us but sadly I have to say no.'

And that was the end of Diana Dors offer.

I must be one of the few men in the world to have turned down the ravishing Diana Dors for £200.

Gerald and Janet Benny at Beenham House were great supporters and used to invite celebrities to stay with them when the Gala was on and all would come along and join in the fun.

Some of the local farmers wanted a Clay Pigeon Shoot and I had hired some traps to fire the 'pigeons' into the air on the command 'Pull' from the shooter.

Neither Gordon who was running the Clay Pigeon Shoot t or I had any experience of a Clay Pigeon Shoot or had recognised that the sit-in traps needed people to operate them who were not 'well endowed'. If they were they were in danger of instant castration as the arm of the trap whipped across their laps. Gordon looked exhausted after the event. I wasn't sure if it was from the effort of operating the trap or from the nervous exhaustion at the thought of instant severe damage to his marriage happiness if he had moved at the wrong time.

By year 3 the event was attracting more than 8,000 spectators and carried on at that rate of popularity raising many thousands of pounds each year for the charity who were benefitting from each year's Gala. We got the Charity to take the entrance money at the gate and to manage the car park. We found that the Charity helpers also fell into the category of 'find the busiest people and they will get the job done'. We did and it all seemed to work wonderfully well.

Over the following years we put together a Committee of our main helpers but carried on as the main organisers running Beenham Gala until we left the village after 7 very happy years.

The 'VILLAGE OF FEAR'
had for us become the
'VILLAGE OF HAPPINESS'.

*

Beenham Players go on 'Wild Goose Chase' with gusto

ILLUSION is part of the stage business, and there is always an agreeable feeling of expectancy as the audience waits for the curtains to part for the first time at a play.

The programme clue to the set at the Beenham Village Drama Group's production of "Wild Goose Chase" (a comedy by Derek Benfield) last week was "The baronial hall of one of the last few remaining inhabited castles in England." When the curtains parted, the set really should have had a round of applause.

I learnt later what a lot of ingenuity had gone into the making of the bare stone walls and the enormous fireplace. The stage is very small and there is minimal space behind it. To contrive four exits, and place so much furniture that the hall looked very comfortable lived-in, and yet not impede the cast to their foreground chases on, over and off the stage, was a major feat in it-self.

The stage manager, set designer and set builders in the persons of Brian Holt, Ron and Sylvia Deacon and Jill Gasking deserve a special mention.

"Wild Goose Chase" was not a play to tax the imagination or the intellect of the audience. Jokes were very obvious and just a bit corny, but it suited my mood on Wednesday, and I thoroughly enjoyed the evident gusto with which most of the players acted.

In a play full of larger-than-life eccentric characters, it is perhaps no stroke a happy balance to portray them...

Chester should be not give them the photograph. A sort of armour (which with the police-man's uniform were the only things hired by the group) proved a splendid hiding place for Chester, and also offered the opportunity for some stage business—the armoured hand reaching out to dial a tele-phone number for the domineering maid, Ada, (played out-standingly well by Ann Marphal, who could not reach the telephone on its high mantelshelf.

Later, there was good synchronisation of lighting, when Chester "disguised" himself as a standard lamp, and one of the gangsters "switched on" the lamp by pulling Chester's tie! The lamp worked!

Peter Bray hit just the right note with his eccentric Lord Elrood constantly feuding with the postman. Stella Neshet who has given some very good performances in previous productions, could, I felt, have afforded to exaggerate the character of Lady Elrood, although on the other hand, Lilian Stephenson as the very old archaeologist, Miss Partridge, who came, Sherlock Holmes style, looking for Nor-man relics, could well have done with being more re-strained.

Jill Gasking as Jenny Gooseet, foresees for the an...

Pictured in a scene from Beenham Village Drama Group's "Wild Goose Chase" are Jill Gasking and Terry Gasking.

PLAYERS TAKE TO THE ROAD

'ESSFUL DRIVE'

PLAYERS had Sales Drive," on a timers, dressed ries cosumes, ough villages in a horse-drawn

same raised such e drama group's es a melodrama, of Maria Marten in the Red Barn," oesday, Mrs. Jill oried yesterday ho play was "er, with the odd of these.

ama begins here four consecutive

g said the group oiles drive before last year's rather roduce had made of about 40 or

it is owned by a Roe, of Ascot, e single Hackney)

Terry Gasking with members of the Beenham Players, who went in full costume using a pony and trap, on a ticket-selling drive on Saturday. The venture was to publicise their next production, "The Murder of Maria Marten or the Foul Deed of the Red Barn," to be staged at the Victory Hall, Beenham, from March 27th to 30th.

THE VILLAGE DRAMA GROUP, BEENHAM
PRESENT
AT VICTORY HALL, BEENHAM

'THE MURDER OF MARIA MARTEN'
OR
'THE FOUL DEED AT THE RED BARN'

A Victorian melodrama adapted by T. W. Gasking

7.45 p.m. on 27th, 28th, 29th, 30th March, 1974
RING WOOLHAMPTON 2482 FOR TICKETS

ADVERTISE YOUR LOCAL PLAY, JUMBLE SALE, WHIST DRIVE, FETE ETC. IN THESE PAGES. *RING* **JANE** ON **READING 580553** FOR DETAILS OF ADVERTISING

LAURENCE OLIVIER.

21st October, 1970.

Dear Mr. Gasking,

It was so very kind of you to send me such a cheering letter. I am immensely grateful.

My thanks to you and all the players of the Village Drama Group, Beenham, and all good wishes for the great success of "Goodnight Mrs. Puffin". I am so sorry that engagements in London and Brighton make it impossible for me to accept your kind invitation.

Yours sincerely,

Terry Gasking, Esq.

SHE WAS POOR .....

But, in the words of the old song, she was honest.

The song may not have been written specifically for Maria Marten, and Beenham Village Drama Group may have changed the words to suit their story, but the song and their latest production are a fitting epitaph to the demise of one of 19th century England's most famous murder victims.

The Murder of Maria Marten played at Beenham Village Hall last week, was a free adaptation by Terry Gaskin of a true murder story which caused a sensation in 1826.

We tend to think of audience participation in the Theatre as a new thing, but of course the Victorian melodrama (not to mention the early silent films), is a good example of this so-called modern innovation.

Beenham had a very successful go at this art form and came out with flying colours. The production had everything, good acting, fine settings, super music and a thoroughly good reaction from the audience who were easily persuaded to play their part by hissing and cheering at approximately right times.

You will be pleased to read, that, of course, in compliance with the Victorian morality, the villain met his just end, on the scaffold, having made a full confession.

I for one shall be very interested to see how Beenham Village Drama Group measure up, in their next production to the extremely high standard set in this one.

By Mike Goss

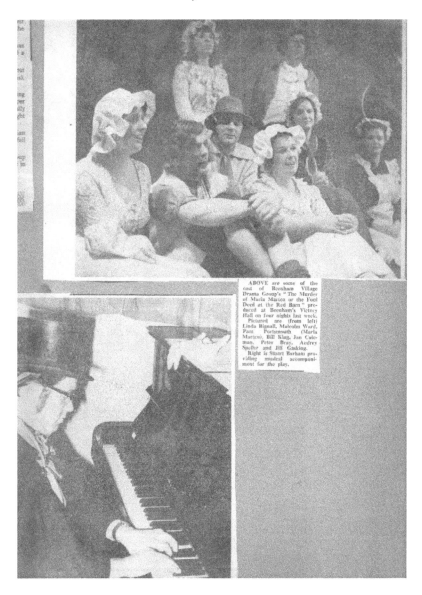

ABOVE are some of the cast of Beenham Village Drama Group's "The Murder of Maria Marten or the Foul Deed at the Red Barn" produced at Beenham's Victory Hall on four nights last week. Pictured are (from left) Linda Bignall, Malcolm Ward, Pam Portsmouth (Maria Marten), Bill King, Jan Coleman, Peter Bray, Audrey Speller and Jill Gashing. Right is Stuart Barham providing musical accompaniment for the play.

enham play worth a longer run

Audience participation was the keynote

The end for Maria Marten (Pamela Portsmouth) at the hands of the villainous William Corder (John Barham) during Beenham Players' production of "The Murder of Maria Marten."

...ER or not there anything in the old ... that seven is a ... member, Beenham Drama Group's production — "The ... of Maria Marten, Foul Deed at the ..." — was certainly successful one. It ... capacity houses on ... nights, and on ... extra chairs had ..., and standing ... the back was also

..., the producer ... the script for this ... to follow theatre ... and portray Maria ... "victim of a ..., although his ... the true story on ... is based showed ... less innocent!

... finally draws the ... with proposal.

... noisest and dancing ... part in this re- ... old story. Added ... enthusiasm by a ... received with ... by an ... has happy to ... the producer's ... of ordeal advice, ... and ugly with the ... family, this was ... evening's entertain-

... have been happy to ... and I suspect ... too, were sorry ... won over. Songs had ... adopted, or ... over the thread ... by the very able ... piano, Mr. ... who played by ... throughout the

... an ambitious play ... did for a cast of ... with, which 12 said, ... of costumes, scene ...

... from opening ... on the village ... in the por- ... and finally the ... few after- ... furniture and ... change of scene

but they were extremely well planned and efficiently done.

Especially effective were the dream sequence in which Maria's mother has a vision of her daughter's brutal murder, and the appearance of Maria's ghost to William Corder in the condemned cell. In each case the sudden dissolution of an apparently solid wall was very well achieved.

The plot is probably well-known to most readers. William Corder, a rich and lecherous young man, already responsible for the death of a young gipsy girl, plans to seduce Maria Marten. The gipsy's mother, determined to avenge her daughter, gives only a half-hearted warning to Maria, planning to use her to bring about Corder's downfall. Maria does not "heed the gipsy's warning," but falls an easy victim to the villain. Later he murders their infant son, kills the gipsy woman, does Maria to death in the Red Barn, and goes off to London with a rich wife.

By a wholly theatrical twist of fate, (of which even W. S. Gilbert could have been proud) the gipsy's son, who had earlier been made to flee the country, now appears as a Bow Street Officer, and thanks to information laid by two other gipsies, is able to arrest Corder and has the satisfaction of escorting him to his execution.

Mr. J. Barham the program... true to early eighteenth century tradition, refer to the cast very formally, and so shall (?), played an exceedingly villainous and unsmiling Corder. His appearance might have been improved for this role, by the addition of a finely waxed moustache which he could then have twirled, Sir-Jasper-fashion, with villainous glee. As it was, his very lack of glee, even when

planning Maria's seduction, made him an altogether more sinister figure.

Mrs. P. Portsmouth, as Maria, was a delightfully innocent and charming victim, and Mr. P. Bray and Mrs. A. Speller made a kindly couple as her parents. The tangible happiness of their early life was well-portrayed by Mrs. J. Coleman, as Maria's half-sister, Anne; Mr. M. Ward as Anne's sweetheart, Tim Robbin; Mrs. L. Bignell as Tim's sister, with their friend Jed Tucker, played by Mr. W. King. Much of the light relief in this play came from these four with a good deal of buffoonery, notably from the cowardly Tim, whose courtship of Anne, made a happy little sub-plot to the play.

The avenging gipsy, Ursula Lee, was played with histrionic fervour, well-suited to the part, by Mrs. L. Stephenson, with Mrs. T. Rigg and Miss E. Marcon as the two younger gipsies, Mrs. J. Gasking, who also choreographed both the country dances and the vigorous gipsy dance, played the role of Corder's maidservant in London. Also taking part were Mr. M. Portsmouth and Miss J. Chorley.

It was a sad occasion in one way for Mr. and Mrs. Portsmouth, as it was their last appearance with the Beenham Village Drama Group, before going to their new home in Bristol. They will be much missed for they have both been very active members, both on and off stage. They gave memorable performances as Waldorf and Belgravia, two shop window dummies in 'Man Alive' in 1971, and Pam also gave an excellent performance as Gillian Holroyd in "Bell, Book and Candle" only last year. Good luck to them both in their new home.

ELIZABETH BLACK

AD-LIBS were at a premium at Beenham Players' production of the melodrama "The Murder of Maria Marten or The Foul Deed at The Red Barn" on Friday—but more from the audience than from the cast.

For Audience participation was very much the keynote at this "world première" as the players billed their production which had been adapted by village drama group member Mr. Terry Gasking.

As requested by Mr. Gasking, the audience joined in enthusiastically, eagerly hissing the villain, cheering the gipsies and country folk, and sighing sorrowfully at Maria Marten's plight. And by the time the final chorus of Maria Marten's lament had been sung by cast and audience it was debatable which side of the stage enjoyed themselves most.

Every scene had its quick repartee from the audience or course jibe from the back rows but this was exactly what was needed to provide the basis "fun for all the family" atmosphere, so sadly missing nowadays.

It took a brave theatre group to branch out in this way. Their first attempt was perhaps a ...

group; her singing voice beyond reproach.

Perhaps Mr. J. Barham as William Corder, the villain could have been more convincingly evil but this was a small point in an otherwise word-perfect performances.

One other thing which could have been more convincing was the transition, as necessary in melodramas, between a member of the cast talking on stage and a supposedly secretly aside to the audience.

A word of praise should go to the stage managing team for an excellent set and scene changes on their first efforts.

206

The Hot Tiara March 1970

Poverty to Peaches

Picture perfect puppies

PUPPY LOVE: Jill Gasking   Pictures by Barry Keith

208

CHAPTER Fourteen
It takes the Biscuit

Whilst living at Beenham my work had proceeded at similar pace to that of my social life. I was still travelling to London Transport but my last minute skid to a stop next to the train at Aldermaston Halt was getting more desperate and the working day plus travel was occupying 11 hours. A bit more time at home in the evening would be welcome and I saw an advert in the Reading Mercury for an Accountancy Clerk needed at a nationally known Biscuit Company in Reading.

My accounting studies seemed to be going well so I applied and got the job. The company was setting up a new Management Accounting System and I was appointed to help out in the section that produced the Management Accounts.

As luck would have it the guy in charge of the section was having difficulties stepping into the demands of Management Accounts as opposed to Financial Accounts and I was soon responsible for the production of the monthly Management Accounts

Whilst still at London Transport I had been studying for an Ordinary National Certificate in Business Studies and I completed it at Reading Technical College. Somehow I had managed to achieve 96% in Statistics and 99% in Accounts.

My other subjects were all good so I was awarded a 'Distinction' at ONC Business Studies.

In addition - thanks to the encouragement of my tutors at Reading Tech, particularly the very attractive one with gorgeous legs who used to sit on her desk whilst lecturing and was thus guaranteed the rapt attention of her pupils (remember it was the days of the mini-skirt!) I had sat and passed GCE 'A' Level in 3 subjects - Accounting, Business Law, and Economics.

Remembering my struggles with studies at Grocers it seemed unbelievably to me that with 3 excellent passes at GCE 'A' Level - Terry Gasking (Little Tel' from 'ackney Downs) was qualified academically to a level that would admit him to University.

University was a rare privilege in my young days only available to the very bright academics amongst the students.

It was even rarer in boys or girls from Olinda Road, Hackney, especially for a boy who went through Grammar School with only a single candle to light and heat his bedroom and see to do his homework – the only room in the house in which he could have studied.

I had passed 3 subjects at 'A' level and it staggered me.

I had no intention of going to University for I had a home to pay for with Jill – my second wife – and paid maintenance for my 3 children from my first wife, so taking time out of work to study was never an option.

The Biscuit Company had an outstanding Group Finance Director who had devised the Management Accounting system. There was also a Chartered Accountant above me as Cost Accountant who's joy was a wall covered in figures from which the entire business could be watched.

At that time I had spent more of my working life outside Accounting than inside and I realised that the joy the Chartered Accountant derived from pouring over pages of figures was shared by very few others in the business and was positively hated by most of the non-financial managers.

With my ONC studies finished the Chartered Accountant and the Group Finance Director tried to persuade me to follow the same line of studies that they had, spend a year or two

'Articled' in a Professional Office and become a Chartered Accountant.

I had no idea if I could succeed and pass 5 years of exams but it didn't seem the right path for me.

I did find a curriculum for the Certified Accountants (now Chartered Certified Accountants - ACCA) that seemed more business orientated so I went for that. It meant I would need to study from home via a Correspondence Course for 5 years but I thought it was worth a try to see whether I really could become a Qualified Accountant.

I was in the Management Accountant Section of the Biscuit Company, the head of the Finance Section was a lovely chap and I got on very well with him. He told me that he had tried for the ACCA and passed all the 5 years of exams except the last when he failed 1 of the 4 subjects involved.

If you failed in any one subject you had to take all the final year exams again and for 8 years he tried to pass his finals but failed one subject each year – often a different one from the previous year. He then gave up and realised that Head of the Finance Section was as high as he would get in Business.

So with some apprehension I started studying for 5 years for a full Accountancy qualification - ACCA (Associate of the Certified Accountants – now the Chartered Certified Accountants).

I started the correspondence course at home much to the chagrin of little Sally Wiggins who just wanted Jill and I to be spending the evenings together.

She really wasn't happy with me in one of our downstairs rooms studying whilst Jill was in the other downstairs room watching TV. Sally would start with Jill and 10 minutes later would scratch at the door between us to be let in with me. Ten minutes later and she scratched the door again to be let back in with Jill. This would go on all evening with our little dog making it obvious that she was happiest when we were settled down together.

In the late 1960s/early 1970s business costs were rising. The production lines on which the biscuits were made were only running for 5 hours or so in a normal 8 hour day. Many of the more exotic biscuits were being produced at a nominal loss just to keep the lines working. The Group Finance Manager had asked us if anyone had any ideas that would improve the situation would we kindly put them forward.

I was out walking our Sally Wiggins and whilst she was sitting so nicely for a biscuit at the end of our walk the answer to Huntley & Palmers problems became blindingly obvious.

We should produce Dog Biscuits on the lines when our orders for biscuits had been fulfilled.

I told the Group Finance Director of my idea and he said I should put together a fully costed proposal and if it was sound he would put it to the Board of Directors.

Off I started with all the zeal of a young man given his head.

Biscuit Manufacture is a plant based operation with minimum labour. Once the plant is installed it can run relatively inexpensively. The cost of the plant was already being written off (depreciated) against the existing biscuits so I need not take it into account.

Further thought revealed that the Selling Costs were effectively nothing for the existing Sales Force could take orders for the dog biscuits as they took orders for normal biscuits. There were no delivery costs to take account of for the companies vans were already delivering to the customer base (Grocery Shops etc) so they just drop off the dog biscuits at the same time.

The result of my costings were that the Company could run the dog biscuits during plant idle time and make a huge profit on them. If they wished they could afford to undercut the existing dog biscuit market and still make a huge profit.

I proudly analysed all this into a Report headed –
'Proposal to Produce Dog Biscuits
In Idle Time.'

I could not see any way this proposal could fail!

I gave it to the Group Finance Accountant who presented it at the next Board Meeting. He had copies taken of my report and they were placed before each member of the Board.

And that was as far as my beloved proposal got!

It appears that the Chairman took one look at the document in front of him, went red in the face and said;

'My great grandfather founded this company and my grandfather and father helped to make it into the finest Biscuit manufacturer in the World' he bellowed. *'Who the hell thinks that I am going to allow this great company to manufacture dog Biscuits?'*

.. in near apoplexy he hurled the unread proposal across the Board Room into the waste bin

That was the end of my great proposal.

It was many years later before I realised that had I loaded the dog biscuits with all the depreciation of the plant, the selling and delivery costs, they would have shown only a slight profit but all our Chocolate Bath Olivers and other 'exotic' biscuits would have returned to a level of profit that they hadn't experienced in years.

My beloved proposal would then surely have pleased everyone on the board and it would have had an excellent chance of being accepted. It would also have done much to enhance Terry Gasking's promotion prospects.

As it was my proposal was never resurrected and it was a very early lesson for me in the art of dealing with and opening the minds of management.

Despite that setback I continued at the biscuit company and was still studying by correspondence school in the evenings. I managed to scrape through the first 2 years of my ACCA when I spotted another advertisement in the Reading Mercury.

*

Courage, the National Brewers based in Reading were looking for a Cost Accountant to run their newly formed Management Accounting Section. The advert specified that the applicant needed to be a qualified Accountant but the job spec. looked remarkably like the one I had worked at for the past 3 years and the pay was 50% higher than I was earning at the biscuit company.

I posted an application and got an interview with the acting Finance Director Bill Jakeman. He was 'Acting' because he was also Finance Director of the London part of the group which by then was the amalgamation of 3 great Brewers - Courage, Barclays and Simmons. It appeared that he was at Reading for 6 months or so to get an efficient Accounting Office working at Courage's.

I enjoyed the interview.

Bill Jakeman seemed a very genuine and honest man who was easy to talk to and as an inveterate talker all my life the interview seemed to go well to me.

Mr Jakeman explained that he had a lot of applicants and this was the first round of interviews.

He would draw up a short list of 3 and have them back for a second interview before making up his mind.

He told me that all the others were already qualified as Accountants so with me only just passed Part 2 of the exams and 3 years studying to go before I qualified (that is if I passed all the subjects every year) it was unlikely that I would make the short list.

The job was that of Cost Accountant and that is very rarely filled by anyone other than a fully qualified Accountant but nevertheless he asked me to phone back the following week to make certain.

Poverty to Peaches

I phoned back the following week to find I was on the short list and invited to a second interview.

Bill Jakeman started the interview by outlining his doubts about how I would be able to overcome the problems I face from my lack of knowledge of the subjects I was yet to cover in my ACCA curriculum and still win over the non-financial and the financial managers.

However he had been sufficiently impressed by my work experience at Huntley & Palmers to put me on his shortlist.

He then started to ask me just how I would set about introducing a monthly Management Accounting System into a Brewery that had only ever had 6-monthly financial accounts with those taking 3 months to produce.

We got into some quite detailed discussions on the structure of Courage and its management and how I would match a Management Accounting System to that structure.

We were well into the detail when I realised that the Financial Director (Acting) might be holding similar talks with all his shortlisted candidates to 'pick their brains and experience' and then hand the job to a tried and tested internal candidate.

I looked hard at Bill Jakeman and all I could see was a very genuine and honest man. I revealed all I knew about Management Accounting Systems in the interview. He thanked me and asked me to phone the following week after he had interviewed the others on his short list. He again emphasised that the job was that of Cost Accountant and he had seen the job as one for a qualified Accountant.

He asked what Salary I was expecting if I got the job. My reply was immediate *'The job is advertised at £14,000 per ann. It is the rate for the job and if I help you to successfully implement a Management Accounting System here I feel I should be worth every penny.'*

'That is a big 'if'.'

215

'I don't think so!' said I *'I have seen one Management Accounting System into a major company successfully and think I learned enough to help this one to similar success. If I do not then it will not be for want of trying on my part but I cannot see why I shouldn't succeed.'*

'I like your confidence' said Bill *'but I still have to weigh up your lack of qualification. However I have been impressed by the knowledge you have picked up when implementing the system across the road* [both companies were based in Reading]. *Now I need to see how the others interview. Phone me next week'*

I phoned the following week.

'I remain very impressed Terry but bear in mind you are unqualified – if I were to offer you the job, what is the minimum wage you will take?'

'£14,000 – I promise you I will prove to be worth it.'

There was a long delay followed by *'I must think about it but what is the earliest you could start?*

A gulp from me - *'I need to give a month's notice where I am and then I'd be free to start.'*

Another long delay, me on tenterhooks knowing I had a chance of getting the job.

Had I been too bold? Should I have stated a lower salary? After a few more moments I got my reply.

'O.k Terry, I would like you to join us. I will put it all in writing and put it in the post. If my secretary can get it in the post tonight the confirmation should be with you by tomorrow.'

'Thank you Mr Jakeman, I really look forward to joining you' and then with a great deal of trepidation I pushed my luck one more time. *'At what Salary?'*

I thought I could detect a chuckle in his voice *'£14,000 a year plus benefits, plus expenses. Just make it work and you will be worth it.'*

This was the biggest rise I had ever had

£14,000 a year was a lot of money to us in 1972. It would change our lives. It would truly be my first step away from the poverty I had experienced throughout the first 20 years of my life.

I had been right – Bill Jakeman was a very genuine and honest man. He also turned out to be the most effective and kindest Financial Directors I was ever to work for.

*

CHAPTER Fifteen
Courage

My first problem at Courage's was my toughest.

I needed to win over all the Brewers, Bottlers, Estate Managers, Sales and Marketing Managers, Transport Managers and so on as well as their Directors.

A Management Accounting System only works if it providing information the MANAGERS want. Most systems fail to be effective because the systems – designed by Accountants - only provide information the Accountant THINKS the managers want – or worse still - only provide information the Accountant wants.

Most – and in my experience the vast majority of non-financial managers (i.e. the people who actually generate the profits within a company) – do not have the experience or financial nous to design a management accounting system. How can they? Their job is not to be playing around with figures but managing and controlling their non-financial sections that are vital to the success of the organisation.

If my system was going to work I needed to find out precisely how each section of the brewery worked and then discuss with its Manager and Director the financial information and costings we can provide to help THEM manage.

Our monthly management report (a summary of income and expenditure that can be logged on a single piece of paper) must be such that it enables them to set accurate budgets and then to manage to them. We also needed my system to give early warnings of any straying from Budget so that THEY – the managers can correct any trends that were adverse and capitalise on any that were advantageous.

To achieve this I needed firstly to tour their section of the business and then to sit down with them and work out how we as Accountants could provide them with the information that would help THEM to manage.

I have used capital letters in the above statements to emphasise the reason for a Management Accounting system i.e. to provide information the Managers want, and how it differs from Financial Accounting System where information is provided for the Shareholders, Accountants and Auditors.

The massive problem at Courage's at Reading was that the omnipotent Brewers would not speak to the Accountants. This had a history that went way back.

The Accountants at the HQ of the Group that owned the Breweries had defined that the whole Brewery should change from brewing the traditional ales that beer drinkers had enjoyed for generations and brew Keg Beer instead.

Keg beer was stored in containers that were in effect very large tins (Kegs) that had a longer shelf life and greater profit than the traditional beers stored and served from wooden casks.

As with nearly all Accountants the figures on the paper drowned out all other considerations and often drowned out common sense.

The Accountants had conducted many Taste Tests where the tasters could detect almost no difference between the new more profitable Keg Beer and the traditional draft ale. Thus the order had been given to change the Breweries over to producing Keg Beer.

Taste Tests try out an egg cup half full of one beer against an egg cup half full of another. The average beer drinker consumes a bit more than an egg cup during an evening's drinking. What may taste the same or similar when drinking an egg cup full turns out to be very different after a pint or two, or three or more (many more the Brewers hope).

The Accountants were not popular with the Brewers and this was never more so than at the Reading Brewery.

The Brewery had lunch time accommodation that was typical of British firms in the twentieth century. The Dining Rooms and Canteens were housed in a large house that was stood in the middle of the Brewery. It had 3 entrances and 4 Dining Rooms.

The top Executives (Board Members and the Heads of each section of the Brewery) ate in the Exclusive Dining Room downstairs, their Deputies including the Financial Accountant and the Cost Accountant ate in a similarly exclusive dining room upstairs and they and any top level guests they might have were the only ones allowed through the Front Door of the House. There was a Staff Dining Room accessible to staff via a side door and a canteen for the workers accessible via the back door. Each dining room had a level of cuisine that the management deemed appropriate to the status of the diner.

The Financial Accountant and the Qualified Accountant of similar status who I was to discover had been previously recruited to see in a new Management Accounting System but had not the experience to progress with it and was full time on the maintenance and production of the Financial Accounts and the Cost Accountant (me) qualified for the exclusive dining room upstairs.

The Financial Accountants were dealing with an ever expanding Free Trade and Tied House customer base and work load. They were processing the accounts for weekly deliveries for more than 2,600 pubs and hotels. I began to understand why Bill Jakeman had plumped for my Management Accounting Systems knowledge over my lack of Accounting Qualifications. He clearly saw in me a person who could perhaps make the implementation of a Management Accounting system happen where more qualified people had failed and I was not about to let him down.

They both warned me not to eat in the No 2 Executive Dining Room (the upstairs exclusive dining room). They had both tried but could not cope with the daily torrent of abuse they got from the other managers. It was led by the forceful and very powerful 21 stone Brewer George but was aided and abetted by all the other managers who were determined to keep their dining room free from the hated Accountants.

Indeed they said that George would never find time to attend meetings with the accountants either in his own office or theirs. I rapidly found this to be true. If I gate-crashed him in his office he immediately went out onto the Brewing floors where admission to non-brewing staff was restricted.

I knew that if I was to be able to design and implement an efficient Management Accounting System I would need to break through that hatred and get these key managers on my side.

Between them all they knew the business inside out. The only thing they didn't know was the way an intelligently designed Management Information System could actually help them to budget and manage their sections and become a key tool of management to them.

I'd been in the job for a week or so when I turned up at the No2 Dining Room for lunch.

The managers sat either side of a very long dining table. The Brewers, Bottlers and key Production Managers occupied the chairs by the entrance and the less powerful sat further along the table.

I walked through the door.

'What the hell do you think you are doing here?' it was the voice of the man I was to learn was the dreaded George. *'We don't have your sort in here, Clear off.'*

'*Hello Chaps* (there wasn't a female amongst them) *I'm Terry Gasking – your new Cost Accountant*' said I smiling.

'*We know who you are and you are not <u>our</u> new Cost Accountant – we want no part of you. You belong over in the Accounts office and make sure you stay there. We don't have Accountants in here,*'

George was a very intimidating figure and his tone was determined and threatening. I silently blessed my Dad for taking me to boxing club in my youth. I have never since been physically intimidated so now it was a case of dealing with the verbal intimidation.

It was my turn to spar -

'*Well that's going to be a bit difficult for you because I am going to be working with you for the next few years*' said I keeping the smile on my face '*and thus I shall be eating with you.*'

There was a silence followed by '*Not if I have anything to do with it you won't.*'

There was a silence as I stood my ground.

*If we have to put up with you today f**k off to the other end of the table. We don't want to see or hear you from here, and don't come back another day!*'

The only empty seats were at the far end of the table so I went and sat on one of them.

The meal starters arrived and a couple of the managers at my end of the table introduced themselves but little was said throughout the meal and no-one spoke to me as I left. This same behaviour continued all week and I knew I had to break up the Brewers verbal control of anything the Accountants in Reading tried to do. They also resisted the missives coming down from the Group Accountants with the same vigour.

There was only one thing for it. I must take George on and win. I arrived early for lunch – no-one was there and I sat in George's seat.

As each senior manager came in there really was shock on their faces and almost to a man they said

'You'd better get out of that seat quickly. If George catches you there will be all hell to pay. That has been George's seat for the best part of 20 years. No-one else sits there.'

Still with a smile each time I gentle said -

'I've got a job to do and to succeed I need George's co-operation and understanding. His knowledge is vital if this system is to be a true help to you all. If this is the only way I can get him to co-operate then so be it.'

The retorts from the manager verged on disbelief to a warning of forthcoming Armageddon.

The door opened and in walked George Troth.

'What the f**k do you think you are doing? You can get out of that seat immediately.

'Sorry George, if you won't meet me any other way then I have to talk to you at the dining table.'

'Not in my seat you don't. F**k off to the other end of the table.

'Sorry George. I'm not moving. This will be my seat until I can sit down with you anywhere and have an intelligent conversation about the way my Management Accounting System works and how you really can help me and my system really help you.'

George was turning incandescent with rage and nearly 6 feet tall and 21 stone moved threateningly towards me.

I really don't know if he was tempted to try to physically remove me from 'his' chair but I was clearly not going to move and continued to smile confidently so in rage George flew out the door.

We continued this scene for 3 or 4 days with me trying to make an appointment to see George in his office. Suddenly he agreed to meet and we met each other with just the two of us in attendance.

I started the conversation with -

'Please hear me out George. I don't mean to be difficult at lunch but it really is absolutely essential that I get your knowledge into the new system.

I will tell you what I am trying to do, how it has worked brilliantly at my previous company, and what we can adapt from their system to suit Courage.

Between us we can design a bespoke system that covers exactly what you feel would help you in the Brewing operations at Courage'.

George did hear me out. He then sat quietly for quite some time.

'Tell me George – what part of the Brewery gives you the biggest problem? The part where you have to spend the greatest part of your time to keep it on track.'

'The daily brew – you idiot – keeping that in perfect condition is the most important part of this entire Brewery. It is not your blasted figures – it is the taste of the beer when the consumer drinks it.

'So what information do you need that will help you achieve that?

Is there any early warning system I can set up to warn of costs going high or low and leave you to use all your skills to produce the perfect pint every day instead of getting side-tracked into the level of support stock you need or have or keeping your eye on the cost increases or decreases or the multiplication of other items that keep you from the brew?'

George looked hard at me for some time and then opened up. He started to discuss areas where he could concede I might be able to help him and outlined a few areas where my type of system might help if it didn't intrude on his number one priority – the quality of the beer.

Next day I arrived early at lunch and sat in the chair opposite George. It was normally occupied by the Assistant Brewer.

He muttered an objection but I felt sure he knew George and I had met. I was also fairly sure that everyone wanted a reconciliation to end the bitterness George had been portraying to me.

George had come into the dining room every day since the first day I occupied his seat and immediately turned on his heel and left. This time, seeing me sat opposite he hesitated and then took his normal seat and even made eye contact with me with a slight nod of the head.

It is incredible that from such a difficult start George and I went on to develop a brilliant working relationship and the knowledge of Brewing he was to share with me played a huge part in the success my Management Accounting System was to enjoy.

There was no doubt we developed a huge mutual respect and I was one of the few Accountants ever to be regularly invited by George to sample that days brew of Bulldog Stout that he brewed for the Belgian and French markets. It was gorgeous!

My Management Accounting System was performing excellently and producing monthly data that was of positive help to the managers. I had designed it on a responsibility basis so that each manager just got one page with the details of the sales and costs for the area they were personally responsible for along with copy of the single page report of the managers and supervisors who reported to them.

Managers were thus not swamped with detail and if my design was right then my one page contained all the data that was vital to them along with variances from their budget.

Adverse variances gave an early warning of things going over cost, favourable variances revealed areas of the business that might allow for greater profitability.

Early in the implementation of virtually every management system abnormalities show up that were not obvious when things were being done 'the way we always do it'. When that

225

happened the manager who is responsible for the mis-performing area gets very upsets and insists the information provided by my system is wrong.

At the biscuit company the biggest abnormality we found was in the stock numbers of Christmas Puddings. These are baked all year round and mainly sold at Christmas. My figures were revealing that we baked many more Puddings than we had in stock – they were disappearing somewhere. *'Impossible!'* said those in charge of puddings.

The figures in my reports inevitably proved to be true.

If I have designed it correctly then they just have to be. Everything is reconciled to actual counts of products and to the costs of purchase. Usually false information is discovered as we are setting up the system

At the biscuit company deeper investigation found that the main storage depot for Christmas Puddings was under railway arches in South London and the local villains had cut out a square of the wooden slats at the back of the arches with such precision that it could not easily be seen.

Each day's batch of Puddings arrived at the Arches in the evening and were counted the next day. Each evening the local lads removed their 'door' had it away with a couple of pallet loads of Christmas puddings to sell around the local markets, replaced their 'door' before they had been counted. Nobody was ever the wise to this scam until the new system showed up the Stock Shortages.

Much the same sort of thing happened at Courage.

My figures were revealing a shortage of Guinness.

Investigation revealed that one Delivery Dray with the aid of a Checker was picking up an extra 6 dozen Guinness every day, dropping them off over a hedge into a field on their route and then returning after their shift to sell them cheaply around the pubs.

An even more audacious fraud occurred when the labour figures in the Bottling Hall and in the Brewery were disputed.

We looked in detail at who the people were that were included in my figures and the Brewer said

'Hang about, this team of 10 guys you show here don't work for me - they are in Bottling'

'No they're not' said the Bottling Manager *'they're nothing to do with me'*

I got their Clocking-in Cards and they were clocked into the Brewery.

'Yes' said the Brewer *'they may clock in at the Brewery but this dates back to when they used to work here. They haven't been working for me for a couple of years. They clock-on with us and then walk over to the Bottling Stores'*

'They may walk <u>toward</u> *the Bottling Stores but they never arrive with us'* said the Bottling Manager.

Sure enough this little team had been clocking on in the morning then disappearing home or to other jobs during the day, then returning in the evening to clock-out and drawing their wages for a full week's work from Courage each and every week.

A new management accounting system is not designed as a thief catcher – such happenings as I describe here are by no means uncommon but they are a by-product of the system. They emerge because of the information we can begin to present to management about how their Sections <u>actually</u> perform and the costs of operation.

At Courage's the greatest challenge to my new system came from the Transport Director.

Bill Jakeman had got me into the Management Board Meetings each month to report on the results thrown up by the new Management Accounting System.

The Board of Directors had previously only had half-yearly Financial Accounts and it took 3 months to produce these.

Managers were used to running their departments and sections using figures and data produced within their own department rather than by a system that used the actual costs as shown in the accounts. Managers had previously had to rely on the cost information the clerks in their departments produced for them.

The Transport Manager was incredibly proud of the system his division used. He could tell the exact cost of running all his vehicles, the cost of tyres, engine parts, maintenance, and differentiate these costs between all the trucks, lorries and vehicles the Brewery used. He ran a most efficient division always within budget and businessmen came from many other companies to see if they could implement the system he used that helped him to such great efficiencies.

Trouble arose from the first set of monthly management data my system produced.

The new system – my baby – was showing a 10% overspend against budget in the Transport Division. His reaction to this was to rubbish my figures thus throwing doubt on the whole system in the eyes of his main board colleagues.

Trouble was the second month produced the same result as did the third.

The Transport managers were not at all impressed -

'People from all kinds of business come to look at our system. It has the highest reputation and impresses everyone. It is copied all over the country by delivery companies', said the Transport Director. *Our in-house system shows that the Transport department are on or below budget and these are the figures I trust. If you say anything different then your figures are wrong and you had better re-design your Management Accounting System!*

Bill Jakeman stepped in, allocated 4 of his senior people from the financial accounting section to look at how the Management Reports figures for Transport were assembled.

Their job was to see if they could determine why they differed from the new Management Accounting System. but they could find no fault in the way the Transport Section assembled their own figures. Equally they could not fault the figures produced by my new Management Accounting System.

Next month the discrepancy occurred again and my figures were rubbished at Board Level.

Bill sent the same 4 over to work alongside the transport clerks who were producing their Reports but again they could find no fault.

Curiouser and curiouser!

Then I went across to transport to examine how their reports came together. There was no point in looking from the bottom up for the financial team had done that and found no fault so I looked from the top down.

Their system seemed perfect.

All the costs for the various vehicles were accurately recorded on a card index system and these were then added together and the total entered on the next level up cards to give a cost per tyres/maintenance fuel etc per vehicle. All excellent and very relevant data.

The cards recording the costs were then added together to give a total cost per type of vehicle (lorries, delivery trucks, motor cars, fork lift trucks etc) and the total was then entered onto a top level card that gave the total costs tyres/maintenance fuel etc for the Transport Section. These were the figures the Transport Manager and the Transport Director used to enable them to run their Division efficiently.

Their system really couldn't be faulted!

I looked again at the problem – something had to be amiss!

It is strange how at such times an insignificant point will often jump up and demand you do something to it even if it seems to have little or no impact on the problem.

Something was fidgeting me and I realised that the totals of the cards that were carried onto the next level were not actually noted on the bottom of the lower level card – the total appeared at the top of the next card up the chain.

Insignificant really but I started the chore of add-listing the lower level cards just to check that the same figure appeared at the top of the higher level card. They were all correct apart from the final transfer.

The figures entered on the final cards were 10% lower than my calculated totals of the cards just below them in Transport's 'hierarchy' of recordings.

I checked my figures 2 or 3 times and sure enough all the totals for the costs of fuel, tyres, maintenance, etc. shown on their final top level cards were 10% lower than the cards they were purported to be from?

Curiouser and curiouser!

I pointed this out to the kindly clerk who compiled them. He hesitated for a while and then confessed -

'That's because we know the figures that come up on the cards run at 10% above the true costs.'

Hold on Terry - take a moment or two to consider the transport's system and wonder if that could be true. *'I'm sorry – I don't understand'* said I *'how do you know they run 10% above true costs?'*

'Experience!'

'Who's experience?'

'Well mine – and the Transport Manager.'

Pause again Terry – is there some significant fact that I haven't found that is outside their recording system?

'What do you base that judgement on?' I asked.

'Years of experience. We know they run 10 % high!' he said and continued *'If I presented the boss with the figures you have calculated from the cards I would soon be out of a job! No – they are not correct - over the years we KNOW that these*

figures run 10% high and so we correct them on the final reports! We have been doing it for years and it's never been a problem. In fact it's never been questioned until you asked'
Pause to take in the significance of this last remark.

'Let me just get this right,' said I *'You have this superb system that accurately records all costs of running this Department in terrific detail, you then analyse them upwards to give wonderful data on the running costs per vehicle but when you produce your Report for the Transport Manager and the Board of Directors of the total running Costs of the Transport Department you reduce all figures by 10%!*

'Yes,' he said *'I suppose we do'*

And that was how Transport department reported their figures 10% below the true running costs of the department.

For years the Transport Division Clerk had been understating the true costs by 10% and everyone was happy.

Now I am going to upset everyone by revealing that the Transport's figures are 10% understated and have been for years. What a dilemma.

It was solved by Bill Jakeman. He setup some private meetings with the Transport Director, convinced him of the accuracy of the New Management Accounting Reports, persuaded him not to come down too hard on the clerk who was only doing what he thought his bosses wanted.

At the next Board Meeting Bill fudged over the reasons for the discrepancies, the Transport Director withdrew his reservations and endorsed the new system and we never looked back.

*

As with all systems there are always a number of idiosyncrasies that get ironed out but once a system is in and working it tends to release some time on its designer and manager. The Management Accounting Reports take away much of the time previously spent on areas that do not need supervision and allow greater supervision of the areas that require it.

Courage's had decided to purchase a Computer to run the financial accounting function of the weekly accounting for the tied and free houses.

The top floor of their offices was strengthened, air conditioning was installed and 'the computer' was loaded through the upstairs windows and put in place.

It was the very start of the in-house installation of computers and nobody in the Brewery organisation had any great experience or knowledge of running a Computer Department.

The Board of Directors decided that Terry Gasking should become Computer Manager whilst still retaining his Cost Accountant duties and title.

They sent me on a 2-week course at Eastbourne University and that was it – 'Little Tel from 'ackney Downs' was Cost Accountant/Computer Manager and still not yet through my Finals at ACCA.

We implemented the Computer System with me learning as I went along.

It is interesting that our processor was 25k (that really is 25k not megabytes of gigabytes now available) and we loaded data off punched cards into the processor and back out onto the massive hard disks you now see on old films.

I am forced into huge smiles when I hear children of primary school age in Computer Retailers telling their parent –

'But Dad – I need 60 Gigabytes.

I am ever so tempted to tell them of how we processed 2,600 accounts every week on just 25k but they would probably think that I was a daft old bugger who didn't know what I was talking about.

Such is the way of progress that even a home computer has massively more power and memory than our first business computer and the modern youngster would only stare in disbelief yet it was only 40 years ago.

*

In the early 1970 Breweries in the U.K. were merging and amalgamating. A few years earlier Courage had merged with Barclays and Simmons and now merged or took over many others including Plymouth Breweries and John Smiths of Tadcaster.

John Smith's of Tadcaster were as big a Brewer in the North as Courage, Barclay & Simmons was in the South and neither company was willing to give up its ways of working in favour of the other.

They ran completely different systems of accounts and the dilemma over which was to predominate was solved by bringing in one of the top 4 companies of Accountants to research all the systems being used in all the merged companies and to build on the one that was best suited to the emerging super-sized Company.

As luck would have it they chose the system I had designed for Courage Central at Reading and built on it to suit all aspects of the enlarged group's Management Accounting Requirements.

The system needed to be introduced and implemented in all parts of the formerly independent companies including all areas of Courage Barclays that were now part of the enlarged group.

I was chosen to be part of the small group of Accountants from the Brewery and from the top Accountant Company to spend the next year or so as a working party to implement the Group-wide Management Accounting System.

Terry Gasking – 'Little Tel from 'ackney Downs' - suddenly had become a Group Consultant implementing accounting systems over the head of experienced ACCA qualified Accountants and even over the head of one or two Fellows of the Chartered Accountants who were in Financial Directors rolls in the various companies - and I still had yet to sit my Final year at ACCA. Wow!

My modus operandi was similar to my early days at Courage.

Make contact with all the Accounting and Non-Accounting Managers; hold discussions with them about the way the Management Accounting System could help them, and then work out a plan of implementation that could be monitored to ensure successful implementation.

There was inevitable objections and resistance but somehow knowledge had got around the group that Terry Gasking was the man who not only took on the mighty George (who's strength, powerful presence and antagonism towards Accountants was known throughout the Brewing Industry) but had become such good friends with George that the Brewer was seen swotting up on Costing Systems out of a book Terry Gasking had recommended.

They might even have known that George had been a significant contributor to the design of the Management Accounts system.

They may not have relished having to change their system to fit into a group-wide management reporting system but I guess they all knew that such a move was inevitable.

Many managers had subtle ways of gaining a measure of revenge.

My modus operandi always required a walk around every part of the Brewery first so that I could get a feel for any physical attributes that might cause problems with the system

I was usually accompanied by a Production Manager and Supervisor and/or Accountant.

At Plymouth Brewery they walked me all around and through the Brewery but left me at the base of the ladder that led up to the Hop Loft,

'We'll leave you to have a look around in the loft and meet you the other side. Walk across the loft and you will see the other set of stairs descending to the Transport Section.'

And suddenly they were gone. I climbed the stairs they had indicated – they were steep like a ships ladder – and there on a small landing was a fierce looking cat.

It was obviously a scrapper for part of one ear had been torn away and its body language was far from friendly. I have always been good with animals and for some reason or other they seem to respond kindly to my voice. This cat made it clear that it didn't want me too near it. It certainly didn't want to be stroked so I smiled nicely at it, wished it well passed by and upwards into the Hop Loft, crossed it and down the other steps to meet the Production Manager and Accountant the other side.

'You all right?' they asked.

'Yes fine, why?'

'Did you meet a cat up there?'

'No, there was a cat on the steps going up. It wasn't very friendly but it seemed all right, bit of a scrapper I would think.'

They looked puzzled. *'Did it have part of an ear missing?'*

'Yes, that's the one'

'And you are all right?'

'Yes fine, so how many days production does the hops stored above represent?

Still looking puzzled the two of them answered my questions as we toured the rest of the Brewery.

The antagonism that often meets the person who has come in to change things will either increase as time goes on or evaporate depending on the personality of the individuals and the success of the changes they introduce. Thankfully I have been blessed with a work ethic that has found over the years that the harder I work the better the results so inevitably finish up on very good terms with most original 'antagonists.

On one of my subsequent visits the guys revealed that the Hop Loft Cat was the scourge of every cat in the area and of most of the humans. The workers would ward it off with brooms if they needed to go up into the loft and their favourite trick was to invite anyone they did not want nosing around to go up into the Hop Loft on their own.

They told me that previous outsider to me to try to get past the cat was an auditor. He got halfway up the ladder toward the landing when the Hop Loft cat leapt off the landing and hurtled toward him, claws extended and hissing as it landed on the unfortunate Auditors head.

It appeared I was the only visitor in living memory who had managed to pass the cat on the stairs without getting bitten and scratched to buggery.

I've stated earlier in this book that I have always had a love of animals and found that I have a rapport with them. I guess this is what the Hop Croft cat felt. Its tolerance of me as I chatted away to it and the way it allowed me to pass without any threat certainly did my street cred no harm at Plymouth Brewery.

Most of my work days were now spent in the various locations of the group – London, Tadcaster, Bristol, Plymouth and Reading along with occasional days at Alton in Hants at Courage's Canning Brewery. Here they also stabled their magnificent Shire Horses that pulled the brewery drays at displays all over the country.

I always enjoyed my visits to Alton. The management there were very sincere and helpful and my day was always complete with a nuzzle with each Shire Horse. These really were magnificent animals 18 and a half hands high at their withers (a hand is 4 inches) meaning its head stood proudly with its ears some 7 or 8 feet above the ground. Most of them were nearly a ton in weight and one or two topped that. Again my rapport with animals showed itself and I was able to nuzzle all of them and chat away to them.

My involvement in Beenham Drama Group was diminishing as I was away during rehearsals so I was very surprised and delighted to get an invitation from the Producer of one of the biggest open-air theatre festivals in Berkshire to play a significant role in their forthcoming production. Timothy West was to direct.

I am a great admirer of the work of Timothy West so was thrilled to accept until I saw the dates. The production coincided with the dates I was due to sit for my Finals of the Certified Accountants ACCA.

I had managed to keep passing my exams each year despite my high work load and even higher social life with the Drama Group and the Gala. If I could pass my Finals then I would qualify as ACCA and could call myself an Accountant.

ACCA was considered to be the second highest qualification for accountants, sitting just behind Chartered Accountants ACA although this difference was to be blurred subsequently.

With my workload in different locations it would be mighty difficult to do the drama and my Finals but I was desperately tempted.

It was the third time I almost threw my lot into trying to make a go of a theatrical career.

The first was in Devon when I attended auditions as an Extra on a film set and finished by being asked to be a temporary Stand-In for one of their stars. They set up the scene and rehearsed the camera runs etc on the Stand-Ins, then everyone else in place we were whipped off the set and the Stars stepped in.

After a few weeks of this I was very confident that I could handle the stars role if someone gave me the chance.

However conversation with the stars convinced me that the way forward was to attend Drama College and with 3 small babies and a struggle to keep my first marriage together that was not an option.

The second occasion I almost gave up all to become an actor was in my early days at London Transport. I was courting Jill and loving the musicals we were doing with LT Players and other leading companies. I saw that the Mermaid Theatre were encouraging newcomers to audition and a few enquiries led to the same conclusion that I really needed to go to Drama School.

I wrote to Rose Bruford School of Mime and Drama and got an audition. The audition progressed well until we each had to individually perform the Shakespeare extract we had been asked to prepare.

I was about the 8th on the list and we could watch the others perform their audition piece. This was a real shock to my system. I had felt I had performed all that had been asked of me so far to at least the standards of the others who were competing for the few places available but now they were acting like cut-down Sir Laurence Oliviers.

Their Drama coaches had obviously schooled them absolutely precisely for their performance of the Shakespeare piece. Chairs were requisitioned as props, every gesture had been rehearsed and perfected, and vocally they seemed completely 'elevated' from the people I had been chatting to earlier.

I had learnt the piece but not thought about all the gestures and emphasis. What on earth should I do?

With my turn getting ever closer all I could do is what I have always done on stage. Play it as though I really was the character and was responding to the events that had been scripted.

I had a few minutes still available to think about how I would use the 'stage' but any movement would need to arise naturally from the emotion the piece created.

I got through my Shakespeare bit and then thought I did quite well on the mime, crawling across the stage, under imaginary barbed wire etc. and that was that – or so I thought. The invigilators were very kind in their remarks and would be writing to everyone when their series of auditions were over.

Back to the day job, in those days I was still at the bottom of the administrator ladder, but a letter arrived from Bernard Miles the Director of the Mermaid Theatre in London. He was most kind about the letter I had written and would arrange an audition if that is what I really wanted.

Without wishing to discourage me he did urge me to consider the fact that even Actors of much renown spend an awful lot of their time waiting for a role to materialise and most worked for less that 30% of the year.

I was reminded of that very fine actress Helen Fraser who's hands I had read when on-set of 'The Brothers' in Devon. She had told me that after co-starring in 'Billy Liar' she had waited months for the offer of another decent role. When it arrived it was in 'The Brothers' with Brenda Bruce, Rupert Davies, Bill Marlowe and many other stars yet this film was never released and lays languishing on some archive store.

The next day a letter arrived from Rose Bruford School of Mime and Drama. I had passed the audition and had been awarded a place with them in the Autumn Term.

What a predicament!

Do I take up the offer of Drama School and try to make a career out of the professional theatre or do I continue to study Business Administration and play at the theatre through the amateur groups.

My Amateur groups did play and fill West End Theatres – something I may never aspire to as a professional. On the other hand I would have loved to try my hand at making a career 'treading the boards' but the voice of Helen Frazer and the letter from Bernard Miles played on my mind and with much regret I decided to turn down my place at Rose Bruford.

I wrote them a nice letter explaining my predicament – I was still paying back the debts from my first marriage and had the maintenance on 3 children to provide for. At that time I was courting Jill and if we were to get together I would need a greater income than that of an itinerate actor.

I had continually been encouraged and complemented on my acting but was I good enough to be a 'star' – I think not!

Rose Bruford School were most kind and even phoned me up to see if I would change my mind but having been in poverty for most of my life until then I just couldn't risk the stage as a career.

That was back when I had just started to study, now 7 years later – (2 years were spent getting a 'Distinction' in my ONC Business Studies and 5 years studying ACCA) I was about to sit my Final exams and suddenly another great temptation was in front of me.

My work and social load meant that I crammed all my studies into the 3 months before each exam which was the period that was needed for word learning and rehearsals of the Shakespeare production so I couldn't do both.

The production would not lead directly to any professional theatre experience but playing under the experienced and very able Director would enable me to gauge whether or not I really had the talent to make it in the professional theatre.

On the other hand these were my Final Exams and if I passed I would be a qualified Accountant and who knows what doors might open to me.

This time it was the voice of the head of the finance section from the biscuit company that played in my head.

Foul up this time and I might go round and round the Mulberry Bush for years – never quite passing all the Final Year Subjects at the same time.

The decision had to be – sit my Final Exams!

I would love to have become an actor but it really wasn't an option.

I sat my Finals and - unbelievably – I passed.

Little Tel' from 'ackney' wiv only 'is candle to heat and to light 'is 'omework - had become a Qualified Accountant.

I needed to pinch myself to believe it.   I think that only someone who also lived through the poverty and malnutrition of my childhood and youth would understand the incredibility I felt.

(The vernacular used in the previous sentence was totally appropriate to my days as a young teenager in Hackney but were now a misnomer. Though never posh nor BBC polished, my accent – thanks to LT Drama - was no longer Cockney.

School dinners at Grammar School were the first regular dinners I had and they had contributed to my growth and service in the RAF had done the rest I was still slim but 6 feet tall and very fit so I guess it was Terry from Hackney in the East end of London who had made it through to Accounting Qualification and maybe was a more accurate description but I still – and always will – think of myself as 'Little Tel from 'ackney Downs'.

At 32 years of age I was to qualify later than those who had gone into accountancy straight from College or University but I was willing to bet that my management and business experience was up there with any of them.

Wow! Terry Gasking ACCA – where on earth was this going to lead?

*

CHAPTER Sixteen
All that Glitters IS Gold

A meeting with the Group FD at Courage had made me aware that the route to a member of the Board of Directors was not an option for me so I looked around and found a job as Financial Director of a family run firm of Precious Metal manufacturers.

At one time the company had manufactured approximately 80% of all the precious metal watch cases and bracelets in the U.K. In recent years – though still a respected name - it held a far lower share of the market and had diversified into gold and silver plating along with a move into a new market where gold was used in medical instrumentation.

They had a work force of more than 280 and a joint venture on plating in Hong Kong with one of the 'Colony's' biggest companies.

Their Financial Accounts revealed that they made adequate profits each year but it appeared that they were having problems with cash flow.

They had Factored their Debts and were paying very high costs for that finance. My first task was to produce a business plan that would secure far less expensive bank financing and restore an overdraft facility that had been reduced and was threatened with withdrawal.

A business plan without me being confident of the quality of the accounts I was using is always fraught with danger but I put one together, negotiated with the bank and secured the finance to ease the immediate situation. I then set about designing an Accounting Management Information System for the company that should highlight why they were suffering Cash Flow Problems.

Their principal business was still the manufacture of precious metal watch cases and bracelets so their stocks of gold, silver and platinum were very valuable.

Buying these metals in a rising market was costly and I thought it essential that pricing of products should be based on Forward Prices rather than the price paid for the actual metal used in the product.

This did not go down well with the Sales Director for it immediately upped the price of all his products.

It was necessary for me to prove that the main cause of the Company's Cash Flow problems was the ever increasing cost of their Stock Holdings. The resultant valuations of their stock also caused a false reading of 'Profits' and disguised losses.

The gold, silver, platinum, etc. that was their stock in trade was continually increasing in price and value. It took time to manufacture and stock in the jeweller's shops before any sale was completed. Even when sold there was a considerable delay in payment being received from the retailers as they traditionally enjoyed payment terms of 90 days or more. Meanwhile it was necessary to buy more stock in order to carry on manufacturing the precious metal products that comprised their trade.

Thus to hold the same quantity of stock at the end of the year to allow you to continue to manufacture required a lot more money than at the year's beginning.

Thankfully my insistence on using Forward Prices did not have the adverse effect on sales that my fellow Board members were fearing for the Retailers and Watch Companies we supplied found that they could pass the intrinsic value of the gold and silver in their products straight through to the customer.

I then started detailed costing of all the products we dealt in. They revealed that we were making modest profits on the precious metal items but losing on our plating operations. It also revealed that the profit shown on the Accounts of recent years were in actual fact Stock Profits i.e. the profit came from the higher value of the Closing Sock over the Opening Stock.. The company was actually manufacturing at a loss.

Their profit was coming from their holdings in Gold Platinum and Silver. They could have packed up manufacturing completely and just bought the raw precious metal at the start of the year, sold it at the end of the year and made the same profit. In fact they would have made greater profits as the stock profits were absorbing the losses made in manufacture.

This was difficult for my fellow directors to accept and took great deal of costing education to prove the point.

In addition we seemed to be majoring on the plated products that had little or no differential from the genuine article and I could not see why this did not harm our precious metal sales and thus our profitability.

In the midst of all this the 1974 Recession hit the U.K. Economy. The FT 100 Index of Share Prices over the years 1972 – 1974 fell 68% from 545 to 154. Newspapers were forecasting that it was the end of the Financial System – wiping out the wealth of the Western World and chaos was about to occur.

The retired owner of the company used to come into lunch and asked me what I would do in his shoes. I knew he had amassed tremendous asset wealth in precious items over his years and boldly suggested he should sell most of his assets and invest in the FT100 shares. When the western financial 'experts' have come to their senses and the index starts to rise he should sell the shares for twice the price he had bought them and then buy back the assets he had sold. If my confidence that the index was correct he would have doubled his wealth and still have all his original assets.

I made this remarkably bold suggestion when the index was still falling and was about 180. It continued to fall day by day for the following weeks and I found all sorts of excuses not to eat in the dining room in case he had taken up my suggestion and was slowly watching his wealth dissipating on a daily basis. Eventually it held at 154 and then started to climb.

'I thought we might see you back now the share index is climbing' said the Chairman. *'On a prolonged diet were you?'* he said tongue in cheek.

The FT100 was to climb like a mini rollercoaster over the years so that as I write this book in December 2012 it has just climbed to 6500 but the relief I felt in 1994 when it did turn upwards was considerable.

The fear of the collapse of the financial system led to people to stop buying plated products on which my company had built a great deal of their production capacities. The type of consumer who would buy our precious metal products instead started to invest directly into gold and silver pushing their prices up and causing us real problems restocking. Also our customers sat on their money instead of paying our invoices so we had money going out to restock, pay wages and pay suppliers but very little coming in.

I knew that we would be unable to pay our wages within a month or two if we failed to act fast and dramatically.

The Sales Director proposed that we gave all our retailers 5% if they would pay their overdue bills. This did not sit easily with me – they were already overdue – why are we giving them an incentive not to pay new orders but let them go overdue when we would give them an extra 5% Discount.

I managed to persuade my fellow Directors that I would send a letter to all our customers advising them that in the tough economic time we were suffering we were imposing a 2% per month surcharge on all overdue accounts and that this will be payable before we could supply any more product to them.

As many of our customers were relying on our products to stock their shops and paid us only when they sold the stock this was obviously something of a shock for them.

We worked the strategy that the Sales Staff would rush around every customer and explain that the company had a new Finance Director and this bastard was insisting on payment of the bill and the surcharge – HOWEVER our salesman/woman could walk away with a cheque to cover all the overdues the sales person would persuade 'the Bastard' to withdraw the Surcharge.

The Strategy worked at least 80% of the time and £millions came pouring in. It saved the company. I learned so much from the success of this ploy that it was to form the basis of *'Terry Gasking Tutors Cash & Management Workshops'* I was to run in many parts of the world in the early 2000s.

Whilst I seem to absorb stress without it showing I began to get breathing difficulties each evening as I drove back to Beenham. We sadly came to the conclusion that the solution was to move to Buckinghamshire to be closer to the company.

We found a bungalow in the Vale of Aylesbury that had recently been modernised. It had a large lounge. The people to whom we sold our cottage in Beenham did not want any of the carpets so we took them with us. We set them down in our new lounge whilst waiting for a new carpet to be fitted and all the carpets from every room of our old cottage were insufficient to cover the lounge floor in our bungalow.

The bungalow was set in just short of half an acre which was good news and bad. It was nice to have the space but it took every moment of our scarce free time to keep the garden under control.

Poverty to Peaches

It saved my journeying at the end of a stressful day and placed us in a most beautiful part of Buckinghamshire with wonderful views of the setting sun.

The agreement the company had made with their Hong Kong partners in the Plating Operation was running out and the Company Lawyer of one of Hong Kong's biggest Companies came over to the U.K. to negotiate a continuance of the contract or its cessation.

As far as we could see the original contract had been drawn up in such a way that with the trading and profitability record of what had actually been achieved the Hong Kong Company could walk away with control and most of the company for almost nothing.

The biggest thing in our favour was our reputation from dealing with watch manufacturers and the Retailers for nearly 100 years whilst the Hong Kong company would need to start marketing and selling from scratch. We had a flimsy stance but at least we had one to negotiate with.

The negotiations lasted two full days and we started on some minor issues. The English born lawyer who represented the Hong Kong Company was very strong verbally on all points but I noticed he lit a new cigarette every time we came to a point of issue that we won.

Since the horrors of my father's death from cancer I abhor smoking but as he was a chain smoker we had to put up with him smoking during the negotiations. It played completely in our favour. He signalled the weaknesses he had in his case by continually lighting up a new cigarette even when he had one already on the go.

In one of our time outs I persuaded my fellow directors never to give in on any point on which he lit up another cigarette so that we could build up negotiating strengths that we might have to concede in the final issue to obtain the best result available to us. And that is precisely what happened.

The Hong Kong lawyer had no idea that his habit and body language was giving vastly different signals from his speech and statements made during the meeting - often quite contrary - and we came away with far more than we had ever hoped to achieve when we had been discussing the situation in advance of the meetings.

The experiences of trying to steer a precious metal company through the travails of 1974 Recession have stayed with me.

When the Recession of the 1990s hit us I did not have a lot of investments but I did manage to double them by relying on a repeat of the history of 1974.

In 2009 I wrote *'Double Your Money'* a small book aimed at helping the individual to do just that and double their money over the 5 years following the 2010-2012 recession (which was also forecast almost exactly in my 2004 book *'Get out of Debt with Terry Gasking'*). Will history repeat itself again? We shall see.

The strategy of being 'tough but fair' on our customers had been difficult to impose on a friendly family run Board of Directors and to their great credit they ran with it and it worked.

All too often companies try to get at the money owed to them by their customers by offering an extra discount if they pay within the 30 days. This always seemed madness to me. If you use that method then the customer is encouraged to continually pay late (longer than 30 days) until you give them a discount for paying on time. Thus you give away 2½ % (or even 5% in worst case scenarios) of your profit for nothing.

I had to work hard to make sure that we did not stop on our insistence of *'Pay within the agreed credit terms or suffer a surcharge of 2% per month'* but our management kept with it and it kept us in positive cash flow.

At times I felt it was a bit of a one man band leading the revolution of Positive Cash Flow especially when the

Managing Director decided he should set an example to all. He cancelled his morning newspaper!

I may be doing him a mis-service but that is honestly all I can remember as his contribution to Positive Cash Flow.

Oh – there was the suggestion that we should take up all the floorboards and staircases in the factory and burn them!

This was in fact an excellent suggestion that the company did every 20 years or so. Their work was precious metal manufacture and as in all manufacturing concerns there is a certain amount of the metal and metal dust that escapes the machines and spreads on the floor to be swept up. Some penetrates the wooden floors and is trodden up and down staircases on the undersides of the workers shoes..

The floorboards and staircases had been in place for best part of 20 years and glistened with swarf of gold, silver and platinum. If burnt and the precious metal retrieved it would pay for a complete re-flooring and leave money over. In the middle of a recession we couldn't afford the close down time it would have taken. However it was a sensible suggestion if all else had been lost.

You see all that glittered WAS gold!

*

CHAPTER Seventeen
The Dynamic world of North Sea Oil

The nice old owner of the Precious Metal Manufacturing Company suffered a Stroke and was incapacitated. This led to considerable conflict and uncertainty as to who was running the company and which direction it was going to take.

A Brazilian Company manufacturing elite watches asked me personally if I would act for them in setting up a subsidiary company in the U.K. At the same time a Hong Kong Company asked if I would look for suitable acquisitions in the U.K. and (just like buses coming along in 3s) a new Watch Retail Company was starting up in the U.K. and asked me if I would act as Financial Director for them on a part time basis.

After much consideration I took the step away from paid employment and into Professional Consultancy. It was 1976 and I was 37 years old and Terry Gasking ACCA, AMIS. (I had passed the Associates entrance requirements of the Institute of Management Information Systems).

I constantly hear Ministers and Members of Parliament exhorting people to start up their own businesses but they have no idea of the travails and tensions involved.

Most MPs have lived all their lives in Parliament or cocooned in a parliamentary support role. It is a mighty big step to give up the security of a monthly wage paying your mortgage and all your bills in favour of marketing and selling yourself. It also demands many more hours in the day than does paid employment.

Poverty to Peaches

I was lucky. I had 3 part-time jobs to start me on my way but they were not without problems.

The Brazilian company used to phone me for detailed discussions most days – their days – usually late into my evenings or even at night. The Hong Kong Company would phone me on most days – their days – usually in the early hours of the morning, and the new Watch Retail Company sailed far too close to the wind in their dealings with their customers for my liking so within little more than a year I was back with the Head-Hunter

He found me a contract consultancy in North Sea Oil.

I was still self-employed as a Consultant but had a 6 month contract it the hugely exciting world of Oil Production from deep under the North Sea.

I was one of a small team put together by the Oil Company (one of the 'Seven Sisters' the seven largest Oil Companies in the world i.e one of the biggest companies in the world with an annual budget spend larger than all but 10% of the Countries of the World).

The team were to investigate why one of the biggest Oil projects in the world was running 12 months late and was £billions over budget.

A couple of years previously the Oil Company had towed the Oil Drilling Platform out into the middle of the North Sea (the oilfield extended under Norwegian and British Waters) took out the ballast and settled it onto the sea bed hundreds of feet deep.

They had designed all the drilling and living quarters in module format and these were being constructed and fabricated in ship-building yards throughout northern Europe.

Each module was about 90 feet long 60 feet wide and 30 feet high and was packed with equipment.

The modules were to be loaded on Ocean Going barges and towed out to the platform where one of the world's biggest offshore cranes would lift it into place.

All the pipes and contacts would then be married up to the module that would be lifted next to it and the whole thing assembled like so many massive Lego bricks into a fully operational Oil Drilling Platform.

The construction was in the hands of one of the world's leading Offshore Operating Companies. They would also operate the drilling on behalf of the Oil Company once all the 'Lego Bricks' had been loaded aboard the Platform and married up.

The Norwegian Oil Corporation realised that they were paying the costs of this entire operation but had no control on how their money was being spent.

At the time of the assembly of our Investigation Team the estimated cost of the project was $3.6 billion ($3,600,000,000) and rising on an almost daily basis and the project was already a year behind schedule.

The Norwegian and to a lesser extent the British tax payers were paying the bills.

The Norwegians insisted that a team of 'experts' be put together to effectively review the entire project and report back. The Oil Company insisted that the team had to be under their control as it would be 'crawling all over the construction sites and Platform' with all the inherent dangers that might have.

1977 was the very early days of North Sea Oil and very few organisations in Europe had the experience of Oil Platform Construction so control of the operation was left in the Oil Company's hands. The Oil Company were instructed to recruit the team of experts to effectively audit the whole operation to date.

On paper the Oil Company recruited experts in Finance, Quantity Surveying, Construction and Contract Administration. In fact they put together a team that had not the faintest experience of oil platform construction.

Terry Gasking ACCA: AMIS had suddenly become the 'expert in financial management' to investigate a $3.6 billion Oil Project but I knew not a thing about Oil or the world of Offshore Construction and drilling!

When chatting to the other members of the team I discovered that the Quantity Surveyor – Jimmy - had a wicked sense of humour but not the slightest experience or knowledge of North Sea Oil or any other oil. His previous task had been building a Motorway.

The 'expert' in Contract Administration had never been in administration but had a Fine Arts Degree and was a charming young man. I could never find out the background of the Construction 'expert' for he seemed to me to be a young man who spent a great deal of time in a world of his own.

We were to be managed by Jesse - a manager who worked as an Internal Auditor for the Oil Company. He too was a nice chap but not a strong character and unlikely to step on anyone's toes, particularly those who were paying his wages.

It was obvious that this was a very rum team of 'experts'.

I think the Quantity Surveyor was the first to realise that the last thing the Oil Company wanted was for us to uncover anything serious. Superficial problems that could be easily corrected were fine and would allow them to report these back to the Norwegian Oil Corporation to show that the project was being thoroughly investigated.

With Jesse's approval I spent a couple of months pouring over the Contract Documents in a London Office to establish precisely what the Operating Company had been contracted to do and then took myself off to the UK Construction site in the North of England to see what they were up to.

I knew from the records I had examined at the Regional Head Office in London that they had been contracted to construct and fabricate 3 of these massive Modules and had about 80 workers working full time on the project.

There on the quayside were three massive Modules looking hugely impressive, surrounded by various pieces of plant and machinery that were obviously waiting to be fabricated inside the module.

The modules were indeed like giant Lego Bricks - more than 3 London Double decker buses long, the length of 2 buses wide, and at least 2 buses tall (my old experiences at LT coming into play). Inside they were full of pipes and mechanical plant but no workers. It was 11 o'clock in the morning and I walked all around the site as is my modus operandi and there were no workers on site.

I found the Site Manager in the Site Office.

'Where the devil are all your workers?' I asked.

'Inclement Weather!'

'Inclement Weather?' I repeated his answer with a lot of incredibility in my voice.

'Yes, Inclement Weather!'

'But there's blue sky and the sun is shining' said I.

'Yes but it wasn't at 8 o'clock this morning' he replied *'at 8 o'clock this morning it was pissing down with rain'*

'Yes but it isn't now' said I *'the forecast was for clearing skies'*

I lied for I had travelled up that morning and hadn't seen the forecast but looking at the sky I guessed it must have said something like that and with no workers on site I was bloody certain the Site Manager had also not consulted the weather forecasts.

'It's no use you coming here in the middle of the morning when you deem to get up' he said belligerently *' you needed to*

be here at 8am and you would have seen the weather was impossible for the workforce'

'That was 8am' said I *'Couldn't you have let them all have a cup of tea or a break for an hour or so and started them at 9 or 10am or even now rather than lose a day's fabrication'*

'No! Their contract stipulates that if there is inclement weather in the first hour of the day they are not required to work. The union would never allow it!' he stated.

I knew this wasn't true for one thing I have always been good at is doing my homework before I tackle a new project. I had been through the contracts in London and knew no such condition existed.

My problem now was what to do?

I did not wish to go into direct confrontation with the Site Manager on the first site I have visited but this was supposed to be the dynamic world of North Sea Oil. It was a world where the Oil Companies paid top wages to get top managers and workers yet no-one had picked up the fact that on this site if it rained in the first hour of the working day the workers all buggered off somewhere and a day's fabrication was lost.

If the other construction sites in this project were like this then it is little wonder that the project is miles over budget and way behind schedule.

My task was investigating the project and reporting back. I was not empowered to be confrontational with anyone so this fact would have to wait for my report after my visit.

I finished my tour and spend a couple of days on site. On the other days each of the employees clocked on in the morning and stayed on until afternoon clocking-off.

Back in London I discussed and filed my report with Jesse – the Oil Company's Team Manager. I had the feeling he was pleased that he has someone who could organise a site visit and make sense of the situation. I wasn't sure Jesse himself could – despite him being an experienced 'Oil-man'.

My next visit to site was in Holland at Rotterdam.

Somehow even to my inexperienced eyes this site seemed to have much more order and industry that their U.K. counterpart.

There were six modules sitting on the quay side partly fabricated and pretty full of the pipes and equipment that were to be fitted to the insides of the modules.

The organisation and management of the site was good and the only real problem I encountered was my lack of confidence that the output from these modules would exactly match the inputs of the modules that were to sit next to them on the Platform.

Although English was the language of Oil Operations it was a second language to many of the people working on the contract and this is always a cause of concern. However - engineering problems were outside my remit so I left such problems to those who were far better equipped to handle them.

I had a few trips to Stavanger offices in Norway in an attempt to marry up Contract documentation and it was proposed that I should visit 3 sites that were alongside the deepest Fjords in Norway.

The sites were extraordinarily attractive. Wonderful scenery with snow covered peaks and deep valleys.

My coldest trip ever was to Boda, 50 miles inside the Arctic Circle where a module was being assembled on an Island just off the coast..

Boda is washed by the Gulf Stream so the water in the harbour had not frozen but the rigging and masts on the boats were deeply covered in frozen snow and frost. The streets were filled with snow and it was the first time I had ever seen mothers scooting their prams along the pavements with sledges replacing wheels on the prams. It was all incredibly beautiful.

This was another efficient site and I was beginning to immensely enjoy my foray into North Sea Oil.

Poverty to Peaches

On the ferry back from the island a stranger stood next to me on the deck and said -

'Are you Terry Gasking, the simple country boy?'

I used the guise of being a simple country boy frequently during site visits when I didn't really believe what I was being told and wanted the manager to clarify exactly what he/she (there were very few female managers in North Sea Oil in the 1970s) was telling me.

'I am, but I'm sorry, I don't remember meeting you on the project.'

'No I work in the back office here at Boda and had heard about you from the other sites you've been to. I was talking about you last time I was at home and my nephew said – 'I know a Terry Gasking he was never a simple country boy but was part of our gang in Olinda Road Hackney. Could it be the same one?'

I spent the rest of that ferry trip in hugely nostalgic conversation about our gang from 'ackney and hearing about a pal from days that were nearly 25 years earlier.

Here was I in a beautiful but remote part of Norway deep in the Arctic Circle thinking I had been the only Englishman aboard the ferry when I am chatted to by the uncle of one of our gang who is still living in Hackney. This type of meeting was to happen to me so many times over my lifetime and it has made me realise that we now live in a 'global village'.

My consultancy contract with the Oil Company was extended by another 6 months.

I was guessing that my critical assessment of the U.K. site along with some relatively minor negative assessments on my initial visits to sites in Holland and Norway was giving the Oil Company reports that they could file with the Norwegian Oil Corporation to show that their team of 'experts' were working efficiently.

I spent a few months in the Paris Offices of the Operating Company where much of co-ordination of the European and offshore operations was done.

I liked Paris.

Wherever I am in the world – at the end of the day I always like to walk back to my hotel and Paris is a lovely City to walk. I particularly enjoyed walks alongside the Seine.

I liked the way all the managers and staff in the Paris offices greeted each other in the morning with a hug and a kiss and then parted at the end of the day with another hug and a kiss.

It reminded me of the lovely group of people who made up the London Transport Players who had made me feel so welcome at a time in my life when I really needed affection.

It is very difficult to feel 'stand-offish' with a work colleague when you greet each other that way each day. I resolved to bring this habit into my future working environments.

The habit also underlined the enormous power of touch.

Touch is one of the most neglected and misunderstood senses! It can convey so many messages and sincerity. It need never extend to any 'rude' touching but as I was to discover from Paris a hug and a peck on the cheek (or a peck on the lips if you were particularly fond of the other person) consolidates a great deal of togetherness.

Lunch time in Paris took me by surprise. The managers would go off to eat at a restaurant and sample the finest Red Wines the establishment stocked. Lunch time would be at least an hour and a half and a fair bit of inebriation.

It would be easy to get hooked on such an enjoyable habit.

My next task was a detailed investigation of the biggest of the Project's Norwegian sites.

It was in a deep valley between high peaks and the only way in was by light aircraft that needed to closely dodge the peaks and then drop almost vertically to get down onto the landing site. Not something I fancied doing in poor weather but was destined to do on quite a few occasions in the months ahead.

This site certainly had 4 modules and a full array of people working on them.

I had researched their contract documents in Paris and their management reports and knew there were on average more than 80 highly skilled – highly paid workers on site.

I don't consciously count workers when I do my walk about at the start of my investigation for they could be in remote areas of the site but something caused me disquiet.

'Have you got any workers away from the main site or are they all employed here?' I asked the site engineer who was showing me around.

English is the international language and as with most Europeans his command of English put most Brits to shame.

'No they are all here in one or other of the modules!'

Jimmy - the Quantity Surveyor was coming to join me in a day or two and I thought it would pay us to just verify the 80 or so workers on site.

Jimmy and I had shared many a joke during our times together on sites and in various offices of the project but it was no joke standing in sub-zero temperature at 6 am in the morning to watch the workers 'clock-in'. We were a little way from the clocking-in hut unseen by the workers we were not able to see what they were doing but were able to count the 74 workers who turned up for work that day.

Before we went into the offices to thaw out our frozen bones we went into the 'Clocking-in' hut and checked all the cards. 84 workers were shown as clocked in that morning. We had only counted 74 so 10 were clocking in 2 cards each.

We repeated the exercise at the end of the day – in equally freezing temperature – and 74 workers went through the Clocking-in hut (now the clocking out hut) but 84 cards were clocked out.

'Dummy workers' is one of the oldest frauds.

In the days of wages paid cash in wage packets it used to need collusion from whoever was paying out the wages. Now most wages are paid by computer directly into Bank Accounts it just needs someone to clock a 'dummy' person in and out each day and get his/her wages paid into a bank account where they can be retrieved subsequently.

The fraud can be easily detected by reasonable supervision of the work force but I was realising the image of dynamic management in North Sea Oil was a myth.

Errors and frauds were being compounded by the massive amount of money being thrown at these projects and the pace at which things needed to progress.

There were 3 major construction sites in Norway. They were situated on the banks of some of the deepest fjords and major offices in Stavanger and Bergen.

A great deal of my time was spent in Norway but my contract allowed me to fly home and back each weekend.

The British Airways and Scandinavian Airways desk clerks got used to 'talkative' Terry checking in on a regular basis and being met from the flight home by Jill and Sally Wiggins both of whom had grown into 'girls' to steal your heart away – be it that one was on 4 legs and the other on two.

We flew through all kinds of weather conditions but the aircrews were first class and delivered us safely to our destination.

There was the aggravation of the Air Traffic Controllers strike in the midst of this period with the worst event happening after we had been sat in the aircraft on the tarmac for more than 9 hours waiting for the next available flying and landing slot in Stavanger. When the Captain was finally allowed to start up his engines we could all hear a banging from the back of the aircraft. Apparently the rear door did not want to lock and on came engineers to fix it. Those of us who had travelled through all the disruption in previous weeks knew that if they couldn't immediately fix it we would miss our flying and landing slot and be back in the queue.

Unfortunately they couldn't fix it in time and back in the queue we went. It was 13 hours of sitting in the aircraft on the tarmac before we eventually were allowed to take off and fly to Norway.

Mostly our flights were excellent but one alarming incident happened on a foggy Friday night on my flight back home to London. We took off ok and had been in the air for about 20 minutes when the aircraft gave a sudden lurch. The Captain's voice came over the radio.

'My instruments are telling me that we have a fire in the port engine. We have closed down the engine and applied its fire hazard operation.

We are returning to Stavanger.'

I was sitting next to an American lady who immediately panicked *'Oh God, Oh God'* she was crying. *'Don't let it happen. God, I'll never see my children again.'*

She was in floods of tears and I tried to reassure her that *'it might be only the instruments giving this message and that fire fighting equipment within the engine should keep it under control until we are back in Stavanger'.*

I had no idea if any of this was true and was not helped by a passenger seated on the starboard side of the aircraft leaping all over us to try to scc thc rear slung engine to see the fire.

My words seemed to have the effect of calming her slightly.

'The cabin crew will be taking all sharp items from you and showing you the crash positions.' It was the Captains voice, *'Please listen to them carefully and cooperate so we can get through this as efficiently and as safely as possible.'*

The Air Hostess appeared beside me *'To get everyone off the aircraft as quickly as possible we will be going down the chutes'* she said. *'I need the first one down to pull the chute out away from the aircraft to let the others slide down safely and get away. Will you do so?'*

With all the pandemonium there was no time to think and I agreed to do so.

'O.k. you will be first down that chute.' She pointed at the door right in front of us. *'Really pull hard on the chute try to pull the aircraft over and stay with it until all the passengers are off'*

The news that we were sitting just next to an escape door and would be first out seemed to calm the American lady. I decided not to tell her that 'our' chute was right in front of the engine that was apparently burning.

The captain brought the aircraft down to just above sea level as we flew back toward Stavanger. It was easy to realise why. If the fire forced us to ditch in the sea he wanted to get it down very rapidly and smoothly.

The flight and the tension went on for some while and then he took the aircraft into a gentle climb. I discovered later this was because we had land in sight and he needed to get the undercarriage cranked down. The loss of one engine had knocked out its hydraulic action. I also discovered that this was the moment of greatest tension on the flight deck. If we now had to ditch in the sea the undercarriage would tip the aircraft on its nose and send it plunging to the bottom, this is why he had delayed the dropping of the wheels until the very last moment.

Stavanger Airport is by the sea so the cabin crew had us all in crash positions with our heads tucked down between our knees as the co-pilot tried to get down onto the runway and pulled up in time to clear the aircraft before the potential disaster explosion or fire devoured the aircraft.

This was the first time I had ever been in such a situation and I hoped would be the last. I could not resist lifting my head to watch what was happening alongside the aircraft as the co-pilot touched down. The runway was lined with fire tenders and those at the start of the runway were already speeding alongside us as we came into land. As soon as we came to a halt the fire officers were up their ladders and ready to douse the aircraft with foam.

I was out of my seat and trying to open the escape door.

The Captain's voice came over the radio. *'Please wait before you go down the chutes. The Fire Officer is reporting terrific heat from the engine but no flame. We are going to try to get you off down the stairs that are already in place'* and they did!

It seemed that the flight deck had reacted to their instrument warning so quickly that they had cut fuel from the engine before the overheated component could set it aflame.

We all met up in the airport lounge where the bar was open and whatever drinks the passengers wanted were free. I was playing golf with Ben in an Open Tournament next day so I turned down any alcohol and steadied my nerves with Coca-Cola.

I managed to get a phone message to Jill (there were no mobile phones then and it was only because I was a regular flyer that I managed to get access to a phone line) and warned her I would be late as they were routing another aircraft up from Sweden to take our passengers home.

There were some pretty drunken passengers on that flight!

I had finally got home, related all the events to Jill and went to bed amazed by how calm I was. I could only conclude that trying to calm and reassure the American lady who sat next to me and who I had never seen before or since that flight had somehow also reassured and calmed me.

Next morning I was up early, breakfasted on toast and cereal and was walking out the door to go to our golf tournament when I felt a little queasy. I got back to the loo (toilet) just as quickly as I could and there threw up and continued to vomit until I thought my entire soul was vomiting down the loo.

I managed to get to the golf course thanks to copious doses of Kaolin & Morphine but my drugged state did not allow for the finest round of golf I have ever played.

In all I served 2 years in North Sea Oil on this project and knew my reports were being received as a mixed blessing by the Oil Company Project Managers.

On the one hand they did not want me to uncover and report on anything serious but on the other hand they needed to convince the Norwegian Oil Corporation that they were thorough and on-going in their investigation of the project.

About half way through the two years a tow rope snapped on the tug towing the barge that contained one of the fully fabricated modules as it was on its way to the middle of the North Sea for loading onto the Platform.

The scene in the Oil Companies Offices was like something out of the TV Series 'Dad's Army'. Fully grown men who had sat at a desk for years and who's figures had grown very round or even pear shaped were desperately trying to get permission to be the one who was to swing down a hoist from a helicopter onto the unmanned barge and affix a tow rope to it.

Most had not taken any real exercise for years and they reminded me very much of 'Corporal Jones' *('Let me be the one to dangle from the rope and tie up the barge Mr Mannering!!')*

The professional seaman got the thing back under control but then there was a race to make sure the barge got to the Platform in time whilst the weather window lasted.

Apparently there were just a few short weeks every year when the North Sea is calm enough for the lifting crane – mounted on a huge flat bottomed barge – to complete the lift of these massively heavy modules.

With such a short 'weather window' when the North Sea was calm enough to lift these modules onto the Platform the Loading Schedule was obviously critical and one tow barge loose in the middle of the North Sea could cause chaos and maybe put the whole project back yet another year.

The whole episode led me to look at the contracts for the specification of the tow-barges and for the lifting barge - and what a can of worms that opened.

Our team had been put together notionally to appease the requirements of the Norwegian Oil Corporation and although we were controlled by the Oil Company they could not deny us access to any of the documentation and records we wished to examine.

Investigating these we discovered that the lifting barge had been the subject of detailed analysis before being hired at a cost of more than $1million a day. It had previously been working successfully in the Gulf of Mexico. However an expert's analysis prior to the contract award had pointed out that the Gulf of Mexico was much shallower than the North Sea with a much smaller wave pattern.

The report emphasised that a flat bottomed lifting barge would not be suitable for the North Sea and recommended a lifting barge built onto the decks of two ocean going ships be used.

Such a lifting crane was available but despite this report the project managers had hired the flat-bottomed lifting barge. Reading this report at length it came as no surprise to me to find that the lifting schedule was more than a year behind schedule.

But why would they hire and use this lifting barge costing more than $1million a day against all the advice they had received?

Why did they not discover that if it rained on site in the U.K.in the first hour of the day a complete day's fabrication was lost but the workers were still paid?

Why did they not discover the 'dummy worker fraud' in North Norway?

Why did they not discover that the managers on site were just pulling any welding certificate to accompany any welded pipe. Thus there was no guarantee that the actual pipes pulled for fabrication on the platform had been checked and certified - without which the project was running a huge risk of pipeline problems or even explosions offshore

There were many more areas of management neglect we discovered and our astonishment came from the fact that North Sea Oil was projecting an image of itself as dynamic, skilful and supremely efficient. We were discovering that it was far from this image.

Before these questions could be adequately answered Jesse asked me to head the team to do an investigation offshore on the Oil Drilling Platform that was still under construction.

Jesse seemed to us to have become disillusioned with performance of his masters on this project and Jimmy noticed that every one of Jesse's trips around and across Europe was routed via Amsterdam in Holland – the drugs and sex capital of Europe.

It was coming up to Christmas and the London Head Office of the Project decided to have a Christmas Dinner for managers and their spouses at the restaurant that sat atop the Post Office Tower in the middle of London.

Our team was invited and I wore my new suit.

I have a great deal of trouble buying new clothes. Throughout my childhood and into my teens there had never been enough money in the family to properly feed ourselves so we could not afford the luxury of new clothes. 'New' to me was a jacket or a pair of trousers from Maurice Jay's Second Hand Clothes Shop and then the 'new' clothes were not worn but were packed away in the wardrobe to be 'kept for best!' This was so ingrained in me that I am the same today.

The new suit I wore to the dinner really was new and had been in my wardrobe for a year or so but never worn. It was sky blue in colour and looked really good on me – or so I thought. I had never been out in it and the neon street lighting picked up some part of the fabric and made it look as if the suit glowed.

'Bugger me Tel', ' said Jimmy as we met up on the pavement outside the PO Tower *'What you driving that suit on - three U2 batteries?'*

The restaurant revolved around the Tower taking 20 minutes to complete the circle and giving diners an ever changing panoramic view of London. This was wonderful on the first circuit when we ordered and sat with pre-dinner drinks but the wonder gradually died as we had completed 3 circuits before the starters arrived and another 2 circuits between the Starters and the Main Course. By now it was dark outside and by the time the puddings arrived another 2 circuits later most of the party were too pie-eyed to appreciate the view or even care.

The dinner had been the first time we had mixed sociably with the Managers on the project and Jimmy's sharp sense of humour overcame many of the fences that had existed previously.

Christmas was soon upon us and on our return to work in the new year one of the English Managers on the project who we had got on particularly well with at the dinner suddenly said to me when we were alone in his office –

'I hear you are going offshore shortly'

'Yes – next week, I am looking forward to it. Many of the Modules I saw on our visits to the construction sites have been transported offshore. It will be interesting to see how they marry-up and what controls they have offshore'.

We were on our own in his office and he suddenly said –

'Do be very careful when you are offshore Terry, a lot of people come to grief from the Platform. The North Sea is very very cold at this time of the year. If you fall in especially at night you won't survive.'

I wasn't sure if he was continuing the teasing ways we had all adopted at the Christmas dinner.

'Oh I'm pretty nimble so I should be ok'

'Well just take care, your reports have caused a lot of grief to some very influential managers on this project'

Before he could say any more one of the very Senior Managers had walked in to call him out to a meeting that was discussing Cost Estimates.

We never did get to finish that conversation and swept up by events Jimmy and I were soon to be found sitting in a Helicopter, wrapped up in survival clothing .

Helicopter Crew warned –

'Survival time at this time of year if we ditch into the North Sea is less than 15 minutes'

The conversation with the English Manager flashed through my mind! The helicopter took off and we were on our way to an Oil drilling Rig in the Middle of the North Sea.

Very many people have visited and worked on North Sea Oil Drilling Rigs since our flight but this was 1977 at the very start of the Development of North Sea Oil. It was exciting and heady stuff. We felt that we were at the forefront of oil exploration and development.

The approach to the Platform was very thrilling. When first seen it looked as though the helipad on top of the accommodation block was far too small to let us land safely but once down there was more room that I thought.

The Platform was an adventure.

It had an Accommodation Block along one side and this was 6 stories high and beautifully equipped. The meals that were available were very high class and there was certainly no suffering when being accommodated offshore. It might be heavy, hard and even dangerous work once the drilling started but it was very relaxed and low key whilst construction was taking place.

It was very interesting that so many of the Modules I had seen on quay sides in various parts of Europe had by now been lifted aboard and to see how they had been integrated together to form a solid structure.

The wave pattern of the North Sea could easily be felt in the small tremors that the Platform was subject to but it really was a brilliant concept and a brilliant construction.

Our main concern offshore was the safety and efficiency of the workers as well as the accuracy of the documentation and the qualifications of the workers.

Onshore we had discovered that many workers had filled jobs they were not qualified for. If this happened offshore and their work proved to be substandard catastrophe could follow now or in the future.

Although English was the language of the project the many nationalities offshore whose first language was not English led to potential problems.

It was interesting to see that the 3 modules we had inspected in the U.K. Construction Site nearly 2 years ago had now been towed out to the Platform and lifted aboard. It was also interesting to note that the offshore workers were working on them to complete the Fabrication of these modules before they could be amalgamated with their surrounding modules. The UK Fabrication yard had failed to complete them within their time allowed on the contract and now they have to be finished at considerable extra cost and time delays offshore.

It was a lot more costly to fabricate offshore and I wondered just how much of the work needing to be done offshore was due to the way the UK Construction Yard had operated its 'Inclement Weather' practice that no-one in management claimed to have been aware of.

We were offshore for a week and the numbers of people on the payroll we had checked in London and Paris did not seem totally compatible with the number of people we could see actually working on the Platform.

When we queried this we were told that at any one time there were a whole host of Engineers working down at the bottom of the Platform's legs some 700 feet below. We attempted to check numbers going up and down but that proved to be impossible. The only way to check was to go down the shaft ourselves. We were told that the lifts were either out of action or required for urgent supplies so that was going to prove difficult.

Because of safety concerns of the Managers in charge of the Platform we had to have an Engineer accompany us wherever we went on the Platform.

We decided to check the night-shift and the engineer allocated to accompany us was one we had never seen before. He was a Mexican-American who seemed to speak little English though I rather suspected he understood far more than he spoke.

Jimmy and I went all over the platform using the lights that were available and the torchlight of our Mexican-American.

One of the Modules was having parts fabricated along its perimeter and so we were walking along the walkway on the outside of the platform with the North Sea crashing and thrashing some 40 feet below us. Halfway along the gangway the Mexican-American stopped, opened a bulkhead door into the platform and ushered us through.

The other side of the doorway was in pitch darkness, no lights anywhere. Jimmy stepped through. I was about to when the words of the Engineer back in London leapt into my mind. I hesitated.

'Don't like this' I said *'let's continue going on the walkway around the platform.'*

'No you cannot,' said the Mexican-American (he did speak English after all! *'We must go this way.'*

'*No! I don't like this way. You go this way, I'll carry on around the walkway,*' said I firmly.

'*You cannot - the walkway stops at the corner. You must go this way*' he told me.

'*No, I don't think so*' was my reply, '*I'll go back the way we came*' and I did.

Jimmy followed me and we never got to see the far side of that module that night.

I will never know whether or not there was a genuine threat or danger if I had gone on through the bulkhead that night but next day I did try to do the trip with a different 'minder' and a little way inside this module there was an unguarded drop into the North Sea and oblivion!

Perhaps the London Engineer really had been trying to warn me of potential danger or perhaps he was just winding me up. I shall never know.

We spent a week out on the Platform before being lifted by helicopter from the helicopter pad that sat on top of the Residential Block.

Back on shore in Bergen, Norway it fell to me to write up the report of our visit. This usually took the best part of a week or so to complete. Our reports were always detailed and factual so there was no room for what might have been a fanciful personal danger and it was not included. The perceived danger had no relevance to anyone but me.

As I put my Report together my mind would keep flickering over the problems our investigations had found on all the construction and fabrication sites across Europe and how they reflected on the enormous increase in costs of the project and the delays in completion.

This was supposed to be the dynamic world of North Sea Oil - the cutting edge of management excellence and efficiencies! Yet a bunch of 30 year-old English lads who had no experience or knowledge of Oil development and production or of the construction of a North Sea Oil Platform kept falling over management failings that were so obvious they surely could not have been missed by even a half conscious management

Our Team would have been quite happy to jog along on the project and pick up the high payments we were getting but the errors and omissions by management were so blatant that they had to be included in our Reports.

The Offshore Report tied up the ends of much of our earlier work and I began to feel most uncomfortable about the whole project.

Wedgie Benn – the Minister of Energy had stood up in the English Parliament and announced that there was just 30 years of oil under the North Sea and we must use it sparingly. We must preserve some of its wealth for our children.

Our investigation was revealing that there was almost certainly 100 years or more oil under the North Sea!

Furthermore there was probably as much under the other Seas that surrounded the United Kingdom.

In addition new Oil Fields were being 'discovered' somewhere in the world every month.

Our facts seem to indicate that there is not – and never has been – a shortage of oil in the world.

We even met one Engineer freshly back from researching the substructure of the Falkland Islands in the South Atlantic. His research left him very confident that the islands sat above considerable Oil fields. I took time out to very briefly research the Falkland Islands to find that 75% of the Extraction Rites for any minerals found in or under the Falklands had been sold to one company many years previously.

The Directors and Shareholders of that company made very interesting reading and for me explained much about why we went to war over an Island that the U.K. had been trying to give away for the best part of 50 years previous.

Poverty to Peaches

It seemed the world was awash with oil that the oil companies were sitting on and denying the true size of the oil fields. There were vast areas of the globe still to be researched. Almost no oil was coming out of Africa and it seemed to us inconceivable that a whole continent was bereft of oil.

On this Project things were turning out to be a long way short of the images projected by the Oil Company and many of the top politicians.

I was feeling very uncomfortable about the real aims of the whole project. I decided I needed a break from the report and clear my head. I caught the Fløibanen Funicular in Bergen to the top of Fløyen mountain (320 metres above sea level). At the top the air was magnificently clear and the views spectacular.

I was hoping the wind would blow away the doubts in my mind but my head was still full of the facts of the entire project.

Finally I shrugged my shoulders and said to myself –

'This all only makes sense if the Oil Company were really opposed to bringing the oil up and were trying to keep it down below the North Sea!'

I smiled to myself and started to walk the well-made path down the mountain. *'This Platform alone will keep Norway self-sufficient in Oil for 30 years or more and it only covers half of the oil field. Another Platform will be needed to drain the other "30 years of oil". This single Platform will also satisfy a great chunk of the U.K's demand.'*

'The oil field this platform is sitting on, along with the many others that we know of – and the ones we have heard discussed but were not for publication – could make Europe into a massive Oil Exporter'.

I continued my descent of the mountain musing that -

Poverty to Peaches

'U.K citizens could enjoy a wealth from the oil beneath their shores that doesn't quite rival the Middle-East Potentates but can certainly banish poverty in the U.K forever if only the government had the courage to take command of its oil and distribute the profits to the poor instead of playing along with the rich oil magnets and making them richer as each day passes.'

I began to admonish my foolishness.

'There has to be a reason why the Oil Companies would put such inefficient managers in charge of a project that has the potential to enrich every person living in Norway and the U.K.'

I walked on down still pondering.

'Is it possible that the Oil Companies really do not want the oil to come up?

I had been talking to myself for quite some time.

I fell silent and forced myself to take in the glorious scenery as I made my descent. The mind is a wonderful part of the human being and I knew mine was still wrestling with that last problem as I carried on the descent.

'Suppose we turn this whole thing on its head!' I said to myself.

'Suppose we think about the massive wealth of an Oil Company allowing it to outbid all others in the auction for Exploration rights and getting charge of a project with the express purpose of delaying production and keeping the oil underground for as long as possible.

Wow this was some thought!

'Then the way this project has been handled begins to make sense?'

I pondered that for much of the descent and then uttered -

'Yes! An emphatic Yes! That is precisely what is happening! But why?

274

'Could it be that if they brought up all the oil they have discovered in the world the price of fuel oil, petrol and diesel, heating oils, industrial oils and all other variations of oil would drop dramatically and their profits could be seriously harmed?'

'That was obviously true but surely the Oil Companies are not being allowed to get away with a procedure that financially cripples many people but that enrich themselves!'

In the U.K. at that time petrol was around £2.50 a gallon (Litres were not introduced until much later). If the Oil Companies convinced the Politicians by fair means or foul that their oil was a scarce resource and should be kept underground so that it wasn't all used up within a single generation I thought that they might be able to create shortages that pushed the price up to an unheard of £3.00 a Gallon.

(The OPEC nations had with-held the supply of oil in early 1970s and its price had shot up but by the end of the '70s they were allegedly 'under control' of the Oil Companies).

It seems that for reasons that are beyond my understanding the oil that is produced from the ground belongs to the oil company as soon as it is extracted. The way the taxpayers of the resident countries benefit is to tax every barrel of oil that is produced and the oil companies are past masters at keeping governments (and individual political leaders) exactly where they want them on this one.

If the Oil Companies can achieved £3 a Gallon for petrol then by keeping new discoveries of Oil underground they could give themselves a massive additional 50p a gallon increase in profit for doing nothing more than they are contracted to do.

Approximately 4 and a half billion gallons of fuel are consumed in the U.K. each year so an additional 50p a gallon would give the Oil Companies an additional £2.25 billion (£2,225,000,000) of profit (less tax) for doing nothing but leaving the oil underground.

In 2012 petrol was costing £1.39 a litre which equates to £5.65 a gallon. Think of the increased profit going into the coffers of the Oil Companies when the projects were originally costed to make a profit at £2.50 a gallon.

Huge companies mitigate the tax they pay in any country by adjusting the transfer cost of their products between locations and ensure the largest slice of profit is taken in a location that has no or very low tax.

(Litres had not been introduced but the cost equivalent is of £2.50 a gallon is 55p a litre. It was inconceivable at that time that petrol and diesel being pumped from the ground to give a profit at 55p a gallon could rise nearly 300% to £1.39 a litre).

Also into the mix of my thoughts was the fact that nearly all Oil Construction Projects were Cost-Plus.

The Oil Companies and their often related International Construction Companies were the only ones with the financial and apparent managerial clout to handle massive North Sea Projects.

It was fairly easy for them to argue that they would be constructing and drilling in the North Sea that had wave patterns and a depth not previously encountered and therefore unpredictable. They could not give a firm quote for total costs for they did not know what they might encounter. They therefore worked on a Cost-Plus basis.

Whatever was spent on the project would be paid for by the Client (in this case the Norwegian and British Governments) and the Oil Company would be take an extra 7½ or 10% on top of each payment as their fee for managing the project.

'It doesn't take a genius to realise that if the Operation or Oil Company delayed the project or ran it at increased costs then they would be increasing the management fee that was payable to them and thus their own profits'.

All this was going through my head as I descended from the mountain. When back in Bergen I began to research the economics of the Oil trade and everything came clear – at least to me!

A book written by a man who had similar misgivings to mine but had access to USA Government Minutes claimed that in August 1928 a secret meeting was held at Achnacarry Castle in the Scottish Highlands. The As-Is Agreement was devised by the 'Seven Sisters' (the 7 largest oil Companies in the world) and formed the basis of what a U.S. Senate subcommittee in 1952 called "the international petroleum cartel."

In 1928, when it was adopted, more than a third of worldwide production capacity was shut down due to oversupply. Owners feared that expanding low-cost capacity in the Persian Gulf would only add to their losses. The As-Is and Red Line agreements retarded the development of Middle Eastern oil resources until after World War II.

It established a pattern for ensuring oil profits by exercising market control

As far as I could see this was precisely what was being repeated with North Sea Oil.

Furthermore this researcher alleged that when Oil was first discovered in Iraq in the 1920s members of the 'Seven Sisters' gained control of all the Exploration and Development Rights.

They then made sure that their 'Exploration Drilling' stopped just above the oil fields they knew to be present. They then declared the prospective oil well to be 'Dry' with no oil present. This kept Iraqi oil underground for decades and kept the control of oil with the massive 'Seven Sisters'

I wondered just how many oil fields in the North Sea, the Irish Sea, the English Channel and all over the world were being treated in the same way.

I am not stating that this is the way Oil is manipulated or that this is the way it works in the world today. Folk must make up their own minds on the ethics and performance of the oil companies and the governments and individuals that feed off them. I include the foregoing details to describe exactly what was going through my mind as I walked down the side of Fløyen Mountain and as I sat down to write my Report of the Offshore Production Platform.

My Report contained the facts and figures of our investigation but I also allowed it to run into considerations of whether it was possible to effectively manage a $multi-billion Project that had two diametrically opposed objectives.

The taxpayers of Norway and the U.K needed the Offshore Oil drilling Platform built as quickly as possible so as to save those countries much of the massive amounts they were spending on the purchase of Oil and they wanted it built as cheaply as possible because they were paying all the bills.

The Oil Company – along with its associated Construction and Operating Companies wanted the oil kept underground for as long as possible and costs to go as high as possible thus increasing their take from the 10% addition to all costs that they enjoyed on a cost-plus contract.

My conclusion was that on this project the Oil Company was winning hands down with induced delays and increased costs and that the taxpayers of Norway and Britain did not stand a chance.

It was quite a hefty report for our Offshore Investigation had revealed the problems caused by many of the shortcomings we had reported on earlier and needed to attach to the offshore section.

When complete I handed my Report to Jesse.

I had noticed of late his hands had started shaking and he had appeared to have 'gone native' in that he stood by our Reports against the best wishes of the Project's Managers.

All of the Seven Sisters Oil Companies were massive, their Directors and Financial Officers controlled incredibly high Revenues and Expenditure - larger than 90% of the countries in the world. Their executives were very powerful men.

The Vice-President Europe and Africa and the Company's Financial Controller of the Oil Company that were running this project were just completing their twice a year visit in which they whistle-stopped on the Projects they had on those two Continents.

It appears that Jesse handed them each a copy of my Report to read on the aircraft taking them back to the States.

The next thing that happened was apparently unheard of in the annals of Oil Companies Directors.

Whilst in mid-flight on their way back to USA they got the Pilot to radio to their destination and have a Chartered Transatlantic Jet Aircraft warmed up and standing by for an immediate flight back to Norway for the two of them.

They had messages sent to every manager on my project and our Investigation Team to stand by for meetings immediately on their return to Norway.

It appeared that my Report had had quite an effect!

There was pandemonium back in the Norwegian offices of the project as the multitude of managers there tried to get a copy of my report to read before the great master got back to Norway. Jesse was frantically photocopying the Report for them.

Talk about 'hitting the ground running' after two consecutive back-to-back flights across the Atlantic the two top executives of the Oil Company were met at the airport and chauffeured straight into their first meeting with the Head of Projects in Europe and the Head of our Project. Meetings then took place with a succession of managers going down the pecking order. It was late on the second day of their return to Norway that I was called into a meeting.

I was on my own as far as the Investigation Team were concerned so it was just me with the two powerful oil company executives and the head of Oil Projects in Europe and the Financial Controller of our project.

I wondered what their approach would be and expected denials and insinuations of mistakes on my part but in fact they were most kind. They asked numerous questions about what our investigations had uncovered on this project and listened intently to my replies.

It was a long meeting as we discussed most aspects of the investigations and the report until the Vice-President of the Oil Company stated –

'This has been excellent work and you are to be commended for your thoroughness and application'

I thanked him for his kind words.

'What do you intend to do from here?' he asked.

'I think I've done my bit and you have got my Report' I replied *'perhaps I should ask you what you intend to do from here'*

'Good question.' he looked at the his companion, *'I think we must now take your report away and figure out a program that eradicates the problems you highlight and get this Project back on track.'*

His companion – the Oil Company's Financial Controller – nodded in agreement.

'I need you to leave this with us now to implement the necessary changes.'

There followed a bit of small talk between the others and then again from the Vice President *'I see your contract is at an end in a few weeks' time. What plans do you have?*

'None really' I replied honestly *'I guess I will just have to see what opportunities show themselves.'*

'We could offer you an excellent full time roll' interjected the Company's Financial Controller. *'We have similar projects all over the world and could do with a guy with your talents acting as Financial Controller on one or other of them'*

I was aware that all three were watching me intently to read in the effect of their statement.

'Yes,' added the Vice-President *'These would carry a six-figure Salary and all the benefits our Managers enjoy. Coming in from outside the oil world you have brought a fresh view to affairs that would be a great asset on so many of our projects.'*

Until that moment I had been quite happy with the way this meeting was going, but now I suffered deja vu as my mind leapt backwards to the meeting with the big bosses at London Transport all those years ago. The stakes were much higher now but the body language of the others was almost precisely the same.

I felt that their body language was revealing their attitude and if I had read it correctly it was saying –

A big salary increase will probably take care of his restless spirit and move this trouble maker sideways into another job in another department (LT) or another country (Oil execs) where he can't do any damage and we can keep him under control.

That is what their body language was saying to me!

Vocally they were full of praise and encouragement and a six-figure salary plus benefits.

For a lad brought up in poverty throughout his childhood and his teens this needed seriously thinking about.

I thanked them for their offer – *'You really are most kind and I am very interested in your offer. I just need to think about it a little more and talk it over with my wife. I will come back to you on it by the end of next week.'*

The meeting ended most courteously.

As I got up to leave they surprised me by asking *'Do you have any copies of you Report besides the one you have brought to this meeting'*

'No, I gave a copy to Jesse and he photocopied it for management but this is my only one.'

'Well - leave everything in our hands. You won't be needing your copy now and we could do with it for our discussions.'

281

They took my copy from me and that was the end of our meeting.

I walked back to the office we were using at Stavanger HQ to be met by Jimmy. *'What on earth have you been telling them'* he asked. *'There has been pandemonium here with the top management collecting all the copies of you report and even been going through every desk drawer in the place in case parts of the Report were lying around.'*

Following my meeting I could not detect any repercussions from the other managers on the Project apart from the fact that they seem to be treating me with kid-gloves.

Jesse seemed to have disappeared from the scene having been posted back to the USA and the Project Financial Controller who had been at the meeting but said nothing took over control of the investigation team.

Six figures – that was at least £100,000 a year plus Benefits gave me an awful lot to think about on my Friday night flight back home.

How could I turn it down?

Why was I so uncomfortable about it?

The thoughts that had filled my head when I was walking back down the mountain after my funicular trip kept intruding.

If keeping the oil underground, delaying Projects, and increasing the costs of construction and production really were the over-riding objectives of the Oil Companies – would I ever be content to turn a blind-eye to whatever project I was working on and allow the abuses we had witnessed all over Europe to take place?

It took a hell of a lot of thinking about.

I was aware that there is something within me that forces me to challenge any situation that I believe to be wrong or unjust and do my damnest to put it right.

I don't seem to be able to rest until I feel the wrong has been righted and fairness has been restored.

These instincts run with me in virtually everything I get involved in so could I really suppress them sufficiently to take the Oil Companies wage and reward. Furthermore did I really want to suppress the instincts that had been the driving force in my life to date?

It was a troubled mind that journeyed back to the U.K. that evening.

Every instinct in me stressed that the conclusions I reached at the bottom of my walk off the Mountain were correct!

Could I walk away from my conscious for £100,000 a year plus benefits (a whole lot of money in the 1970s).

My early life was spent in abject poverty so this was a terrific temptation to say yes to the Oil Company's offer.

It was time to talk it over with Jill!

I was met at the airport as usual by Jill and little Sally Wiggins and we drove home without a mention of the potentially life changing thoughts on my mind. I walked the dog. Walking my dogs has always been a great time for me to think things through and often come up with solutions. On this occasion I needed to talk the whole scene over with Jill.

Back home and I did precisely that.

'Will you ever be happy turning a blind eye to wrongdoing?' she asked.

'We don't know that it is wrongdoing' I replied *'it is just that the scene I have mapped out just seems to exactly fit the scene I have found throughout this North Sea Project'*

'Terry – once you have worked things out you are seldom wrong and I have never known you not charge in and try to put things right. You're the same in our social life – look at the way you changed Beenham Gala, and the Drama Group. Look at how you measured out the Golf Course in an effort to get them to introduce alternative tees for the second 9 holes instead of playing from the ones they used first time around. Look at all your jobs. You're great skill is in seeing what is

283

wrong and how to put it right. I can't see you stopping that now – not even for £100,000 and benefits'

I knew she was right.

'I don't want to find myself a Widow in some remote country because you had a fatal accident when on site'.

I slept on the decision for a few nights but I think I knew from the outset what it would be.

I turned down the Oil Company's generous offer and walked away from North Sea Oil

But what to?

I had no job lined up. I didn't know what lay ahead.

My life so far had been full of adventure. What on earth was my life going to be from here?

*

CHAPTER Eighteen
Catastrophe – back in Poverty

We had some savings from my spell in North Sea Oil and Jill's 21 years as a Teacher so we could chance a move into a different career.

When we had moved to Buckinghamshire the Education Authority could not come up with a job for Jill but she got herself a Teaching post at a prestigious Private School in Chesham.

It meant she had gone from a start in Teaching as a Primary School Teacher in the days when her first class contained 54 children; through to teaching in a Secondary School where she was Head of Needlework when I first met her, then onto a temporary post in a Tottenham School whilst we married, then back to secondary education at Theale in Berkshire for the first few terms after we were married followed by 6 very happy years in the Village School at Beenham.

After 21 years of Teaching Jill was keen to try something different. She was not happy with the way education in the U.K. was going. A lack of discipline was creeping into children and many parents. Educational theorists and politicians – most without an iota of experience of the classroom - were beginning to determine the curriculum and the methods to be employed.

I had become fascinated by the new 'home computers' that were coming to the market. They were the size we now call laptops but they had far more processing power than the computer I used to run the accounts of over 2,600 Pubs and

Inns in my Courage days. I felt sure these 'home' computers could be programmed to run the accounts of small businesses and set about trying to prove it.

We found a shop we could rent in Wendover in Buckinghamshire and Jill occupied the ground floor with a wonderful stock of stationery, writing papers, wrapping papers and other stationery. I turned the two rooms upstairs into small offices and started to design a small business accounting management system that would run on these new computers.

The Computers that interested me most used BASIC as their programming language. I had never been taught to program computers but managed to pick up enough BASIC to complete rudimentary programs.

I decided to major on one manufacturer and I took on an agency to sell the computer along with word processing and spreadsheet software that ran on it.

We were doing well, the Stationery sales and the sales of the computers were paying the rent and allowing me to design an 'easy to use' accounting system for small business.

Suddenly – out of the blue - I got a totally unexpected phone call from my first wife.

'We are having terrible trouble with your youngest daughter. She needs to get away and have a change of home for a few weeks. She needs the time to sort herself out. Will you have her for a term?'

I hadn't seen my daughters for a number of years.

Each time I had visited them it had a severe emotional effect on me. I found it almost impossible to get them to open up and talk to me. I was fearful that my first wife had resorted to the lies and deception the Police Superintendent had revealed all those years ago at Peel House and that she was inventing stories that would put the girls off from ever wanting to visit or stay with Jill and I.

On the way home from these visits I had to constantly stop the car to vomit into the kerb as the impact of having left 3 glorious little girls and the hopelessness of my situation hit me.

If I went to the authorities and told them that I thought my first wife might be filling the girl's heads with lies what could I expect them to do? I just had to hope that the girls would find the real me once they had grown up and find out for themselves what Jill and I were really like.

The girls were growing up but at each visit they still clammed up and wouldn't talk to me. Now I am suddenly asked to house my 15 year old youngest for a term.

How can I refuse? Why would I want to refuse?

What was so awful at her home that made my first wife and her husband contact me for the first time in more than a decade telling me they were having trouble with my youngest and asking me to house her for a few months?

I talked to Jill and she agreed that if youngest was in trouble then we should give her a home for a few months and see if she could sort her life out.

It was strange to suddenly have a 15 year old girl living with us at home. She was intelligent but seemed to live behind a lot of baby style talk. We had contacts with the local school through a golfing companion and got her a place for the Autumn Term.

It was a mixed school but she seemed to be having trouble making friends with the other students. She told us that she had never been allowed to have any boyfriends and when there were school events or dances her stepfather would always take her and bring her home. He was a teacher and she attended his school. She claimed to be a little scared of boys and that she knew nothing about sex.

This presented a problem to Jill and I for we had always found it easy to mix with either sex but we solved it by having a word with the Teacher who was responsible for the welfare of the children. We knew her well for I had produced and directed a couple of Pantomimes in Aylesbury and the musical opera - Die Fledermaus that had apparently been highly rated by Halton Players where she was a leading player.

Knowing the Teacher at her school was very helpful for Jill and I for she advised that our youngest had a vivid imagination and the other children thought she was constantly spinning tales that were inconsistent and probably untrue.

The school also discovered that youngest had been a continual absentee from her school back home and that struck all of us as odd as she claimed that she travelled to school every day with her stepdad who taught there.

Her teacher felt the many stories youngest told might be a sign of insecurity and she was playing the part with whoever she was with that she thought might make the biggest impression.

Despite all this she seemed to have settled in reasonably well.

She would keep repeating that if only her stepdad and her dog was also living with us then life for her would be perfect.

She had come to us with the idea that she would like to become a cook or a motor car repair mechanic when she left school. These seemed to be diametrically opposed goals to us but she impressed on us that they were the careers her parents thought her best suited to and she agreed.

The school had an excellent Drama Section in which she revelled and impressed. After 3 months her aims had changed and she really wanted to take up Drama.

After much discussion we agreed that if she worked hard at her studies to make up for the ground she had lost due to her constant absences in the past so that she actually qualified for Drama School then Jill and I would find the money to pay her way through college.

It was a far different younger daughter of mine that I put on the train back to Lancashire. She was vibrant and excited. She couldn't wait to get back to her parents and tell them of her Drama ambitions.

Her stay with us had been a distraction and it coincided with a drop in my businesses profits as our manufacturer continually reduced the sale price of its products. When we first took on the Agency they would compensate us for the stock we held and had purchased at the higher prices that operated prior to the price reduction but now they had stopped that practice. We needed their stock for our programmers to work on and to sell.

If we were to complete and market our Golf Club Management System; Small Business Management System, and our Restaurant Management System we needed additional finance and it was very difficult for us to raise. We were in danger of going broke for a mere £25,000 but the bank would not play ball and advance us a loan or extend our overdraft.

Our Computer systems could earn us a fortune if we could complete them and successfully market them – they were in advance of anything on the market. If we ran out of cash before they were complete then they would earn us nothing.

After much soul-searching Jill and I decided there was no alternative other than to sell our house, pay off the mortgage and use the balance of the house sale to complete our software systems.

It is a very tough decision to sell your house, rent accommodation and bury all your capital in the business but we couldn't see any alternative.

We rented the top of a house in Back Street and ploughed on.

We had arranged that my youngest would return home to live we also arranged that she and her sisters would come to us in the holidays.

Thus I found myself driving north to meet their stepdad and the girls at a service station on the M1 where I would pick up the 3 girls and return so they could have a short holiday with us.

I arrived to find the 3 girls and their stepdad already there. The girls including my youngest were back to their uncommunicative ways and there was a very muted hello. Worst still was the body language of my youngest had gone from the exuberant and vibrant girl I put on the train at the end of her stay with us. It was back to downcast and dull.

Whilst at the Service Station we stopped for a coffee and some cakes and sandwiches when out of the hearing of the girls their stepfather said to me. *'I am aware that you have been ill-treating her and warn you to cut it out, don't do it again'*

I didn't have a clue what he was talking about.

'What on earth are you talking about?'

'It's all right I haven't told your first wife – she would go berserk. Our youngest confides in me and told me you and your wife have been ill treating her'

'We bloody well haven't!'

'Well she said you have'

The girls were now sat in my motor car and ready to go. The statement had so shaken me that I was uncertain of my next move.

Their stepfather was waving them goodbye and telling them to behave themselves. I decided I should get them away from him as soon as possible. I got into my car and drove home in silence as I tried to make sense of this last event.

After my terrible inquisition by the Police Superintendent that cost me a career in the police I had grown to accept that my first wife found it impossible to tell the truth when a lie suited her better. Had this behaviour spread to her second husband – the children's stepfather? And what of the girls, have their values been similarly corroded?

Poverty to Peaches

I couldn't solve these questions whilst hurtling along a motorway – they would have to wait until I got home.

It was a tough, tough drive home.

When home I told Jill about the Stepfather's remarks and she responded – *'You need to sort this now. Twenty-one years of teaching tells me that you need to confront your youngest in front of her sisters and give her the opportunity to repeat her accusations. That way we can find out whether it is her or her Stepfather that is inventing tales'.*

I felt she was right. We must nip this story in the bud before my first wife embroiders it even more.

That evening after the girls had settled in and we had eaten I brought the subject up – Jill was with me so I had hoped it would be a kind of family discussion.

'When we were loading the car your stepfather accused me of ill-treating you when you were here. Where on earth did he get this story from?'

The girls remained silent. My youngest seemed uncomfortable so I addressed my next remark to her.

'He told me that you had told him that Jill and I had been ill-treating you, is that true?'

No answer was forthcoming.

'You have your sisters here to support you so please tell us what you have been telling your stepfather'

We waited for her to reply until she suddenly said –

'I'm not letting you bully me like this. They always said you were a bully. Fancy trying to tell me I might go to Drama School and become an actress. I'm going to be a cook'

'Never mind about Drama School. What have you been saying to your Stepdad?'

'I don't want to talk about it. I'm going to phone my dad'

And with that she phoned her Stepfather. Next morning he arrived at our door and all 3 girls got into his car and were gone.

I had waited years for my girls to find me and now within 24 hours they were gone. It was heartbreak time.

All I could do was to throw myself into work to try and build up some savings to get a mortgage and get back into a house of our own. Get some stability back into Jill and my life and hope that the girls might try to find us when they were old enough to act under their own volition.

About this time our beloved Sally Wiggins died of cancer of the jaw. It was a shattering experience! I would never have believed that the loss of a scrap of a dog could be so devastating.

The death of Sally Wiggins was so shattering to both Jill and I that we declared we couldn't go through that grief again and it was the end of our dog ownership!

Ten days later Henry arrived!

Henry was a cross between a black Labrador and a Whippet and covered the ground at an incredible speed. He turned out to be a magnificent dog, kept all the other dogs he met under control without ever being in a fight with them and became a magnificent friend of Jill and I as well as a dog.

We used to walk at the same time as many other dog owners and the dogs would be allowed to run as a pack. If there was the slightest altercation anywhere Henry was there like a shot and peace was immediately restored.

Over the years I tried to watch how he managed to do this and gain absolute control despite many of the other dogs towering over him including a massive Bull Mastiff and - on one occasion - an Irish Wolfhound. I found that he immediately fronted the newcomer and just would not let him/her join the pack until it acknowledged Henry as the leader. You could actually see the body language of the other dog bristling as it considered the option of 'taking out' this boss dog and the fronting would go on for some time.

Poverty to Peaches

On rare occasions Henry would raise his hackles during this confrontation but in every case you could see the new dog physically relax as he/she accepted Henry's authority at which point Henry's body language would relax and the new dog happily joined the peaceful pack.

The lessons I learned from watching my beloved Henry during his lifetime caused me to make a study of human body language and was a contributory factor to some tremendous successes for me that were yet to come.

Jill loved Henry but stated that the only thing she missed in dog ownership was bringing up a puppy so into our lives came Primrose – a 10 week old yellow Labrador.

She was lovely – everything a yellow Labrador puppy should be with that incredible unique sweet smell that only a puppy can give off. She retained all her lovely traits as she grew older.

We had read that you should allow a bitch to have at least one litter so when she was 3 years old we thought that it would be nice to ask Guide Dogs for the Blind if they would like us to breed a litter on their behalf.

We had not realised that they had over 30 years of brood histories and thus balanced their litters very carefully – only using 'outside' bitches or stud dogs when they might improve the strains of dogs they use. We had pedigree papers for Primrose and were asked to send copies to the Leamington Spa breeding centre. If the head breeder - the wonderful Derek Freeman – liked the dog enough then he might use her.

I think it is true to say that Derek became a fan of Primrose.

He did use her with his selected Guide Dogs stud dogs and the three litters she bred that Jill fed and raised went to Guide Dog Schools all over England and to Guide Dog and Seeing Eye Schools in Canada, Japan, Belgium, France and Holland. Even to this day we still get letters from the grateful managers of these schools who invariably used our puppies as breeding stock when they were old enough.

We always kept at least one puppy to continue the line and Primroses descendants have continued to breed incredibly lovely puppies. We have always restricted their broods to 3 in the lifetime of the mother and in that way most of our dogs have lived a full and very happy life.

Breeding our Bitch with Guide Dogs of the Blind Stud Dogs and then donating all the puppies to Guide Dog Schools in the U.K and overseas led to a good rapport with the managers and staff at the GDBA Breeding Centre.

Our experience at running charitable fetes and shows led to us helping them at their annual Open Days. We heard that a group of them were organising a Sponsored Walk across Scotland to raise money to buy an electronic wheelchair for the son of one of the Managers. His son suffered from Cerebral Palsy so I was delighted to be allowed to join their walk.

We all met up at the point when the waters of the Irish Sea wash up Loch Linnhe to Caol and the plan was to walk the 72 miles from there to the North Sea in 3 days.

Ralph and I had walked part of the Pennine Way (the backbone of England) during some leave we had when we were naive Aircraftsmen in the RAF.

At that time we knew nothing about walking in the hills and had had a few practice walks on the South Downs of England. We were reasonably fit and easily managed to fit in the journey to and from the South Downs and a walk of 15 miles a day in our practice walks and so confidently expected to cover that distance each day on the Pennine Way.

It was the first year the footpath had been opened and navigation was by compass and map. There were no trail arrows pointing the way. We did well by and large except that we had stuffed our kitbags so full of spare clothing and tinned food we had a great deal of difficulty lifting them – let alone carrying them for 200 miles. In addition we each carried a small tent – a bivouac – to sleep in.

We struggled to make 8 miles a day!

We had failed to take account of the fact that the South Downs has wonderfully springy turf that is mainly grass and that we were carrying light haversacks that only carried a bottle of water and our sandwiches. On the Pennine Way we were ploughing our way along unmade tracks, often through thick mud, and carrying a pack that contained just about everything but the kitchen sink.

On my walk across Scotland we were hanging around at the start for 40 minutes or so waiting for one of the party who was late. The atmosphere was good as each of the half a dozen walkers had brought their wives and families up to Scotland for the 3 days and they had all gathered to see us off so it was a carnival atmosphere.

I was eager to get started as we needed to complete nearly 20 miles a day to complete the walk in 3 days and my Pennine Way experience had stayed in my mind but everyone else was very relaxed. They all worked together at GDBA and I was the outsider joining them.

The first part of the walk is along the footpath that runs alongside the canal to Gairlochy. As we finally got under way some of the wives set off in their motors to have a picnic ready for us at Gairlochy but 2 wives, with children running free and in pushchairs joined us for the walk to Gairlochy – a distance of about 6 miles.

It was a made up footpath alongside the canal but have you ever tried to get family groups, wheelchairs and young children moving at 4mph which was my estimate of the speed we needed to get to the to complete the first days scheduled walk in the light?

I couldn't seem to convince everyone that we needed to step it out, particularly if we were going to stop for a picnic after just 6 miles.

'Relax Terry, chill out, we know this area well, it's where we holiday, we've done this journey loads of time, we'll be o.k.'

So on we went in our carnival atmosphere with the children dancing along and racing ahead for the first few miles before they started needing carrying.

Eventually we met up with the advance party who had blankets spread on the grass, containers of food and the kettle boiling. Well it wasn't exactly boiling as they didn't put it on the primus stove until they had greeted their partners and husbands.

Once more the whole party took on the atmosphere of a carnival as they sat around, played with the children and showed no inclination to get cracking on the 15 miles that lay ahead. By the time we eventually got going I estimated that we had about 5 hours of daylight left. That equates to 5 hours of walking at an average of 3 mph if we were to finish the day in daylight.

Three miles per hour does not sound much but if you are a non-walker try walking at that pace for 5 hours without a break. If you stop for a drink or a bite then 30 minutes pass without you noticing it and you need to progress at 4mph thenceforth to keep to the time schedule.

I tried without much success to keep them going at a reasonable pace but all too soon darkness began to descend on the glorious scenery we were walking by the attractive Loch Linnie. We were soon tripping over the roots of trees we couldn't see in the darkness caused by the canopy of leaves and much muttering was coming from the group behind.

The women folk were to meet us at Invergarry to drive us back to our accommodation. Some of our party were looking in quite a bad shape for what had been a reasonably easy terrain of the last 20 miles.

'Didn't think it would take us this long' said one of the party with feeling.

'I'm bloody exhausted!' said another.

'We've got two more days like this' said a third *'I may not be able to make it'*

The carnival atmosphere had evaporated.

'Can we stretch it out a bit and spend 5 days on the walk instead of 3' suggested someone.

'No' said the leader *'we only have 3 days leave'.*

There was an air of despondency settled over the party.

'Don't worry too much' said I *'I can set a pace to make sure we get through the next two days a bit easier and in the light'*

This didn't seem to cheer them much.

I suggested it might be because we got away to such a late start that caused the problems but it turned out that they had no idea what it was like to walk 20 miles in a day at a reasonable pace.

'But you holiday here and have done this journey loads of times' said I echoing their words at the start of the day.

'Yes but we've never walked it' came the reply. *'We've driven it dozens of times and it only takes 20 minutes in the car to complete each stage.'*

There was nothing I could say. These were all my friends from the Guide Dogs for the Blind Association and they had kindly let me join them on their walk.

I had over £250 worth of Sponsorship if I finished the walk so tomorrow I must walk at the pace that will get us through the 27 miles to finish that stage if possible in the light.

The next morning two of our party could not make it to the start line – the first day had exhausted them.

We set off from Invergarry alongside the beautiful Caledonian Canal and linked up with Loch Ness to

Drumnadrochit – the legendry home of Nessie – the Loch Ness Monster!

I was walking at the front of the group in the hope that they would feed off my pace. They did for most of the morning but the lunch time stop took the wind out of them and they gradually dropped back – leaving me to finish the walk on my own someway ahead of the group. It was just as well I did for I was met by the pick-up cars for the party who had been anxiously looking for their husbands and I was able to send them down the route to a spot about 5 miles short of the finish where they completed their day's walking.

Only John McKay and myself finished the walk at Inverness on the third day alongside the waters of the North Sea.

It is a glorious walk now known as the Great Glen Walk and I can thoroughly recommend it to every able bodied reader of this book but – be warned – either take 5 days to do it, or put in some 20 mile a day training in the weeks before you start.

Another great walk I was to do a year or two later was to walk across England with my great chum – Ralph.

We used 'Wainwrights Walk' that starts on the West Coast at St Bees Head then goes over the startlingly beautiful Lake District, the Pennines and then the North York Moors.

It is about 194 miles and takes about two weeks. Ralph and I used the Caravan to stay at strategic points but by far the best method seems to be to book into the series of Bed and Breakfast places across the route where you can get your luggage transported from location to location and thus walk with just your days food, drink and maps (a GPS system is recommended!). Again this really is a magnificent walk to do and both the crossing on foot of Scotland and then England were a wonderful uplift to my spirits and soul

When back working on my computer software systems I got approached by the Vice-President of a group of independent

Hairdressers who had some excellent ideas for a complete Hairdressing System that we could sell to all his members.

I would need to finance the writing of the software and fully recover these costs from the early sales before paying him a Royalty for systems he sold to hairdressers outside his group.

He was confident of getting at least a 75% take up from his members and at the price we agreed that would give my little outfit over £1,000,000 profit from the sale of the computers and the systems.

We were beginning to build the business and I won a trip from the manufacturers for selling the most systems relative to my 'catchment' area.

The trip took me and a number of similarly successful computer dealers on the Orient Express from London to Venice then onto grandstand seats at the San Marino Grand Prix before flying back to London.

The journey was wonderful. It was April and the train travelled along and sometimes above the snowline in the mountains and routes across Europe – it was breath-taking.

Sadly I think it was also the beginning of the end of the excellent relationship I had with the computer manufacturer.

Some while previously they had brought out an update of their laptop to act as the 'small business computer'. It was a development from the original but much more versatile and powerful.

They had now replaced that with the newly designed business computer that had had different operating systems to their previous products.

We had sold a few of these business models and they were very impressive computers. I wondered about transferring our software onto them and they offered to bundle our accounting program as part of their offer package.

I couldn't see any way of financing the system rewrite so we stayed with the updated original computer after further assurances that it was to stay on the market for at least the next decade.

The marketing people at our computer manufacturers advised that it would take that long to recoup the costs of the fully automated line that was producing the computer we were designing our systems on.

Though I could construct simple programs and design a full accounting system to run on the machine my ability did not run to fully programming it. I was lucky to find 2 super chaps who were computer experts in the RAF and fancied a shot at completing programs on our preferred computer.

They were excellent and we soon began to sell the computer with our own software for Golf Club Management, Restaurant Management, and Small Business Management.

We were beginning to make money and I took on a chap to look after the administration of the business to free me up to design and sell our own software. He bought his way in by providing £20,000 of capital that helped to pay our programming costs.

We were deeply committed to the development our business software when our manufacturer brought out a brand new 'Home' computer with a completely different user interface.

The new computer was hugely impressive and as far as I could see the only thing that stopped it being suitable for business applications was its small disc storage. It did not have a 'hard disk' for maximum data store as did their other computers but used the new small 'floppy' disc that would not hold enough data for our requirements.

During my trip on the Orient Express the Marketing Director of the manufacturer stopped off at each of our individual cabins to find our view of their products and where we thought the market was going.

I took the opportunity to interrogate him about the plans for their new computer. I told him it would be ideal as a small business computer but it needed a hard disk connection.

He assured me that it would never be fitted with a Hard Disk connection as it would impose on the market they had reserved for their other computers. I persevered with the theory that the new 'home computer' was the ideal computer for small businesses but he convinced me that if they were to fit a hard disk port to their new computer they would undermine the huge market they already had for their existing brands.

He assured me that the computer we were using for our software systems would never be withdrawn in the near or even distant future as they had a fully automated, state-of-art factory producing them by the thousand in California.

I told him that I thought his company's strategy was mistaken but I had no alternative but to take him at his word and commit every penny I had behind the writing our system we had designed on the computers we were using.

His body language suggested that he resented my hard questioning over the marketing plans for his company but he was pleasant enough although a little distant to me throughout the rest of the trip.

Out of the blue came an invite to Jill and I to attend my Eldest daughter's wedding.

I talked to her on the phone with an offer to pay for the wedding as used to be the way in days of old but she said that her mother (my first wife) and her stepfather were determined that they would pay for it and didn't want me involved except as a guest.

It was a pleasant wedding in Lancashire with a reception in a very pleasant Working Men's Club. The thing that caused Jill and I most problem was the apparent normal habit locally whereby all the men stood together at the bar – with no females amongst them, and all the women sat in a group at the other end of the function room. Occasionally one or other would peel off from a group to get another drink for the lady but that was it. There was virtually no conversation of mixing between the two groups.

Jill and I eventually settled for sitting together in the middle of the no-man's land and chatted with my new son-in-laws parents. My daughter's stepfather and my first wife were clearly running things.

Back at work we were still selling computers and Jill's stationery was gaining ever wider recognition and trade.

Suddenly a phone call came from my Youngest daughter inviting us to go to the christening of the baby daughter she had just had. There had been no contact between us and the altercation over alleged' ill-treatment' and we had no idea that she had a husband or was pregnant let alone a mother at the age of 18.

Despite all the previous problems we knew we had to go.

The Christening was in Lancashire and my first wife and the children's stepfather were controlling events. There was no father either at the Christening or on the birth certificate. My first Grandchild and not a father to be seen!

My Youngest daughter had obviously thrown her lot back in with her mother and stepfather.

A year or so later my Eldest daughter phoned me to say that her husband had been made redundant. He had been a maintenance Electrician at one of Lancashire Cotton Mills.

The Mills were all closing so there was no work for him in Lancashire. Could they come down and stay with us whilst he found work in the South of the country?

He could but failed to find work so we took him into our business and taught him as much as we could about the computers we were selling. We gave him a job and sent him out on any maintenance jobs we had. He was a problem to us.

I had never before worked with anybody so work-shy. I had come from a background whereby if you wanted or needed anything then you rolled your sleeves up and worked as hard as you could to earn enough to get what you had desired. My son-in-law obviously came from different stock. He seemed devoid of any work ethic. His daily routine seemed to be to shirk his way through the working day.

He learnt enough from us to eventually get a job maintaining computer testing equipment that a local major company was importing from Japan. It was a job with great prospects and opportunity and his employers even sent him to Japan to train on the equipment.

Then my Middle daughter came to stop with us. She had finished training as a nurse and got a job in Wendover nursing at the Abbeyfield home where Jill's mother was being looked after.

Things were progressing well apart from the Administrator of our business effectively sacking a very loyal secretary who had been with us from the start and replacing her with someone he had worked (and maybe played with) in a previous employment.

I had been leaving all dealings with the manufacturer to our administrator. It was taking a lot of weight off my shoulders and he had done a deal with them whereby we could have one of their trained sales team to work with us for 3 months to boost sales.

Our administrator was out one day and the manufacturer's Sales Representative stopped off as he was going through Wendover. I hadn't seen him for a long time so I took time to have a chat with him when he said –

'We're having another of those Stock Bonuses. Stock-up with our latest product next month and another £200 could be yours'.

'*How do you mean ANOTHER £200? I haven't seen the first £200 yet*'

'*You must have. We paid it out at the end of last month.*'

'*I never saw it and nothing went through the books*'

'*That's because you always get paid cash*'

'*How long as that been?*'

'*I dunno, certainly for as long as I've been your rep. Your partner requested it. I personally paid him £200 in cash last month.*'

'*How much else has been paid out as Cash bonuses?*'

'*I dunno, I could look it up and let you know*'

I took this matter up with our administrator when he returned but he tried to pass it off, saying he was keeping the money to pay all the staff a bonus at the end of the year. As none of these payments had gone through the books there was considerable doubt in his story.

Even though it was a terribly crowded work time for me we decided that his days in the company were over but he would not leave without 'selling' me back the investment he had made when he came.

'*The business is worth a lot more now than when I came in*' he claimed '*You've been freed up to write all that software and that could sell and make you hundreds of thousands of pounds. If you want to get rid of me it will cost you £60,000*'

Lots of discussion took place around a suitable figure for him to leave but I was beginning to think that the longer he stayed the more damage he might do to my business. So he got his £60,000 severance pay but it was to be paid out of the future profits of the software.

Despite that setback things were going well for us financially and I was keen that we got back to owning our own house. We found a delightful but small cottage in a quiet village in the Vale of Aylesbury just off the Chiltern Hills.

Poverty to Peaches

It was a 2 up 2 down plus kitchen and had an old dilapidated barn in the garden that had once stabled the local coalman's horse and cart. It was made of Witchert (or Wychert) which is a compound made from mixing the white chalky clay found in the Vale with straw from the stables and forming it into 3 feet square blocks that were served as the base of the wall. These were left to dry out in the sunshine and when hard another layer was laid on top of them and so on until the cottage was complete.

It is a marvellous material for the thickness of the walls acts as to suppress extraneous noise from outside the cottage. More importantly it absorbs heat from the fires in winter to throw the heat back into the house by acting like a heat brick. In summer it absorbs the heat from the sun so the cottage avoids ever getting too hot. There are a number of Wychert Cottages built around this part of the Chilterns with most being built before 1724 that we believe to be when ours was constructed.

The business was doing reasonably well and whilst I was waiting for the chaps to complete the programming on the Hairdressers system I could turn my mind to other things.

I had done numerous lectures to staff on the U.K.'s forthcoming Decimalisation in my Courage days and from somewhere came an invite to talk to the students at the new University College at Buckingham. It was the first Private University founded in the U.K. for many a year and I was asked to hold 3 lectures and follow up Tutorials On 'Costing and Management Systems'.

With the systems I had installed in the major companies early in my career and with the hundred or so small businesses to whom I had sold and installed micro-computer systems I obviously had extensive practical knowledge of the subject. I also had an ACCA and AMIS qualifications to legitimise my teachings.

UCB (the initials of the University) had revolutionised the usual University year by fitting in Four Terms instead of three.

By tightening the curriculum slightly it meant that we could get as much teaching into 2 years as the 3 years of a normal university degree.   At that time the college appealed to students who were willing to work hard for their degree and these and a slightly older group of student's met me at my first lecture.

They obviously enjoyed my ability to pull actual examples from real life in answers to their questions and I soon developed a great rapport with the students. My lectures and tutorials were always very well attended and the undergraduates prospered.

The following term I was asked if I would put together a course on Management Accounting and spend one day a week teaching on that subject and on an Introduction to Computers.

We also ran this latter course to outside business men and had a lot of success with it.

From my lectures I was asked to run some seminars on the *'Future effects on Society of the Micro-computer'* and these proved to be very interesting to me and very challenging to my audiences.

I had seen the effect of computers on a big business where a book-keeping staff of 142 people was reduced to 12 after the computer was installed and implemented.

Typists would disappear they would be replaced by these new Word Processing programs running on micro-computers.

In fact the executives and managers would learn to type and amend their own letters and memo's. (In the late 1970s when I was giving these seminars the preceding thoughts were so far into the future as far as most businessmen were concerned that they could not conceive of such a way of working and very few people believed me)

Poverty to Peaches

Similarly on the factory floor computerised machines working faster and more accurately than the human were replacing the human being.

If we failed to change the traditional ways of labour relations then there was no way that I could visualise full employment in the U.K. in traditional skills once all businesses took advantage of the speed and efficiency of these new machines.

All of this would result in mass sackings or redundancies of the staff and workers no longer needed. I felt that this would be a recipe for disaster.

'The Devil makes work for Idle Hands' is a very true statement.

It is a human characteristic that we try to better ourselves and/or our quality of life. The legitimate way of doing that in the western world is through the rewards we get from work. If a person has no hope of getting a job or a decent salary then you have a recipe for chaos and anarchy.

Wide scale implementation of the micro-computer must mean that there would no longer be enough full-time jobs for humans and a method of job-sharing would need to be introduced.

Companies and organisations would be able to make and sell just as many products and services after the computer had been installed as before it so instead of 'laying people off' (redundancy) why not keep them on the payroll at the same wage but for only half-a working week as there was only half a week's work for them?

The organisation's profits would be the same but their workers would have more time off for leisure or whatever they wished to spend their time on.

It was this point that was the real stumbling point to employers for it went against the grain in them to pay the same wage for less work but this was a crucial part of the solution.

Pay them the same wage and their spending power stays the same, recession is avoided and the demand in the economy is maintained thus the companies will continue to sell their products.

Sack them, lay them off, or make them redundant, or whatever term you wish to use and their income drops or disappears, there is less money spent on products thus the big 'sacking' companies see their sales shrink and their profits sink and the whole economy goes into a downward spiral.

In addition the country will be forced to support this increasing number of people for whom there is no longer a job. Welfare costs will soar. Governments will be forced to 'invent' categories of out-of-work people to prevent them being recorded for what they are – the Unemployed.

We will see the school leaving age extended. It has nothing to do with giving people a better education and everything to do with getting them off the unemployment register. Everyone will have the opportunity to go to university, or become cannon fodder in the Army for the same reason.

People will be classified as 'disabled or unable to work' so that the government can keep them off the Unemployment Register.

All of this will happen because the government and big business are unwilling to see 'outside the square' and consider different rules of employment (viz – full pay for working half a week – or one week a month) that will absorb those losing their jobs because the human had been replaced by the computer.

The stumbling point for many 'key' employees be they directors, professors, or working people, was the disbelief that anybody could 'share' their jobs.

They considered their contribution to their organisation was unique and could not be replicated by anyone else – however well they were qualified.

I ended these lectures with the thought that if society failed to make this fundamental change to the way we operate labour relations then the growing mass of people who were unemployed - and who had little or no chance of ever being employed - or of bettering their station in life by working hard and climbing up the career ladder - would take matters into their own hands and there would be anarchy on the streets of our cities and towns.

Many of those living in despair of ever improving their life through fair means will resort to foul.

Sadly – almost without exception - the decision-making politicians and ministers have no clue what it is like to be poor or to live in or even just above poverty.

Most ministers have an Eton or equivalent schooling and hugely privileged upbringings. They have no idea how to manage the poor and most have no willingness to make the rich contribute a fair share of their wealth to helping the poor.

Tax dodging and avoidance schemes abound and not only is a blind eye turned to them by those in power but many politicians actually embrace such schemes.

So went my lectures in the early 1980s and now – 30 years later I am watching my warnings materialise.

I was beginning to enjoy life with my dual role in academia and in business when another bombshell hit me.

My Middle daughter had her fill of looking after the old folk at the home and she came into the business to take over as many of the roles formerly held by the administrator as she could. I began to admire her fortitude and desire to succeed and was delighted to have her working alongside me.

My children had never been open about their childhood at home and I had never pressed them about it. I felt that my task was to open some windows in their lives and let some fresh air in to overcome the closed environment they had been brought up in.

On this occasion we were talking about the problems I had on visits when they were children and teenagers. I said -

'I just couldn't get any of you to talk to me.'

'Well we weren't allowed to'

'Why not? Why did your mother and stepfather not want any of you to talk to Jill or I.'

There was a long pause and I could see she was wrestling with something.

'Dad, I have to tell you something! Our stepfather has been having sex with us since we were 12 years of age.'

This was a tremendous shock to me and knocked all the breath out of me.

I had never ever suspected that this could be the reason for them not talking to me. I had thought their silence was down to untrue stories being told by my first wife to turn the girl's minds against me.

She continued

'He has had sex with me and the others girls regularly since we were 12. He is still trying to make us do it with him even though we have all left home.'

I was shocked to the core of my soul. It is impossible to describe my feelings at that point it time!

There was no doubt I was suffering massive guilt on my part for not having detected the abuse and massive sorrow for my poor girls but it was far worse than that.

Bad enough their father leaving them within the first 5 years of their lives and then paying only fleeting visits.

Bad enough that my first wife had built a picture of me in their minds as so horrible that they had been unable to confide in me about their stepfather's abuse.

My girls were now 20, 19 and 18 years old and he is continuing with his assaults?

I comforted my daughter as best I could and asked her to give me a little time to work out what best to do. We talked on for a while and when I got home I talked it over with Jill. We decided we needed to talk to the other two girls to see what their attitude would be toward the any actions we might take.

My eldest lived in Buckingham. I was there next day –

'I have a difficult subject to broach with you' said I after a cup of tea and some small talk.

'I need to come straight to the point. Your sister tells me that your stepfather has been sexually assaulting each of you since you were 12 years old.'

There was a stunned silence.

'Is this true/' I asked in as sympathetic tone as I could muster..

My daughter burst into tears.

'Is that yes or no' I probed gently

'Yes' she sobbed

'This is awful. I said and bearing in mind my middle daughter's information that he was still trying to carry on with the abuse *'How did you bring it to a halt?'*

She looked at me through eyes full of tears and then burst into massive tears as she said *'It's still going on, he hasn't stopped'*

Jeez, I thought this is getting to be beyond my comprehension.

My Youngest daughter aged 18 has had a baby with father unknown but we now highly suspect that her stepfather might be the father of her child; my Middle daughter is brave enough to tell me that her stepfather has been abusing hcr since she was 12; and my Eldest was married and still her stepfather is abusing her.

I knew that I would stop it from happening any more but should she tell her husband? What effect would it have on her marriage? Would it be fair to husband to be kept in the dark? How are we going to break the news to him?

I stayed with her until her husband returned from work. She was in tears as soon as he walked through the door and blurted out the whole story to him.

'*I always thought there was something funny about her relationship with her stepdad*' he confided in me '*but as he is a champion body builder I have never dared ask. I will look after her from here.*'

I reassured eldest daughter that I would find a solution to this whole situation that brings it to an end in a way that best protects all 3 of my girls.

How I was going to do that I didn't have a clue at that moment in time.

I left them coming to terms with the news.

I had a feeling that my Eldest might have been relieved that the terrible skeleton was now out of the cupboard – at least as far as her husband was concerned.

'*What a mess!*' I thought to myself on my drive back home. '*What an unholy mess!*'

The next day I was in a car to Lancashire to meet the headmaster at the school where the stepfather taught. I was hugely concerned that with his 3 stepdaughters gone he might turn his attentions on one or more girl pupils.

The Headmaster was non-committal but he would set up an investigation.

I went to the local Police HQ and had an interview with a Police Inspector to make sure he was put on a list of child assaulters. The Inspector wanted to know if we were going to press charges but I couldn't tell him. At the age my girls were now it was their decision.

I returned home and tried to pick up the pieces of my life.

I was there for my children but I still had a living to earn.

We were coming very close to the launch of our hairdressing system and the V-P of the hairdressing chain claimed to have received many advanced orders.

We launched it through a series of demonstrations at locations around the country and picked up 20 orders for immediate delivery. Added to the advanced orders the V-P had it meant we were already well over break-even and possibly on our way to our first £1,000,000 profit.

My eldest daughter's husband wanted an urgent meeting with me and we arranged to walk around the cricket field whilst he got what was worrying him off his chest.

'My wife is distraught' he said. *'She has been in tears since you went on about the abuse. Her stepfather is threatening to commit suicide. He has committed himself to a Psychiatric Hospital in Burnley but says he will jump off the cliffs when they let him out.'*

'Sounds like a bloody good solution to me' I muttered.

'It's all right for you but he has been your daughter's dad for 15 years and she doesn't want to see his life destroyed. She wants you to let up on him'.

I walked in silence for a while.

'Son-in-law', I said, *'you are making it sound as if I am the villain and you are defending the man who has abused your wife since she was 12 years old. He has such a hold over her that he is still abusing her even though she is married.'*

We walked on together further round the cricket ground.

'Just think for a moment what her stepfather has done to her and then think that all I am doing at present is making sure he cannot go on abusing my girls or anybody else's girls. If that means he jumps off a cliff when he comes out of Psychiatric Hospital so be it. That's his choice. When my girls were 11 years old they had no choice. They just obeyed 2 very strict 'parents' who were bringing them up and then suffered sexual abuse throughout their teens. Now where do you think your sympathies and loyalties should be?

We walked further before he said -

'You are right. He has such a hold over all of us that we are all feeling sorry for him instead of the victims of his abuse.'

Apparently a few days later stepfather arrived at eldest daughter's front door and demanded to be let in telling them that he just wanted to talk to them. Son-in-law was at home and refused to allow him in, slamming the door shut and keeping every bolt on as stepfather tried to break the door down. Both son-in-law and eldest daughter were apparently scared out of their wits but eventually stepfather left and didn't return.

My youngest daughter had left home with her baby and was living in a B&B establishment on the Welsh Coast where the family had stayed on holidays in previous years.

Because of the seriousness of the stepfather's abuse of all 3 girls I managed to contact the specialist who was been treating him at the hospital. He told me that stepfather was the type of person who tried to gain power over others.

A Svengali type personality. He will lie and manipulate others until he gets control of them and then not let them out of his control.

It was therefore essential that we break the link and control he has over the 3 girls. He was discharged from hospital and he and my first wife fled to Portugal.

Whether she had also been involved or had knowledge of the abuse we were never to find out. They had gone to Portugal and so were out of my daughter's lives so we never broached the subject again. The last thing I wanted was for my 3 daughters to have constant reminders of the abuse. I also did not want to somehow renew the strings he had that he used to manipulate to control them.

Almost immediately we were into the task of loading up the computers with our new software when I got a phone call from the hairdressers V-P.

'You been to your manufacturer lately?'

'No, I've had a few family problems to sort out, why?'

'My friend in California has just phoned me to say that there is a rumour going the rounds that they have stopped production on the computer you are using and are dropping the product!

'Oh no! They can't be. The Marketing Director UK has promised me that their production line will continue manufacturing for the next 10 years.'

'My pal is pretty well up on these things. You'd better check the rumour out. My members are not going to spend thousands of pounds for a system running on a discontinued computer.'

I couldn't believe the rumour to be true after all the assurances I had got from key managers at our manufacturer.

This would be a disaster if it proved to be true. We had invested all the money we had in the completion of the hairdressing system and already have enough orders to pay us back tenfold. If the computer is really being withdrawn then there is no way we can finance the changing of our software to another machine.

With our scarce human resources it would also take so long to change all our systems that we would lose our advantage of being first in the field and the better capitalised computer firms will scoot past us.

The rumour turned out to be true.

The hairdressing group cancelled all their orders. We were left with all our systems made useless, and a whole stock of computers that we couldn't sell.

We were wiped out.

I had to put the business into voluntary bankruptcy and face paying off my creditors and my former administrator.

The law on voluntary bankruptcy of the individual had not been softened in the mid-1980s but I chose not to go personally bankrupt.

This meant that I owed well over £100,000 and my income was gone with the ending of the business.

I was massively in debt – could see no way of paying it all off and had no income.

At the age of 45 I was back into Poverty!

'How secure is your marriage?' asked the Liquidator.

'Hopefully – very secure. Jill is full of support despite the fact that I have lost all we were working for.'

'That's good because in most liquidations of this kind - the marriage ends up in the Divorce Court'

'Oh please don't tell me that. I feel really beaten. If I lost my Jill I don't know what would become of me.'

'The bailiffs have cleared your ex-business of every asset and they tell me that you were honest with them and co-operative. It can be a very traumatic time.'

'That is an understatement. I am distraught.'

I really was uptight with tension. I felt so guilty for losing everything Jill and I owned after all the faith she has always shown in me. I had no money coming in to pay our mortgage and my ex-administrator was pushing me so hard to pay him the £60,000 cessation payments that he was taking action to seize my house. I didn't know which way to turn to ease the situation.

Jill and I were looking to rent a mobile home on a mobile home park near Wendover if he won his action against me and we lost our cottage. How could I stop him? I have no money coming in and he wanted full payment to stop his action against me and he wanted it now!

'There are some papers I would like you to sign' said the Liquidator pushing some forms in front of me.

'You and your wife are entitled to a redundancy payment from the Government.'

What redundancy payment? I had no idea such a scheme existed.

'You will receive £1,200 each.'

The news came as such a shock that my heart gave a lurch. £2,400 would allow me to make small payments on the mortgage and to ex-administrator that would stop them succeeding in taking action against me for full immediate payment.

It might also give me time to find an income to pay for a roof over my head and put food on the table.

After nearly making it to millionaire status and having it snatched away from me when it was practically in my grasp I had come to realise that the only financial goals that are really important are to put a roof over your head and food on the table.

For total fulfilment you could add the need for an opportunity to 'make something of yourself' as the old saying goes.

Part payment staved off any actions against us and I needed to find work to repay both big debts and get back on our feet again.

Circumstances helped by three or four unscrupulous players had knocked us flat on our backs so it was time to get off the floor, dust ourselves down, and see what we could make of the rest of our lives.

Jill was an absolute rock. No man could have been given better support and encouragement. She had every entitlement to admonish in the strongest possible terms - *'Terry! What on earth have you done? How could you bring us down to this destitution?'* but she never did. She never admonished me in any way. She just rolled here sleeves up and supported every move I made to try to get out of the mess I had got us into.

What a wonderful wife!

*

Poverty to Peaches

Poverty to Peaches

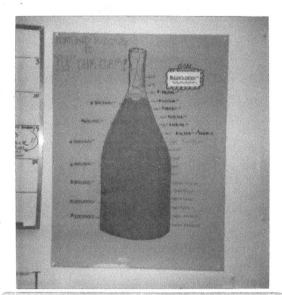

Portland, OREGON
CASH IN: $796,545 / Debtor Days - 30

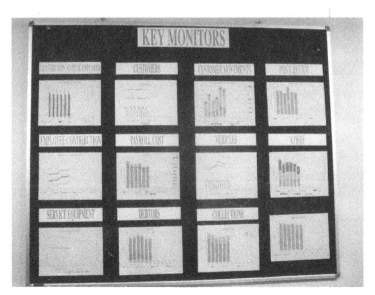

Poverty to Peaches

Poverty to Peaches

Poverty to Peaches

CHAPTER Nineteen
'A roof over our heads and
Food on the table'

I still had occasional work from University College at Buckingham and my lectures, seminars and tutorials were going very well. They were being very well received by the students so UCB stepped up my role to cover Management Accounting, and Introduction to Computers.

This latter subject was also available in specialised seminars that I ran for business people and was bringing a lot of businesses in touch with this new and growing University.

I had bought an old battered van for £250 and this got me up to the University and back. If anyone thought it odd that the lecturer teaching them drove such a decrepit vehicle they were either too polite to mention it or it didn't bother them.

Outside lecturers were paid quite well and I was beginning to pay my way and have a small amount left over to make instalment payments to my ex-administrator and on my mortgage. It was sometimes touch and go but we kept our financial heads above water.

There is a hugely prestigious Management College in the Chilterns that was rated in the top 6 management colleges in the world.

They used to run 1, 2, 3 or 4 week courses on management, finance and behavioural sciences. They were planning to start an MBA (Master of Business Administration) course and as this is a semi practical academic qualification they were in contact with UCB to see if they could do some kind of linked course.

UCB were kind enough to arrange for me to go along and see if there were any joint courses we could do, or alternatively whether we could use some of each other's lecturers and academics to work jointly on their courses.

Ashridge Management College has an ambience that takes your breath away.

Set in a fold of the Chiltern Hills it has magnificent rhododendron covered gardens that were so good that the late Queen Mother was frequently driven through them to admire the plants and the scenery. It has sunken gardens, arboretums, spring flowers plants and blossoms, hanging baskets, all surrounding a magnificent building that had once belonged to the man who built many of the English canals.

It sits in Ashridge Park a beautiful natural area where the ancient Kings of England would go hunting. Deer herds consisting of hundreds of these lovely animals roamed free in the park and could be seen by night and by day, but in their hundreds at dusk.

Walking through the front door of Ashridge Management College was breath-taking! Unbelievably here was I – 'Little Tel' from 'ackney Downs' (as explained earlier at 6feet and half an inch tall - I was no longer little. Drama had taught me not to drop my 'h' but throughout my childhood and my early days at Grammar School I really was half the height and less than half the width of many of my contemporaries. Thus throughout my lifetime I have always thought of myself as having emerged and evolved out of 'Little Tel' from 'ackney Downs').

Here was I in some of the most splendid surroundings I had ever visited to meet the guy running the Financial Management courses to talk about some joint lecturing.

In fact it proved to be a one-way journey. Ashridge had just received certification to run its own MBA courses and no longer needed the link with an Academic University.

However my meeting took place and the man I was meeting turned out to be a terrific guy.

At Ian's kind invitation I started to lecture on some of his Financial Management courses at Ashridge.

My lecturing income from UCB had kept our heads above water financially and now there was the occasional course at Ashridge on which I was invited to work. We were beginning to work our way out of the mire my foolishness in taking my eye off the ball in my business had caused.

An accidental meeting I had with the former secretary of the chief rival my now defunct computer company had led to her revealing that the demise of my company had been set up by our rivals and a marketing manager at the computer manufacturer.

The manufacturer's salesman that had been lent to us to help boost sales of the defunct stock we held as a result of the manufacturer ceasing to manufacture the model we had built all our software on was apparently put into us with the orders to get hold of all our customer base and pass it on to our rivals in High Wycombe. Apparently the manufacturer's marketing manager had an 'arrangement' with our rivals.

This would explain how our rivals had won 2 or 3 prizes in the National Draw held by the manufacturer for all their dealers. The prizes were of considerable value including a luxury motor car.

It was time to talk to a solicitor and get advice.

We assessed the losses that had been caused by the liquidation of my company along with the loss of profits on known orders we had received but could not fulfil due to the withdrawal of the computer by the manufacturers without notification to us and it came to more than £6million.

We sued the manufacturers for that amount.

That started nearly 2 years of frustration and dissatisfaction as the manufacturer employed every technical and legal excuse they could to delay bringing the case to court.

We had developed our case to a level where we presented for assessment to a leading QC and he was sure we would win but could not guarantee how much of the £6,000,000 we would be awarded.

The manufacturer thereupon changed their Solicitors.

My solicitor was very unhappy. This would not only allow them to delay the case yet further whilst they instructed their new solicitors but the new solicitors they had appointed were the ones used by the pharmaceutical companies and they knew every trick in the book to avoid liability.

The new solicitors immediately raised more technical issues that served to keep the case out of court.

I had a visit at home from one of their new solicitors to discuss the case. While with us he asked to go to the toilet which was at the other end of the house and I thought nothing peculiar about the request. Two weeks later our partial Legal Aid was stopped and from then on we must fight on totally with our own money.

On challenging the Legal Aid Board they produced a photocopy of my income. It was a photocopy of the document that I had been working on in my study when the solicitor had called. His trip to the toilet was obviously a cover to search my house. Trouble was the income statement had not taken account of all my travel and programme development costs so showed Gross Income and failed to show my net income.

I now seemed to be working solely for the benefit of the Lawyers. All the spare income I could muster was going to fight my case.

We nearly got them into court but they claimed they had a document in the USA that proved they had notified all their software writers 18 months in advance of the intended withdrawal of the computer we had been assured was in production for the next decade.

They then delayed and delayed producing this document until the Recorder at Court gave them 14 days to produce. 18 months later they were still arguing technical issues of confidentiality that they claimed prevented them producing their 'evidence'.

Jill and I were only able to cover our food and accommodation with all the rest of our income going to the lawyers.

The manufacturer's solicitors came through at this stage with an offer to cover all our legal costs if we dropped the case.

We really felt bad.

We had the Opinion of the QC that we would undoubtedly win the case but without stating how much we might be awarded. We had enough proof to show negligence on the part of the computer manufacturer; and probably enough to show their Marketing Manager's conspiracy with our chief rivals to take us out; but we just couldn't afford to go on fighting the case. The lawyer's fees were taking up all we earned.

There really was only one decision we could make.

Goodbye £6,000,000 (or whatever proportion of it the judge agreed); goodbye to the gravy train for our solicitor for the costs had been considerable; but hello peace and an enjoyment of our earnings from that moment on.

My earnings had grown from UCB and the increasing number of lectures I was doing at Ashridge Management College.

The clients of Ashridge Management College were mainly the managements of leading U.K. companies. They also had a number of Open Courses that individuals could sign themselves onto or get their company to send them onto a course.

I felt that my battered old van was no longer appropriate so I sold it for £50 and bought an equally old but far more charismatic Morris Minor.

Ian turned out to be the kindest and most considerate guy I ever worked with. He was meticulous in his preparation and went out of his way to help his clients and the lecturers he had working on the courses he was responsible for.

How such a kind and considerate man could become such a monster on the golf course was always beyond me but his kindness at work made his mood on the golf course tolerable - as long as you ducked in time to miss the golf club whistling through the air after he had hit a poor shot.

I began to also lecture at Ashridge on the Open Introduction to Management courses along with Introduction to Finance and soon progressed onto tutoring some of Ashridge's client's courses. On these I would have overall responsibility for the working of the course even though specialised Lecturers would handle their individual subjects.

It was great fun and I seem to be able to rapidly gain a rapport with the delegates from any country, creed, religion or colour. Perhaps the greatest demonstration of that was a client's four week General Management Course I tutored that had 22 delegates from around the world speaking 18 different first languages. There I picked up the technique of sitting the delegate with good English next to one with poor English and allowing them to develop a rapport and often close friendship as they helped each out with anything that was difficult to understand.

I would always handle the Financial Management Section of the courses I tutored and as with the Open Courses every delegate scored each section of the course out of 10. I was lucky enough to invariably score very well, often achieving the top mark from most of the delegates. On one occasion an attractive lady who was a partner in a rapidly expanding company in the West of England scored me at 11.5 out of 10 and my colleagues all wanted to know what extra services she was scoring but in truth I took my tutors role seriously and felt I had a vicarious responsibility for all my delegates.

This vicarious responsibility stayed with me throughout every seminar, lecture, tutorial, and management workshop I was ever to run and often got in the way of some very tempting offers from which I always walked away – often regretfully.

About this time the Village Cricket Team got fed up with my comments when I walked my dogs around the ground that they should be putting the kids (14 and 15 year olds) on to bowl an over or two instead of batting them at 9, 10 and 11 and never giving them a bowl even when the friendly 2nd XI game was all but lost.

'You want the kids to bowl so start a Colts cricket team for us' came the reply from George who had been a magnificent Chairman of the club as well as an outstanding player.

I had not played cricket since my knee was damaged playing South Western League Football at Falmouth Town many moons before. However I thought I should see if there was any interest amongst the youngsters for a Colts Team.

We started with just the 3 they needed to complete the adult's Second XI in the club but by the end of our first season we had 52 boys turning up each Tuesday Evening. Second Year and we entered them for the Under 17s League even though our average age was 15 and they were hopelessly outclassed by experienced Colts Teams. The boys stuck at it and by year 3 we made the Finals of the Oxfordshire League Cup and got our first boy into the County u/17s team.

I was asked if I would run Buckinghamshire's County u/17s and agreed. Buckinghamshire were a Minor County in cricketing world. In practice this mean that the cricket 'big wigs' pretty well ignored and disparaged them. The Minor

Counties only played against other Minor Counties with little or no ECB funding.

I was to learn that the u/17s squad was comprised of all the boys who had represented Buckinghamshire at under 11s and through to under 15s had won less than a handful of matches in all those years and had won no games at all as under 15s.

Representative cricket in the 1990s had little to do with how good you were but a lot more to do with what school you went to.

The only way I could see to overcome that was to invite every village and town side in Buckinghamshire to send their best under 17s to free nets I was running at various locations in the county.

I drew up a list of 30 of the most promising lads and invited them to a week-end at Stowe School where we invited some ECB coaches to run some sessions and a top Sports nutritionist. I did the sessions on 'How to be a Winning Team' and then we selected the 17 players who were going to make up our squad for the forthcoming year.

It was quite a revolution for the same group of boys had represented the county as under 11s right through to under 15s (there wasn't an under 16s) and they – and their parents and coaches – expected them to form my under 17s squad with perhaps 1 or 2 others.

Less than 1/3 of the previous squad made it into my u/17s. Their former captain who had given me the impression that he thought of himself 'the bees knees' never made it.

I have noticed over the years that people who have gained control of organisations or committees have enormous trouble accepting a newcomer who might be brimming with bright ideas but is almost certain to upset (or even kick over) the applecart.

So it was with many of the people running English Cricket. Even though my County under 17s had a marvellous year –

tying with Northants (a First Class County) and beating Surrey and Sussex there was no way forward for Terry's Methods and they were positively blocked by the former Surrey County Cricketer who was appointed Buckinghamshire County Captain.

I didn't need to see all my good work spoiled so I left my voluntary unpaid role as Manager of the County Under 17s.

Sadly I had to leave it in the disastrous hands of one who could only understand the traditional methods of English Cricket at a time when we had the worst National and County sides in cricket. He didn't even take the trouble to find out how we had transformed Buckinghamshire's constantly losing youth teams into winners. He was only interested in imposing his own methods. I don't think the county youth squads ever won another game under his management against First Class Counties.

I was still working at Ashridge Management College and was picking up a great deal of work. I was earning more in fees and tutoring more clients as an outside consultant than I would have done had I been a full time Tutor with them.

Ashridge had a finance lecturer who had been with them for years and he handled all their overseas clients who needed a finance course. He was a very good lecturer and knew his subject well but some of their clients wanted a new face who might take a different approach. I was asked if I would like to run a seminar in Abu Dhabi and jumped at the chance.

The client was the Abu Dhabi Oil Company. I don't know whether it was my earlier time in North Sea Oil that gave me credibility or the fact that I just like people irrespective of creed, race or religion but my week of lectures was very well received by the delegates and their management.

My course combined Introduction to Management with Introduction to Finance and ended with a computer simulation of a business that delegates had to manage in teams of 6. In was great fun to lecture on and seemingly great fun for the delegates, many of whom personally thanked me and claimed that I had really stimulated their interest in the subjects and in successfully managing the assets of their country.

Every time I have worked abroad I have done my best to read up the background to the country I would be working in.

When in the countries my greatest interest outside work was visiting the original or ancient culture from which the present society had grown. If you could throw in the odd game of golf as well I would be in my element.

I was very lucky in Abu Dhabi. I was accommodated in the hotel that housed the President's visitors quarters and I was one of the few visitors allowed down into the ground floor area where the President's held his minister's meetings.

The staggering thing was that everything was clad in gold or was solid gold, even the lift that took you down into these quarters and the chandeliers that lit up the 'conference' room.

Although I am not Muslim – being a rare attender at Quaker meetings - one of the delegates on the course was kind enough to take me to a prayer meeting in the central mosque. He introduced me to all and sundry and I was treated by them all so well and invited to listen in as the children quoted the Koran. When quoted in Arabic the Koran has a lovely rhythm to its words and content.

If you remember my childhood I played my junior soccer in multi-cultural football teams so visiting the places of worship of the different religions has always seemed to me to be the sensible thing to do. It provides an insight to the way different parts of the world behave and I was later to visit the places of worship in China, India, the USA, Canada and most parts of Europe.

On about my 3rd visit to Abu Dhabi the Executive who was the Head of Training in the Oil Companies took me to see the beach on which he was brought up in a house made of palm

Poverty to Peaches

leaves before the oil was discovered. Wealth had come to Abu Dhabi in my lifetime and its nationals had gone from being nomads to millionaires in one generation.

On one occasion I was sitting in the lounge close by the lift that descended to the President's floor when one of my young delegates came in with his elderly grandfather on his arm.

He introduced me but grandfather didn't quite know how to greet the visiting white 'professor'. He was reserved and spoke no English and I spoke no Arabic so our contact was enacted in body language only.

He was tall and upright but had a face that was lined and blackened by a lifetime as a nomad and I gathered this was his first trip out of the desert and into the modern city of skyscrapers that is Abu Dhabi. He walked with the aid of his grandson's arm and a stick and grandson took him over to the exclusive lift that was large enough to house up to 20 or more people at a time and that connected to the Presidential suite below. The old man was not allowed in the lift and an attendant was constantly on duty to make sure no unauthorised people entered it but was happy to let people look at the solid gold décor.

I was watching the old man's face. He was completely bewildered by such a proliferation of wealth. His eyes roamed all around the lift. He gave a nod that was more of incredulity than approval and then turned and walked away.

It was clearly the youngsters who admired such incredible wealth. The old man's body language suggested his life would be totally fulfilled if he could get back to the few goats and chickens he constantly moved around the desert in his Bedouin existence.

Jill hated flying but she did join me on one of my trips to Abu Dhabi when the Head of Training gave her a warm welcome. He did us proud – booking us the Penthouse Suite that occupied the whole of the top floor of the Hilton Hotel's exclusive block that was a little apart from the Hilton Hotel and its exclusive beach.

They made us terrifically welcome and it was a marvellous stay. Perhaps Jill's favourite story was of the bed that we slept in the Penthouse. It was so wide that if she stretched all 5ft4ins of her with her arms as high above her head as possible she still couldn't reach either side of the bed. She wondered if it bedded all the concubines at the same time but we didn't like to ask.

Abu Dhabi is a wonderful place to visit. It is a secular state. Alcohol, drugs and pornography is strictly forbidden and women wear the burka that covers them from head to foot but they have a tolerance of other cultures. So alcohol is allowed in the Western Hotels, but not allowed out in the street. The exclusive beaches that front the hotels are surrounded on the land side and alongside by high natural fences that keep out the view of the bathers but inside the surrounds swim suits can be as brief as you like. I certainly enjoyed the site of pretty women in the skimpiest costumes I have seen in public on their beaches.

On my last visit the Jet Ski had been invented and an awful lot of local young men seemed to be jet skiing up and down the sea in front of that particular beach.

I knew a little of the history of the Emirates from my reading before my first visit and the Head of Training was delighted that I had tried to learn about their culture. When I left at the end of that visit he presented me with a copy of the Koran printed in English and Arabic.

I didn't read the Bible until I was an adult and since then I have several times read from cover to cover as the Christian's holy book that has influenced the Western Cultures for hundreds of years.

Now it was my opportunity to read the Koran from cover-to cover and do you know what – I was struck not by the differences but by the similarity of the message. The secret of life and of true happiness is to love your neighbour as you love yourself and to help those less fortunate than yourself.

I have now read the holy books of many other religions and note the same similarities of the message. I am still an occasional Quaker as it seems to be the right religion for me but what a marvellous understanding of other cultures my leisure time in these countries has given me.

I wonder how many of the leading politicians of this world who rain down bombs on any religion that is not their own or how many citizens and media editors have taken the trouble to even read the Koran let alone see how it is enacted? I can't help but feel the world would be a better and safer place if they had.

Lecturing at Ashridge was continuing apace and soon we had caught up on payments on our mortgage and were well on our way to paying off our ex-administer.

I got a personal invite to put together a Management Training week for the clients of a private educational and training company in Kenya

It was my first assignment under my own name that had no connection with Ashridge, or University College at Buckingham, and I didn't know what to charge. I thought Ashridge were charging £600 a day for any of its lecturers working on an outside course so I plumped for that figure to be my fee. Ashridge probably also charged their client for course preparation and research but I felt I would be pushing my luck if I tried for that so £600 a day for when I was in front of the delegates plus travel costs and out of pocket expenditure became my charge for private courses.

It was a high fee for my Kenyan client to pay but my Management Workshop went so well they seemed happy to pay. They invited me back several times as word of the successful Terry Gasking Management Workshops spread around the companies trading in Kenya.

I didn't want to reduce my day fee having got it established so instead I donated a tidy sum to Kenya Society for the Blind.

The money was invested by the trust in my father's name (remember he was blind and I thought he would be looking down from above with full approval). The income from the investment was to be used to provide huts for the blind people's family to live in and for the purchase of food crops that he/she could be taught to grow and tend over future years.

Back at Ashridge I was having a lot of success when tutoring the 4-week management courses of a massive (£3.5 billion turnover) group that had world-wide interests. Ashridge fed their delegates excellently every day but on the last night of this course there was a formal dinner that would be attended by one of the group's Directors. He and I would then make a speech after the dinner – me to summarise the course – he/she to inform the senior managers on the course of the group's plans and progress.

We always had a lot of fun on these occasions and my speech was always a light hearted affair. On one famous occasion I was interrupted by a Salvation Army lady making a collection and forced to dig into my wallet to make a donation. Whilst I was doing so I realised that the Salvation Army lady was shedding her clothes much to the delight of all the delegates.

I was to discover that they were all in on the jape and longing to see how much she could phase me but apart from having a naked very attractive lady sitting on my lap it didn't phase me at all, indeed I was able to make many interesting references to her attributes and even managed to verbally connect them to aspects that could connect with the profitability of the client company.

I few years previous I had been asked individually to look at one of the companies in this group that was turning over £170 million in sales in the U.K. and making profits but was demanding too much additional finance to keep going.

By that time using a combination of spreadsheets on my laptop I could run the management accounts of clients and produce the factors that were critical to success. The system is the basis of my book *'Accounting Keys for Success'* that I went on to write when I had retired. It enabled me to identify the dozen or so critical factors in the way the company was performing. Get those right and performance improved – sometimes startlingly so.

My system also dramatically simplified and graphically displayed the management accounts so that key managers could focus on the parts of the business that needed improving or/and build on the parts where progress was possible without going through pages and pages of accounting figures and trying to make sense of them.

After visiting a number of the company's locations to check the authenticity of the results my system had revealed I reported my findings to management.

The biggest problem of this company was the amount of Working Capital they needed. They were providers of workplace clothing. This meant that they purchased all the clothing with the clients motif on and then charged the client a hire fee and laundry costs over the lifetime of the clothing.

It required a lot of front money to provide the clothing that was recovered in the hire and laundry prices over the long run. As they expanded their sales they needed ever more 'Working Capital' to keep going.

The essentials for such a company is to keep your stock (inventory) to an absolute minimum and get your invoices paid by your customers as soon as humanly possible, whilst negotiating longer pay dates with your suppliers.

Whenever you go into detail with the directors of a company about the problems you have found and the way you would propose to solve them there is the danger that the prospective client takes all your research to use for themselves and they show you the door. Such was the case here.

My consolation was the £1,200 I had charged them for 2 days on sites and my Report and presentation to management.

It was now 3 years later and one of the directors of the group that owned the company asked me to go back in and see if I could achieve what I had forecast.

I explained that without the co-operation of the company's directors and top managers it will not happen.

'Don't worry, Terry,' came the reply *'the management team have no alternative but to co-operate! This will be their last chance of survival. We can no longer finance them and if we have to sell the company it will be sold without any of the present management'.*

I got the company's last 3 years of management accounts, put it through my system and as clear as a pikestaff it was flagging up excessive Working Capital as the major problem.

Working Capital is in the main made up of the stock you have in raw materials, or that you are working on, or that is in your warehouses or on your shelves. The money owed to you by customers also makes up part of the 'Working Capital'.

To reduce both of those needs you to change the way the company has worked in previous years and to change the mental attitude of everyone involved – directors – top managers – middle managers – supervisors and foremen, the people working on the line as well as those actually selling the product. The tribal behaviour that is part of all big companies along with the inherent resistance most people have to change made this almost impossible to achieve 'in-house' when using companies managers or staff.

This is where the Terry Gasking Management Workshops made their name. This was to be my first and it was two intensive days of instruction and involvement for a group of 30 to 36 employees from the whole spectrum of the management chain.

From Operating Directors down to stock controllers, managers and supervisors and included half a dozen from Accountants – the Financial Director down to the Credit Controllers. I started them at 8 am on the first day and knew that I had until lunchtime to capture their interest and imagination. This took the whole gambit of skills I had picked up from my days in drama and skill at working an audience but I always achieved it. I knew that not to have done so would result in a failure to improve the performance of the company.

I also knew that this was the period of time that demanded every bit of skill and experience I had ever acquired. It was extremely unlikely that anyone in-house would have the varied experience and background that would enable them to acquire the skills of capturing and stimulating an audience to change the way they worked.

Having captured their interest on the first morning then with their undivided attention and focus we moved onto the ways we can measure success and then finally the ways we can enhance that success within a company.

I had prepared case studies and they worked in syndicated groups of 6 mixed disciplines and these were vital to the success of the course. On the last afternoon each group presenting their solutions in financial terms using a Balance Sheet, Profit & Loss Account and Cash Flow to the rest. The presentation had to be made by the non-accounting managers.

Over the years an amazing number of non-accounting managers shook my hand vigorously at the end of my Workshop

'Terry I can't thank you enough! I came up through Production [or Sales or Admin or PR or any management discipline other than Accounting] *and I control substantial budgets* [often $multi-million]. *I sit in Management and Board*

348

Meetings and have never really known precisely what the Finance Director/Accountant is talking about. They use jargon, obscure words and meanings that often seem to be the reverse of everything I have learned [Debtors and Creditors are often quoted]. *Your workshop has made it all clear. For the first time in my life I feel that I can confidently sit down with the Accountant and get them to do what I want in my Department instead of me being forced to always accept their recommendations because I don't really understand what they are saying.'*

On the first day of my Management Workshops we packed up for dinner at 6 pm and returned at 7.30 pm to work on the case study material I had thus far given them.

Once each group had control of their own Case Study in the evening after-dinner session and could bounce ideas off me as I moved through the groups they became completely hooked on the task in hand – determined to bring the best set of results to the whole group the following afternoon.

This never failed in any of the 306 Terry Gasking Management Workshops I was to run in multi-national multi-million pound/dollar companies over the next 20 years.

It was common for me to go off to the bar for a drink before bed at 10 pm with everybody still working on their case study. I would normally have to drink alone as they were all still working but occasionally one group or other would break off and join me. After one drink they were all back into their syndicate room and I was off to bed.

My delegates seldom finished their self-imposed work schedule before mid-night and it was often the early hours before they turned into their beds. The latest I heard about a group finishing their first day was 4.30 am in the morning and all of them were back in the lecture hall by 8 am the next day.

Many wise directors realised how I was able to achieve these results and it was succinctly and accurately summed up by a director of the £3.5 billion company who sat through more than one –

'Terry this is not a Finance Workshop – nor is it a Management Workshop per se. You succeed because you capture hearts and minds from the outset and then set them tasks that they can handle and understand. It's brilliant. It has turned around an awful lot of our companies and there are a lot more who could benefit.'

There were - and thankfully the work came my way and they made up many of the 306 Terry Gasking Workshops I was still to do.

The company that I was going into were the providers of workplace clothing. In the 3 years since they had turned me down they had been haemorrhaging cash that the group who owned them could not afford.

In the 3 years they had failed to reduce the cash they needed for Working Capital – indeed they had needed nearly £2million of extra cash just to keep going. Their presentations to the owning group management meetings were always along the lines that these controls I had suggested were ok for other companies but just could not work in their industry. They had tried everything and the task was impossible.

One or two of the owning Group Directors who had seen me working at Ashridge had insisted that they put Terry Gasking in there and see how he does.

So after putting their last 3 years figures through my monitoring system - in I went with my Terry Gasking Management Workshop

Within the year following the first Terry Gasking Management Workshop (first because I returned for a one-day workshop at 6 months and again after a year) Working Capital had reduced and the company had an extra £30million in the bank and profit was up by 7%.

Poverty to Peaches

The success achieved through the Management Workshops I was running allowed my clients to self-finance their expansion. With the expansion effectively costing their owners no extra investment came increased profits.

No wonder I started to get numerous requests to run a Terry Gasking Management Workshop in multi-national companies in so many parts of the world.

In fact so many requests came in I was getting to the stage that I would be working flat out on the research and monitoring as well as running the Management Workshops.

My interview with one set of Directors had not gone so well and I knew they didn't really want me in their company. On the other hand they were part of the group I was doing a lot of work with so I didn't want to be seen to walk away.

I decided to price myself out of their company by doubling my fee to £1,200 a day.

A month later they were back imploring me to run my Management Workshop.

It seemed that their banks were refusing them any more credit and they were desperate for cash. I ran the Workshop and had a fully focused group of 33 delegates. They had all heard that their company was in danger of folding and that Terry Gasking had turned around a number of companies in the same plight.

They thus implemented virtually everything we recommended and £millions of pounds rolled into their bank accounts on an almost immediate basis.

This story was repeated over and over again. My fees therefore rapidly increased on all future contracts to £1,200 a day and then to £2,000 a day

This was the later 1980s Recession and banks were closing down credit lines. *'Banks lend you an umbrella when it is sunny and take it back when it rains'*

This is precisely the way banks worked with a huge number of companies in the 1980s and so my Management Workshops

351

were in great demand. My doubled fees had not deterred any potential clients.

By the time I retired my fee was £3,000 a day, all my travel first or business class, first class hotels, limousine pick-up and drop from and to airports and 1/2% of the cash generated in the 12 months following my first workshop.

In every case profits increased.

Profits can be measured in a multitude of ways so I did not get mixed up in how my clients portrayed their own profits.

With Cash – either you've got it – or you aint!

If you've got it then it can be counted accurately.

If you haven't got it then how much you owe can be measured accurately.

On a number of occasions I was put into $multi-million companies by the owners when they had decided their subsidiary should only be given 6 months before being sold off.

I was usually able to pull more idle cash out of the company than the sale price that had been provisionally agreed and in all but one case we (we - being the delegates who had attended my Workshop) turned their company around so efficiently that it was retained and often received additional investment by their owners.

'Little Tel' from 'ackney Downs' had come a mighty long way.

*

Poverty to Peaches

CHAPTER Twenty
Adventures & Kindness

I love Africa. I ran Management Workshops over a 3 week period 3 times a year in Africa for about 7 years and loved every trip.
I stroked a fully grown 'wild' Lion, had a fully grown Leopard purr at me, rode an Elephant for a morning through the bush, was chased by an Ostrich flapping her wings at me with her family in close pursuit after I had accidently disturbed them, jumped out of my skin when the bush beside me moved and a massive Rhinoceros came out to see what I was up to, played an 8 iron to the green with a Warthog grazing 5 yards behind me, missed a putt when an unseen Water Buck emerged from a water hole alongside the green, Had a 'wagon load' of monkeys fall out of a tree alongside a green and gambol all over my line of put, as they then played with my golf ball I guess it didn't make much difference what the original line was, marched off Mount Kenya with just an Umbrella in my hand to move a Buffalo out of the path of the straggle of executives who were descending behind me only to discover that the buffalo was the greatest killer of humans in Africa (I guess that is if you exclude human killers), sat in a small boat yards from a herd of 150 wild Elephants drinking with the Nanny Elephants constantly lifting the mischievous youngsters out of the water and onto the bank only for them to immediately jump straight back in again, listened to Hippos playing close by as I tried to sketch them and the multitude of Gazelles, Zebras, Gnus, and other animals of the bush,

disturbed the line of Giraffes until I changed my shirt from red to brown, had a strong smell of buffalo in my tree platform only to be advised by the scout that none were in the area and what I had smelled was a black mamba somewhere in the tree with me, and had a conversation with a 6 foot long Komodo Dragon that was camping under my hut on a Game Farm.

All of these incidents and the other marvellous adventures I had in Africa and around the world would take another book to explain but really they all occurred due to my love of animals and my irresistible urge to talk to them and try to communicate with them.

Watching my lovely dog Henry throughout his lifetime had taught me well on communicating via body language and I really did get on wonderfully well with nearly every animal I met. So successful were Henry's tactics that I imported them into my Management Workshops and understanding and using body language in humans became an integral part of them.

The Komodo Dragon incident was very interesting.

My major client owned a leading holiday travel organisation in Eastern Africa and asked me to see if the 'Terry Gasking Magic' could work there. Amongst their companies was a joint holding of a prestigious Game Farm where the Royal Princesses had stayed before one of them ascended to the throne. Now I was booked to stay there for the week-end in between my Workshops. Somehow having 'Little Tel' from ackney' staying for the week-end failed to have the same attraction to the owner as the Royal presence.

The owner was the original owner of the Game Farm and had sold out his majority holding to my Client. Much to his disgust he had been ordered to attend my Management Workshop the following week and you didn't need any knowledge of body language to tell that he was not happy about it.

His Game farm had all kinds of indigenous and imported animals including the Komodo Dragon who had escaped his enclosure and taken up residence under one of their Guest Huts. The animal was about 6 or 7 feet long really did look like a dragon. It would come out by day and bask on the grass alongside.

Who do you think got allocated the hut with a Komodo Dragon under it?

Yep, that's right – 'Little Tel from 'ackney Downs'

Most of the other huts were occupied by Air Crews on a few days break before their return flight to wherever but its allocation to me was a clear reaction from the owner at being ordered to attend my Workshop.

The only problem for the owner's tactic to scare me off was that I have been a talker all my life and have a huge love of animals. Put those two attributes together and it is inevitable that I have a strong desire to talk to every animal I meet including a Komodo Dragon!

That and the communication skills taught me by my beloved Henry Dog had me sitting on the grass alongside my hut trying to persuade the dragon to come out and say hello and have a conversation with me. I almost succeeded and there was never any fear or threat in the eyes of the animal so we just chatted away with him facing me about 2 feet away. We did this a number of times whilst I was at the Game Farm so the former owner's tactics lost out big time.

There were many adventures everywhere I went in the world but one in Zimbabwe defies explanation. I went for a half day horse ride accompanied by the Manager of one of their very large game Farms and the native Zimbabwean who looked after the horses. We passed in front of an 'amphitheatre' made by the surrounding cliffs that overlooked a vast plain. The cliffs had some trees that had taken root on them but I got an uncanny feeling I had been here before.

'Do you mind if I stop for a moment?' I asked *'I have an uncanny feeling I have been here before'*
I stared up at the ridges made by the rock formation of the cliffs.

'You are going to find this strange but I have this very strong vision of me sitting on that ridge a long, long time ago – listening to the Chief of Chiefs making a speech to all the clans that had come from all over the surrounding Plains and gathered in this valley. There were thousands of warriors and families who had come in peace to listen to the Chief of Chiefs.'

The Manager looked upon me with a kind of stifled tolerance of one who is used to putting up with visions of fanciful guests. I was still rooted to the spot, sitting astride my horse and visualising the various tribes who were there countless years ago when the Zimbabwean horse man who was with us said something to the Manager in Shona.

'My man doesn't speak English' said the Manager *'but he has lived here all his life and is excited by your pointing. He tells me that he discovered some wall paintings in a hidden cave on the side of the cliff. He has never shown them to anyone but will take us to them if you want.'*

'Yes please' said I and we rode our horses a little way up the cliff before tethering them to a tree. As we proceeded on foot the Manager said

'I don't know what he is on about. There is certainly nothing recorded anywhere about there being any cave paintings anywhere near this part of Zimbabwe.'

The Zimbabwean led us through a narrow gap in the rocks. The manager was looking quite nervous. *'Got to be careful of a Cobra'* he said. *'They sit at the front of the caves and grab a Cliff Rat to eat. They also grab humans. The rest of the rats tolerate them as it keeps the bigger predators away.'*

We carried on under an overhang and into a sheltered cave and there – sure enough – was a wall covered in wall paintings looking as if they had been drawn by primitive man thousands or even millions of years ago.

All three of us were astounded by the conviction I had when first encountering the amphitheatre of rocks and by the discovery of the cave paintings.

There was absolutely no way I could have known they were there yet I was certain I had been there thousands, perhaps millions of years ago!

There are many events that defy rational explanation!

Nearly all my clients were so very kind.

I had the Managing Director's car and driver throughout my stay in Shanghai and the most marvellous banquet of Chinese specialist foods there and in Shenzhen. Magnificent Indian gourmet in Mumbai and the most hair-raising and dangerous taxi ride I ever had to Pune. I enjoyed the most marvellous hospitality all over the United States with stretch limos as my transport at each location and golf courses provided my relaxation on my rest days.

A Dhow trip across the Arabian Sea to a lobster and steak Picnic on a remote island was another highlight as was sailing a hired yacht off the coast of California.

All of these were enjoyed in the last 15 years of my career when I ran a total of 306 Terry Gasking Management Workshops on behalf of my clients.

I got all this work through the kindness of my clients recommending me rather than them taking personal credit for the success their companies had achieved.

I had run my Management Workshops in the U.K. end of my multi-national client and they had been very successful. They asked me to look at subsidiaries of theirs in Kenya and Zimbabwe. They operated throughout eastern and Southern

Poverty to Peaches

Africa and again the Management Workshops were very well received and very successful.

A few years later I got a phone call out of the blue from a Director of the biggest conglomerate in Zimbabwe. They owned 16 major companies in all kinds of trades and operated throughout Zimbabwe, Botswana, and the northern half of South Africa.

They invited me to their Zimbabwe HQ and a look at their accounts and operating methods convinced me that the Management Workshops would work very well. They put me into one of their companies and the results were so good I finished up working with all 16 companies they owned.

Where I was very lucky throughout my life is that people who were in a position to give me considerable help in my life continually appeared. When asking my new client where he had heard of my Management Workshops he reported that it was from the Chief Executive of the Transport Company I had worked with a few years earlier.

Apparently my earlier client had won an award from all his fellow business men for running the most efficient and successful company in Southern Africa.

At the presentation ceremony he answered all the questions about his progress to this success by telling his peers that if they wished to enjoy similar success they needed to get a visit from Terry Gasking.

He could have easily taken all the credit but persisted in pushing my name as the catalyst that had made it happen with the result that 17 more clients were chasing me for Management Workshops.

I was to learn that a similar thing had happened with my biggest client. They had a sales turnover in excess of £3.5 billion but no cash. Their Director of Purchasing and Personnel had been the Director attending a last night dinner at

Ashridge a number of times and had sat in on the Management Workshop I ran for them in Atlanta Georgia USA.

I heard from a fellow Director of his that every time their Board of Directors met to devise strategy to reduce the cash dependency of their businesses he would just say and repeat *'We need to get Terry Gasking into these companies.'*

It led to 15 very happy years working in more than 54 Cities spread around 5 Continents.

Each Management Workshop brought tremendous success for my clients, and I am delighted to record that none of them failed.

Three of my workshops revealed the Directors working to a different agenda to their owners. I was pretty certain that each of these were legitimate companies owned by the Mafia and being used to support other sides of the mafia trade in various parts of the world so I guess they are best not discussed here.

What had helped me to get the contracts with my biggest client was that the Group had a new Chief Executive and Financial Director. Their predecessors were all very Public School and I suspect bringing in a lad from Hackney Downs Grammar School with no University to his name would have been very infra-dig even though he was by now a Fellow of 4 major Professional Bodies -

Terry Gasking FCCA: FIMIS: FIMgt: FRSA:

The new CEO and FEO of the Group were American and South African so not steeped in the need to have gone to Eton, Harrow or the like, and then onto the Oxbridge Universities.

Indeed when they first recruited me I loved the CEO's comment on seeing my quotation at £2,500 a day plus travel and subsistence costs door-to-door (soon to rise to £3,000 and a share of success).

'Terry, I know you come with a great reputation but tell me is this quote in Yen?'

It wasn't – it was in sterling and despite the odd good natured grumble he agreed the fees and was kind enough to write an introduction for the financial management books I was to write when I retired.

Mother was in a care home by this time and I would visit her on my return from different countries I was working in.

'Terry, do you have to traipse all around the world like this?' was her regular question. *'Can't you get a job locally in a factory? That way you could earn a regular wage and still be home by 5 o'clock each night'.*

'Mum, I'm doing all right. I love working in different countries and cultures, my clients look after me well and I am earning fabulous fees.'

'You've always been a worker but they can't be paying you enough to make it worth all this travel'

This was coming from a woman who was brought up in an era when the family's only travel was by charabanc from the East-end of London to the Hop Fields of Kent once a year to spend their holiday living in sheds and hostels, picking hops for the farmer for a few shillings (10p) each day.

'Mum, I know it sounds unbelievable but I am earning £3,000 a day!'

Mother knew I wasn't lying. We had been brought up in a totally truthful household and would not think of lying to each other or anyone else. In the same way every word in this book is totally true without invention or exaggeration. It is word-for-word how my life has unfolded.

The look on Mum's face as she tried to come to terms with her Terry earning £3,000 a day revealed that she just couldn't grasp the magnitude of it. She has spent a lifetime working for a few shillings an hour to keep the wolf from the door and had done so successfully all our lives. Most years she would have been lucky to have earned £5 a week that she would invest in saving stamps to buy second-hand clothes, pay for a holiday at a seaside B&B usually on Canvey Island, help pay the rent and help feed the family alongside Dad's earnings (£6.50 a week) from the National Institute of the Blind's basket makers Workshop.

I first started running seminars, lectures and management Workshops when I worked for Courage and they got me to run a series of 'teach-ins' around the U.K. on the forthcoming 'Decimalisation' of the currency.

I then put together an Evening Class on Book-keeping at Misbourne where Jill was on a typing course to help in our business, later came lecturing and tutorials at University, seminars on the Future Social Effects of the Home Computer, 7 years of tutoring and lecturing at Ashridge Management College, and 15 years out on my own with the Terry Gasking Management Workshops.

In that time slightly more than 20,000 people - Directors, Managers, Supervisors, Staff, Workers and Students - have been my delegates and I can truthfully say that I have enjoyed the company virtually all of them. I believe that all but a few have thoroughly enjoyed the lectures and the knowledge that acquired. Many have become personal friends.

It leaves me convinced that if the running of countries was left to the people then we would live in a wonderfully peaceful and friendly world.

Sadly the politicians and religious leaders who gain control of the countries and religions are almost unanimously driven by the need for personal enrichment and/or power. They and megalomaniacs behind them who are pulling their strings are the reason we must suffer wars, murders and disputes.

The very rich truly rule the world.

The really sad thing is that with very few exceptions they rule it with the sole aim of making themselves even richer without regard to the harm they bring upon nations, cultures, creeds, religions and the ordinary people of the world.

Poverty to Peaches

I believe the run on the Euro that caused so much consternation in recent years and dragged down the economy for hundreds of millions of people was caused by the rich shorting the currencies so that they became even richer!

I have no problems about anyone becoming a millionaire or even a billionaire – indeed they have my huge admiration - but I can never understand the motivation when someone has $billions of personal wealth why must they continue to pursue tactics that will make them even more $billions rather that give everything over $1billion away.

When I walked off Fløyen mountain in Bergen in 1979 I worked out a theory about the control of oil when the price of oil at the pumps was 55p a litre (USA 34cents) and the Minister of Energy was standing up in English Parliament stating that there was only 30 years of oil under the North Sea.

Now – 34 years later – the Oil Drilling Platform I worked on is still producing oil and there are many, many more drilling rigs in the North Sea and 45 new areas for exploration have just been given licences.

Around the world there are more 'discoveries' announced on a regular basis.

As I write I see that the Norway has just commissioned the development for yet another massive oil field that has been discovered – 'the largest development in the North Sea for a decade' 93 miles off the Shetland Isles that will create more than 700 jobs and produce oil for (how long – yes you've guessed it) 30 years!

It would seem that there is a mass of oil under the earth and seas. Enough to enrich the whole world.

If my theories were correct then we should all be enjoying an era of cheap fuel throughout Europe and the World.

The Platform I investigated was costed to return a profit when the price of petrol at the pump was 55p a litre.

Poverty to Peaches

This Platform has been fully depreciated many times over its lifetime and though it has maintenance and repair costs they are a fraction of the costs of construction and towing and lifting the modules aboard.

The cost of producing the oil should therefore be dramatically lower than 34 years ago and yet I have just paid £1.38 a litre. It should be well below 55p a litre!

With fuel at the pump less than 55p it would allow for a dramatic fall in the cost of living and with it a vastly improved lifestyle for virtually everyone.

You could fill the fuel tank of your car for less than £30 instead of the £90 it is costing me at present. Heating Oil and the fuel needed for production would be a fraction of today's costs. The economy of the whole world would be buoyed.

Instead the people who own the oil companies have got immensely richer over those 34 years and have such a tight control of oil they clearly intend to go on getting richer.

How did the old song go?

'It's the Rich that gets the pleasure but the Poor what gets the blame.'

Alas I believe it will always be so!

I was extremely lucky to have found a career that I was particularly good at. In every case my success came in companies that had tried everything they knew to 'turnaround' their performance and had not succeeded.

How did I succeed to a level that was far beyond my wildest expectations when I started the Terry Gasking Management Workshops?

For the answer to that question I think I have to look to the experiences I have enjoyed throughout my life. My Modus Operandi had become -

I would first make a presentation to the full Board of Directors to discuss how the Terry Gasking Management Workshop worked. I needed to gain their commitment to allow my delegates to pursue the assignments that came out of the Workshop.

The delegates would complete these assignments whilst still managing their normal work (in every case the assignment would be a change in the way they handled their normal work. The change would have been worked out by the delegate with his/her colleagues in the syndicate groups).

I would then enter into my computer the results shown on my client's top level monthly management accounts for the last 3 years. These would be pushed through my analysis program (see 'Accounting Keys to Success'). This would highlight the areas of weakness and strengths and allow me to work out achievable goals for that particular client.

Next came site visits to their principal operating centres and offices for me to check that the situation on the ground confirmed the Accounting Keys to Success results.

If the results were confirmed by my site visit (and they were in nearly every case) then I would request a balance of staff at each Management Workshop that comprised –

A Main Board Director; Operations Director and Manager; Site Foremen and Supervisors; Stock Controller and 2 Assistants; Buyer and Assistant; 2/3 Product Managers; Credit Controller and 3/4 from Credit Control; Sales Director and Manager; Sales Area Managers and 2/3 top Sales People; Financial Director and Accountant; 2/3 Site Accountants; Administrator

I would leave it to the company to fill any empty places up to a total of 36 delegates.

Even though they all worked for the same company many of my delegates had never spoken to or met many others so the introduction to my workshops was all important. Throughout the Workshop we worked only on a first name basis. The body language of some members of staff revealed that they started the Workshop in total discomfort at calling their bosses by their first name. The occasional top manager or director showed the same discomfort but this was all lost as the Workshop progressed and many a close friendship resulted across status boundaries that had been sacrosanct previously.

The first morning was all important. I had to have captured their interest, imagination, and involvement by lunchtime and it was the lessons I learned from Drama about how to capture and work an audience that served me here.

Understanding body language was a vital ingredient of the success. Without knowing it my delegates were revealing exactly what they were thinking as they progressed. About 60% started the workshop hugely defensive and it was always a joy for me to see them all gradually lose their negativity and become involved in the Workshop.

The case studies I set them were an equally important ingredient. Accounting Keys for Success allowed me to set case studies that were totally relevant to the individual client and finally it was that most neglected sense – the power of touch that was vital.

The case studies were handled by groups of 6 in syndicates that I had put together as the Workshop progressed. They were cross-discipline, cross management levels, and contained an even balance of positive body language with negative.

I would walk around the syndicates in the after dinner session (scheduled as 7.30pm – 10.30 but usually going on past mid-night). I would spend 10 minutes or so with each and whilst standing with the group I would casually rest my hand on the shoulder of the nearest delegate. It had a similar effect to my days in the RAF when reading hands. The touch broke down any barrier the delegate might have with me and I was immediately aware of what was really bothering him/her. I gradually steered the syndicate's discussions to their area of concern and encouraged them to express their views – prompting them if necessary.

Poverty to Peaches

This was always amazingly successful as through the evening I could make sure that every delegates reservations had been discussed and resolved by the group themselves. Little wonder none of them wanted to pack up till gone midnight.

At the end of the Workshop all the delegates would set themselves assignments that they would complete over the next 6 months.

Six months later I returned to conduct a one-day Follow-up at which every delegate presented their results.

I had received the top level results for those 6 months and they had been passed through Accounting Keys to Success so I knew the overall effects my Management Workshop had achieved but I did not know who the achievers were.

When I walked into the lecture room it was immediately apparent. The successes were on their toes, their body language so positive as they couldn't wait to tell me and the Workshop what they had achieved. Those who had not achieved had really negative body language that was getting ever more negative as they looked around them at the majority.

I used to find that about 10 delegates from the original workshop had found it impossible to change from their old way of working, about 18 would have completed their assignments and have improved their results – some startlingly so, and the rest would be somewhere between the two extremes.

I used their body language to put 2 or 3 positives up first to reveal their success on the Overheads. In each case I got the whole Workshop to congratulate them and did my very best to make them feel a star (a tool of motivation that is so often missed by managers and directors).

I then put up the most negative body language I could see and sure enough they had achieved nothing. Answers given to my probing made it obvious to all that the delegate had done nothing and failed to change the way they worked – hence the lack of success.

Whilst they were still at the front of the Workshop I would start to compare their performance with the 2 previous 'stars'. I would then ask the Negative if I should ask his/her Director to place him/her under the control of one of the 'stars' for the next 6 months so that he can learn how to manage successfully.

I never did make such a request – never had to. The negative body languages never wanted to suffer such humiliation again.

When I came back for my second follow-up in another 6 months there were almost no negatives. One or two had left the company but all the rest had succeeded and the company was many $millions wealthier in Cash Flow and increased Profits.

The results displayed in the last collection of photos in this book outlines the achievement of one talented woman who took the lessons of the Terry Gasking Workshop back to her branch in Portland Oregon, USA.

Over the whole of the United States this group gained multi-millions but this result shows just what was possible for one positive, enthusiastic, and hugely likable manager to achieve.

I began to realise that my Workshops were using skills I had picked up from the hugely eventful life I had been fortunate to lead. It seemed to me that no experience is wasted and its lessons can be applied to events as they unfold.

Americans have a great saying *'what goes around – comes around'* and that for me sums up how I was able to achieve success with so many companies in so many parts of the world.

China; India; Middle East; Kenya; Zimbabwe; Botswana; South Africa; Italy; Spain; France; Germany; Belgium; Norway, Sweden; Denmark, England, Scotland, Wales, Ireland; USA, and Canada.

Poverty to Peaches

Over the years I have had some marvellous quotes from Directors of huge international companies –

> *'I don't care how busy you are; get yourself along to work with Terry Gasking. You will learn more from him about Finance and Accounting than you will from virtually any other source'*
> *'The only way you can fail to learn from Terry Gasking is to be asleep or unconscious throughout your time with him – and he will not let you sleep'*

> *'One of his most outstanding characteristics is his great insight into these* [finance and related business disciplines] *and how they relate to business situations. He has an uncanny way of effectively teaching complex concepts in a simplified very understandable fashion'*
> *'I was one of the lucky executives to be trained, in Terry's unique way, in the art of financial and cash management'*

> *'Not long ago media comment about my company frequently started with the phrase 'debt laden'. Barely twelve months and $1billion of debt reduction later that prefix will need to be changed to 'debt free'.*

> *'Terry was not only responsible for saving millions of dollars in cash flow and related profit enhancement , but he also helped hundreds of our non-financial employees gain a strong comprehension of basic finance concepts thereby making them better employees and developing them personally.'*

A top Director to the CEO of a world leader –
'Have you met Terry Gasking? He is one of the world's finest consultants in Sweating the Assets and Self-Funding success!'

Not bad for
'Little Tel' from 'ackney Downs'
wiv only a candle to do 'is 'omework

CHAPTER Twenty-One
Strictly Peaches

I loved working in different parts of the world. Every trip was an adventure. Every client was a fresh challenge.

My final client was another multi-national and for them I ran my Management Workshops in 3 European Countries as well as 1 in Hong Kong, 2 in China, 1 in India and 3 in USA.

It has been a very eventful life and career that I think owes much to my wonderful father.

Though he died when I was 17 years old he was a real inspiration to me.

Life threw a really dreadful hand to Dad. Extreme poor sight as a boy that deteriorated to complete blindness, an eardrum that was perforated as a child and left him completely deaf on his left side. Never-the-less he trained himself to tap-dance to such a high standard that he played virtually every Music Hall in the U.K. until 'Talkies' and blindness finished his career.

Bombed, evacuated, years in poverty, and finally forced to sit on the floor making baskets for 8 hours every day for the last 10 years of his life, he remained terrifically cheerful and supportive of everything Julie and I wanted to do even when he was suffering untold agonies of poorly treated cancer that finished his life at the age of 59.

My courage to walk through the various and many doors of opportunity that have presented themselves to me in life comes from the example of my father as does the work ethic he inspired in me. Doing nothing and accepting the choice of living on Welfare was never an option for dad.

Dad knew that if you did nothing but accept charitable donations such as Welfare Payments and the like then nothing very interesting, exciting or worthwhile will ever happen to you.

Embrace every opportunity with a relish and you may fall flat on your face from time to time but over a lifetime you will come out of it vibrant and fulfilled.

Without ever reading 'The Wastelands' by T S Elliott dad had come to the same conclusions as the author. He endowed in Julie and I ethics that ensured we would never spend our lives wandering in the wastelands. It is a lesson still to be learned by the architects and managers of the Welfare State.

Government Ministers constantly headline statements and make decisions that reveal they have not the faintest idea of what it is like to be poor or of the incentives that drive the individual to improve the lot he/she has been dealt in life.

Welfare as it is operated and managed in the 2000s condemns millions of people to a life wandering the wastelands of life. The privileged Etonians that govern the UK and the massively wealthy who run the USA have absolutely no chance of understanding the problem or the motivations that would bring an end to poverty. Sadly their egos do not allow them to hear the voices that could help. They may listen (and many fail to even take that step) but they do not hear!

I still have a yen to work in Australia and New Zealand, South America, and Southern Asia but with no contacts in those areas I felt it was time to call it a day and write about my adventures.

I started by writing books for non-financial managers and students that revealed the methods I had used to bring such phenomenal success in all kinds of trades in so many parts of the world.

If I could achieve such a success surely the intelligent student or manager could duplicate that success. I also felt that i would be a pity if methods that proved to be so successful went to the grave with me.

In 1991 I had been commissioned to write *'How to Master Finance'* by a Publisher who never followed up the initial orders and eventually parted with the rights to another leading Publisher. They got me to write an updated version to sell internationally. I did and before they got it to the market their American subsidiary with the rights to my book went belly-up so I had no outlet for the books I was then writing.

Eventually the company's liquidator discovered that the rights to my books returned to me. Never short of a work ethic I decided to publish them myself as TwigBooks and they began to sell around the world.

A great friend of Jill and I who had been one of the gorgeous girls in the dance troop for *ShowBoat* said she had always wanted to write a book but didn't know how to.

I asked if she had anything interesting to say and discovered the most wonderful background. She was in the dance troupe at *Hackney Empire* at the age of 14, danced at Britain's number one variety theatre – *The Palladium* at 16 years old, summer season at Blackpool, dancing in London as the bombs fell in World War II – called up in ENSA (the British Forces Entertainers) and was in shows that followed the War Front Line up through Italy and then Down through Europe.

Boy did she have a story! I edited and we published. Barbara Stewart became an Author at the age of 83 –

'Barbara Dancing through Life'.

Then I heard about a teacher at Hackney Downs Grammar School who had been an avid letter writer all his life. He had died and left all his letters in the hope that they would one day be published.

His greatest claim to fame was that he had been the inspiration to Harold Pinter. Harold Pinter won the Nobel Prize for Literature and had been a student at Hackney Downs about

5 years before I got there. He was very keen for the letters to be published

The indefatigable 'Willie' Watson edited them and we published *'Fortune's Fool'* –letters from Joe Brearley's life from leaving University and teaching in Germany in the 1930s (incidentally his letters home gave me the first insight as to why the Germans let Adolf Hitler take command of them).

The book also covered Joe's return to England after the War and then his retirement in Germany where he fell madly in love for the first time in his life.

A few years later we also published his wartime letters in *'Seen from the Wings' Part 1 and Part 2* also edited by 'Willie' Watson.

'Willie' also typed a hand written book by Alfie Dodd - an old boy at Hackney Downs in the same year as me -

'Alfie's Yidl' is an autobiographical account of a boy growing up in post-war London of the 1940s and 50s - Memories of an East-End family in the 1940s – 50s

With my 5 Management Books we suddenly had 9 books published and numerous requests to publish others.

Occasionally whilst walking my dogs Saffy, Thyme and Taggie, I was joined by a delightful young lady walking her dog 'RB'. She was coming up to her exams and telling me about the stress of modern day schooling,

'Hang about Robin, it may be stressful but you've got an awful lot more going for you than your parents had, or particularly your grand-parents did.'

I started to tell of wartime children, evacuees and the stress they and their families must have suffered. It was clear that the schools were completely missing this period of English history despite its dramatic impact on all who were involved.

Many of my friends were evacuees.

Poverty to Peaches

I got their stories from them and found a number more ex-evacuees to pen a brief note of their experiences. The result was a lovely little book I edited and we published –
'Evacuees the Stories of the Children'
This has led to a constant demand for us to print interesting books and these include –
'Travels with Ernest' by Ryan Keith – Travelling around the North of Ireland on his trusty old Vespa. It is a very nicely written book.
Two Books by an old friend from school who used to run the team that represented Egerton Road Synagogue for whom I played in goal –
'Everything you wanted to know but never bothered to Ask' by Brian Ariel – A Curio shop of a book with treasures of knowledge waiting to be found – and
'Songs of the 20th Century' by Brian Ariel – Songs; Composers; Lyricists and more –
Then there was a sweet book by my sister -
'Little Nessie' by Julia Mowery. A lovely book based on Loch Ness is ideal reading for children aged 9 to 99
And our first Novel
'Kranzweg Castle' by Julia Mowery – a theatrical troupe playing leading theatres in Europe in 1939 receives an invitation to entertain German High Command in Kranzweg Castle. War is declared and they find themselves trapped. In a brilliant development of the plot Julia takes them through twists and turns that leaves the reader eager to read on and find out what their fate will be.
And now **'Poverty to Peaches'**
When you have been brought up in poverty and find that fate, Guardian Angels – or a god somewhere on high has given you the energy and fitness to work your way out of that poverty then you never lose that work ethic.
I hope to go on writing or editing for the rest of my life.

I think my days of running Charity Events are possibly at an end. Over our life time Jill and I have always helped or organised and run dozens of events in aid of one charity or another. Most have attracted many hundreds of people and a few many thousands of people. They have all made money for the Charity which was just as well as I have never had the privilege of Sponsors or Backers and have supported the events with our own money. We never put the Charity at risk.

Sadly in 2011 the record of always making money came to an end and a loss on 3 Sponsored Golf Tournaments in aid of Medical Detection Dogs cost Jill and I a lot of money. We cancelled the events because of a lack of entries months before they were due but sadly the golf courses refused to return our deposits.

The loss is either a sign that the Austerity imposed upon the U.K.by the two chumps at the top of the Government* caused severe distress to charity giving, or that I am losing my touch – or both. Either way Jill and I will probably content ourselves with helping others rather than running the show.

*(see *Double Your Money'* that was written in 2009 for the methods that would have completely avoided the Recession. It also contains my letters *'Dear Prime Minister'*)

Medical Detection Dogs are phenomenal. The charity has discovered that it can train dogs to 'sniff out' cancer in urine samples, or to give early warning of impending dangerous blood sugar changes in diabetes sufferers, or to help sufferers from a number of life threatening problems. With a very tightly run administration no money is wasted and it really is worth all effort to raise funds and gain publicity for them.

A few years ago I did a number of Regional Radio and TV live interviews for the Sleep Apnoea Association as they battled to get recognition by the National Institute of Clinical Excellence that it was cost effective to give sufferers a CPAP rather than leave them untreated with the high risk that they will suffer high blood pressure, strokes or even heart attacks.

I even managed a 20 minutes audience with the Minister of Transport at the House of Lords as I tried to get him to make all Heavy Goods Vehicle, Public Service Vehicles, Pilots and Train Drivers take a Simple Sleep Apnoea test every 3 years.

I was thwarted by and large by his PPC who kept trying to turn my 'evidence' against me personally but by then I had many years experience of handling difficult delegates at the start of my Workshops so was soon able to overcome his objections. However inertia at the Ministry was always going to be a stumbling block.

I had a good hearing from the Minister but nothing came of it and still folk are falling asleep at the wheel and causing massive disasters on the motorways.

The interviews I did live in the media for Sleep Apnoea Association led to my one and only live interview on my own subject – 'the future of the British Economy over the years immediately ahead'.

It was on BBC World News and scheduled for mid-morning. Unfortunately for me it was the day when masses of people were phoning the BBC to protest at the appalling behaviour of two overpaid and uncivilized 'celebrity presenters' who had insulted on air a kindly TV figure.

There was I warning of a massive Recession about to hit the U.K. in the years 2008-12 and advising the methods we could use to avoid its worst ravages. There were they – the presenters and producers – interested in little other than the rapidly growing number of people phoning the BBC to protest about the two D.Js.

The story of the DJs was repeated every few minutes during the broadcast and the rest of the day.

Terry's attempt to save the U,K, and world economy was shown live once and then never heard or seen again.

Oh well – such is life.

Writing, editing, publishing, walking my dogs, playing golf and ballroom dancing are now my main occupations.

I have wanted to ballroom dance for a number of years but I only learned 3 dances as a young man. Unfortunately jigging up and down on the spot replaced the sheer joy of moving across a ballroom with a lovely girl in your arms.

Thankfully Strictly Come Dancing has rekindled interest in the gracefulness and joy of 'proper' dancing and a number of Tea Dances are emerging (or perhaps re-emerging).

Jill has had a few Heart problems that have led to stents in her arteries and also has had two half knees replaced so her dancing days are over and bridge, reading and TV are now her greatest hobbies.

Jill was a great stage dancer in her time appearing in amateur shows in top theatres in the West End of London for many years. She was part of the super troupe of dancers that I first met when I was drafted in for a part in Showboat.

At that time her stage partner was Ivor and they had been paired on stage for 10 years or more. A year or so before I joined the Players they performed Brigadoon (by all accounts one of the favourite shows of most who were involved).

An excellent Scottish dancer called Rita joined the group for Brigadoon and stayed on for future shows. She went on to marry Ivor.

Sadly Ivor died quite suddenly 20 years ago and we all realised at his funeral that we had moved into our own lives and hadn't seen Ivor for many years. We had all been such a tight knit and extremely happy troupe that we resolved never to allow such a gap to occur again and Bertha's Tuesday Class Reunion was born.

It is open to anyone who attended Bertha's (the producer and choreographer at LT and many other top groups) Tuesday Class. We meet once a year – all bringing food and drink that goes onto a central buffet table to be shared by all. The atmosphere is always terrific - fun and laughter throughout the afternoon.

A couple of years back at one of our reunions Rita was talking about how she had managed to fill her life after Ivor's death with her work as a Nursery Nurse and by helping look after her grandchildren when needed. Now she was retired and the grandchildren had moved away she was finding life a bit lonely.

Jill and I invited her to have a break from normal routine and spend a few days with us. While she was here I managed to persuade her to go to a Tea Dance at the next Village. It is run every two weeks by the delightful Mary.

Rita was reluctant to go as she only knew how to dance 3 ballroom dances. As luck would have it they were the same 3 that I knew – Waltz, Quickstep and ChaChaCha so off we went and found a terrifically entertaining way of keeping fit and having fun. Now a year later we can dance all the ballroom dances thanks to a DVD by Len Goodman that gives you the basic steps of each dance onto which you add the steps you see others perform at each tea dance.

Sequence dancing was completely new to us but is proving to be great fun and equally entertaining. Rita and I really are enjoying our dances and the dinner for all 3 of us at the Bottle and Glass afterwards allows Jill to have the vicarious pleasure as she listens to the mistakes and successes we made in the afternoon tea dance.

Rita found a wonderful group at a tea dance in her region of Berkshire that she had invited me to. We always feel very privileged in the way the excellent dancers at Hartley Wintney have welcomed us and helped us join in the sequence dances. We can't make it to the lovely Sylvia's lessons as I live too far away but they are all so kind to us in allowing us to follow their moves.

Poverty to Peaches

Bertha's training at Tuesday Class really does pay off for we can often pick up the sequences sufficiently well after watching two dances and get round the floor more or less correctly and without putting the others off.

I had a hip replaced a couple of years ago and when I restarted golf that little white ball had a mind of its own. In my first 9 holes I lost 5 balls, in the next I lost 4. It was looking as if the game was going to get very expensive but I am gradually improving and watching my handicap slowly reduce. It would be nice to get my golf handicap down to single figures once more but I must confess I am thoroughly enjoying the game again and will do my best.

You can see from the foregoing - life has been a really great adventure for Terry Gasking and is continuing to be so.

I have to believe that all my Guardian Angels and all the gods have pulled for me in this world for mine has been a Peach of a Life!

- I was brought up in an extremely happy home
- I was allowed to play unsupervised
- I found a wonderful wife at my second attempt
- I have had a Peach of a career
- I have a Peach of a Dancing Partner.
- I have an absolute Peach of a wife.
- and now I even grow Peaches in my garden.

As a result I now have this wonderful line to greet my guests with –

'Hello – would you like to stroke my Peaches?'

At 73 years of age I have to admit that they realise my words are in jest as mine so often are but wouldn't I have loved that line when I was a teenage virgin longing to be laid?

But then again I would have been far too shy to have ever used it!

It really has been a Peach of a life from ***Poverty to Peaches***!

Poverty to Peaches

Poverty to Peaches

I hope you enjoyed my book
Terry Gasking

ABUNTU
I am because we are

Other books from TwigBooks –

Evacuees – Stories of the Children
The heart-warming stories from 18 WWII Evacuees
Edited by Terry Gasking ISBN 978 09560618 05:
First published 2009

BARBARA – Dancing through Life - Palladium Dancer, Dancing in the Blitz, following the Front Line thru Europe in ENSA, then TV Extra - By Barbara Stewart ISBN 978 09547236 75: First published 2007

Alfie's Yidl by Alfred Dodd ISBN 978 09547236 99: Memories of an East-End family in the 1940s – 50s
First published 2009

Travels with Ernest by Ryan Keith - Around the North of Ireland on a Vespa ISBN 978 09560618 81 a beautifully written book - First published 2011

"Fortune's Fool" The man who taught and inspired the Nobel Laureate Harold Pinter. Compiled from his letters home 1931-1977 by G.L.Watkins Introduction by Harold Pinter; ISBN 978 09547236 82: First Published 2008

Seen from the Wings 1 A Second World War Journal - England to the Middle-East 1942-1944 Edited G.L.Watkins ISBN 978 09560618 43: First Published 2010

Seen from the Wings 2 A Second World War Journal - Change of Duty then Home 1944-1946 Editor G.L.Watkins ISBN 978 19079535 21: First Published by 2011

Thanks for the Boblet wartime Letters Home of David Ogilvie ISBN 978 1 907953 55 2: The story of evacuation and separation from his parents for the six-years of the Second World War. First published in 2012

Little Nessie by Julia Mowery ISBN 978 09560618 36:
A lovely book based on Loch Ness; ideal reading for
children aged 9 to 99 First published in 2010

**Everything you wanted to know but never bothered to
Ask** by Brian Ariel – A Curio shop of a book with
treasures of knowledge waiting to be found ISBN 978
09560618 74 First published in 2011

Songs of the 20th Century by Brian Ariel – Songs;
Composers; Lyricists and more - ISBN 978 09560618 98
 First published in 2011

<u>**Books written by Terry Gasking
for the Manager and Student**</u> –
Available in Paperback and as EBooks

HOW to MASTER FINANCE ISBN 978 09547236 13:
First published 1991. The rewritten and revised
International Edition Published in paperback in 2006

PERFECT FINANCIAL RATIOS ISBN 978 09547236 44
First published as a paperback in 1993

GET OUT of DEBT with Terry Gasking ISBN
9780954723606 First published in paperback in 2004;

ACCOUNTING KEYS for SUCCESS
ISBN 978 09547236 68 First published as a paperback in
2010

'CASH & the Art of Successful Business Management'
ISBN 978 09547236 51: Published 2008

DOUBLE YOUR MONEY! ISBN 978 09560618 12
First published in paperback in 2009

Poverty to Peaches

And a delightful novel written
by my sister Julia Mowery

Kranzweg Castle by JULIA MOWERY
A troupe of theatrical performers are playing leading
theatres in the Cities of Europe in the late 1930s. They are
invited to the Medieval Kranzweg Castle to entertain
members of the German High Command. War is declared
and they find themselves entrapped. In a brilliant
development of the plot Julia takes them through twists and
turns that leaves the reader eager to read on and find out
what their fate will be. ISBN 978 1 907953 51 4:
First published 2009

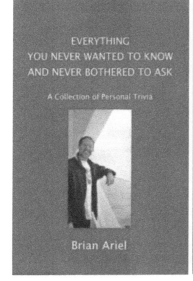

Poverty to Peaches

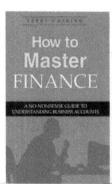

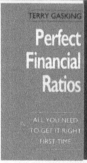

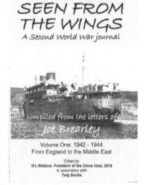

Books are available from leading Bookshops, Amazon, Kindle, most
IPlayers and other Ebook readers
For our latest publications
Please go to www.twigbooks.com
TwigBooks; 1-2 Biggs Lane, DINTON, Aylesbury,
Buckinghamshire UK, England HP17 8UH

Lightning Source UK Ltd.
Milton Keynes UK
UKHW011846210422
401860UK00001B/2